Secret
Child

Gordon Lewis and
Andrew Crofts

Secret Child

1950s Dublin – a young boy
hidden from his family

HarperElement
An imprint of HarperCollins*Publishers*
1 London Bridge Street
London SE1 9GF

www.harpercollins.co.uk
www.secretchild.com

First published by HarperElement 2015

1 3 5 7 9 10 8 6 4 2

© Gordon Lewis and Andrew Crofts 2015

Gordon Lewis and Andrew Crofts assert the moral
right to be identified as the authors of this work

A catalogue record of this book is
available from the British Library

ISBN 978-0-00-812733-6

Printed and bound in the United States of America by
RR Donnelley

Find out more about HarperCollins and the environment at
www.harpercollins.co.uk/green

Chapter One
Going Home

The flight was delayed but none of the passengers milling around the lounge seemed to mind too much. There was something of a party atmosphere at that end of the terminal at JFK that day, which added to my own sense of excitement at my impending adventure.

I felt strangely nervous considering how many times I had boarded flights before. This trip, however, was going to be different to the usual round of international business meetings and holidays. This was literally a trip into the unknown, back into a past filled with dark secrets.

It seemed like the whole flight was going to be packed with Irish Americans heading home for the St Patrick's Day celebrations, many of them wearing something green for the occasion, and some of them already cheered by a couple of pints of Guinness, taken to pass the time. I deliberately avoided eye contact with everyone, wanting to keep myself to myself, protecting my thoughts, preparing myself for whatever might be awaiting me at the other end of the trans-atlantic flight. The last thing I wanted was to fall into a conversation where someone started asking me questions about my plans for the next few days.

To give myself something to do I pulled the small envelope out of my jacket pocket and stared for the hundredth time at the modest collection of black-and-white photographs it contained. I had stared at them so long and so hard over the previous few months I knew every faded detail by heart. It was like looking into a different world; one that should have been joined to mine by memories and stories shared by previous generations, but was in fact quite alien. I might as well have been looking at pictures of strangers, and those pictures on their own were never going to give up their secrets, however many times I studied them.

'American Airlines flight to Dublin, Ireland is ready for boarding.' The announcement made me jump and raised a jovial cheer from some of the revellers at the bar. 'Will First and Business Class passengers please proceed to the boarding gate.'

I slipped the photos back into my pocket and stood up, walking through to my seat without talking to anyone, only half hearing the conversations going on around me and gratefully accepting a glass of champagne from the smiling stewardess as I settled down and stared out of the window at the tarmac, wanting the flight to be over so that I could get my adventure started. I realised that my nerves were partly caused by fear of what I was about to find out and partly by the thought that I might not find out anything at all. I did not want to have to return to New York none the wiser as to the events surrounding my birth and the early years, which my family seemed determined to keep shrouded in mystery.

Going Home

Extracting even the barest facts from my cousin, Denis, had been an agony. Anyone would have thought I was trying to pull his teeth out rather than ask a few questions, as each one was met with a sigh and the barest of monosyllabic answers that he could get away with. If it hadn't been for the fact that I was buying him dinner and that he was bound by politeness to stay at the restaurant table for the duration of the meal, he would have made his excuses and left the moment I raised the subject of the past. When I finally had to let him off the hook he swore blind he had told me everything he knew, but I was not at all sure he was telling the truth. That generation seemed to find it an agony to talk about anything personal or emotional, however far in the past it might be. Maybe he had buried some things so deep he had actually lost them for ever.

'What do you want to be digging up all that old stuff for?' he wanted to know. 'It's so long ago.'

'That's why I want to know,' I persisted. 'What harm can it do?'

'You don't want to be going over all that again,' he muttered, 'best to let sleeping dogs lie.'

'I've been trying to piece together what happened,' I went on, 'and there are a few gaps that I need to fill in.'

I had refused to give up with the gentle interrogation, however much he evaded answering, and I doubted he would be accepting another dinner invitation from me for a long time. I pulled the pictures out again as the cabin crew went through their familiar rituals and the plane roared into life and lifted off from the runway. Despite the few things that Denis had reluctantly divulged, I was still having trouble getting a clear picture, which was why I had decided I had to make the trip back into the past for myself. I had to actually go to the streets where it had all started to see if they would jog my own memory, unlocking some of the doors in my head.

I had received the call from Patrick Dowling in Dublin two days before and had booked the flight immediately. He had been meticulously careful not to raise my hopes by making any promises, but I had grabbed at the straws he was holding out with all the desperation of a drowning man. He worked in some sort of public relations capacity for the Children's Courts, and as a younger man he had also been a social worker in Dublin, so might know more about the sort of place that I had been kept for those early years. I felt sure the Court must have records from the time when I was born. Patrick was the best lead I had at the moment.

'If you were to come in to see me next time you are in Dublin,' he had said, 'we could see what we can find out.'

I'm sure he was just being polite, hoping to put me off from what seemed to him like a lost cause. He certainly didn't expect me to ring back a few hours later and tell him that I had booked my flight and would be with him in three days' time.

'I can't promise anything …' he'd said quickly, probably horrified to think he might not be able to help me after I had travelled all the way from New York to see him.

'I understand,' I assured him, 'I'm just grateful that you are willing to help.'

I did understand how slim the chances of success were, and how little information I was going to be able to give him

Going Home

to go on, but that didn't stop me from being ridiculously optimistic – and nervous.

I was aware that the Dublin taxi driver was watching me in his mirror and I tried to avoid his eyes, not wanting to be drawn into the conversation that he was obviously keen to have.

'Can I ask,' he said eventually, ignoring all the signals I must have been giving off, 'do I hear an Irish or an American accent?'

'Probably a mixture,' I replied, giving up all hope of being able to remain alone with my thoughts for the duration of the ride from the airport into the city centre. 'I've been living in New York for a long time, but I was born in Ireland.'

'I thought as much,' he crowed, obviously pleased with his own powers of perception. 'You dress like a Yank, in your smart suit, and you have that American twang about your voice. But then I thought you must be Irish with those deep blue eyes and your looks.'

Believing that the ice had been broken between us he continued to chatter and I was able to drift in and out of the conversation as he pointed out local landmarks and buildings that he felt had probably arrived since I was last in the city. I could see there had been a lot of changes, but the essence of the city remained the same, with street after street of red-brick houses, every corner seeming to boast a pub. What surprised me was how small everything seemed after New York. The buildings had seemed so huge when I was a child, the roads so wide.

'Is this your first time at the famous Shelbourne Hotel?' he enquired.

'Yes,' I nodded and smiled at him in the mirror. It wasn't completely true; I had been there before, more than fifty years ago. Although I had only been visiting for tea, it was an event that was etched deeply on my memory. It was the day when I first met Bill and realised that everything in my life was about to change and that nothing about my past was quite as I had believed it to be. I had never experienced anything like that tea before, and wouldn't again for many years. It had been like arriving unexpectedly on a different planet.

'Hello and welcome to the Shelbourne Hotel,' the young receptionist beamed, 'may I have your name, please, sir?'

'Gordon Lewis,' I replied, handing over a credit card.

She scanned her screen with well-practised speed. 'Ah, yes, Mr Lewis, we have a nice suite for you, overlooking the park.'

I didn't need a suite, but because I had booked at such short notice it had been all they could offer me. She signalled a bellboy to take my case up.

'How long do you plan to stay with us, Mr Lewis?' she continued as she typed.

'It's a little open-ended,' I confessed, 'I will know better in a few days.'

'That's fine, Mr Lewis,' she said. 'Enjoy your stay with us.'

I walked to the lift with the bellboy, looking forward to being alone behind a closed door with my thoughts. Once the bellboy had gone I pulled back the net curtains and stared out at the green of the trees opposite. Even though I had been living in the nicest parts of New York and other cities, the little boy in me was still impressed to find myself in the best hotel on the south side of the river in Dublin.

Going Home

I had thought I would rest a little and then go out for a walk to acclimatise myself to the city of my birth, maybe find a noisy bar where I could lose myself in a dark corner and allow my mind to wander back over the years; but as the rain started tapping gently on the elegant old Georgian window I seized the excuse to stay where I was, turning on the television to watch the St Patrick's Day parade. I would be spending plenty of time in the coming days pounding the streets and sitting in the bars as I tried to unearth the truth.

The next morning I rose early, too wired to sleep despite the time difference with New York. The rain had lifted and sun streamed into the room as I pulled back the curtains and ordered breakfast. An hour later I was down in reception, struggling with a map of the city.

'Good morning, sir.' I looked up to find a bellboy smiling at me. 'Do you need any help? Do you know where you want to go?'

'Yes,' I said, a little too quickly. 'I know where I'm going. Thanks all the same.'

I folded the map into my pocket and walked briskly out of the hotel, hoping that I looked like a man who knew where he was heading. I didn't feel like sharing any information with anyone, however well-meaning they might be. The habit of secrecy was too ingrained for me to be able to shrug it off that easily after so many years. The boy's accent had brought back unsettling memories. My friends and I must have sounded exactly like that when we were the little 'unfortunates', running wild on the streets of north Dublin. Anyone who comes from Dublin knows the difference between those from the 'north side' of the River Liffey and those from the more prosperous 'south side'.

Once I was out of sight of the hotel I slowed down, my heart still thumping in my chest as I forced myself to stroll at a more leisurely pace towards the O'Connell Bridge with its ornate stone carvings and elegant Victorian street lanterns. I believe it is the only bridge in Europe that is as wide as it is long. Half-way across the bridge I stopped amid the bustle of people and traffic. Little had changed, except for me. Last time I had stood there, waiting with my mother for the meeting that was going to totally alter the course of my life, I had been too small to see over the side, peering through the stone balustrades and jumping impatiently up and down, wanting to get a better view of the detritus of the city as it drifted in the waters flowing under the bridge.

I leaned for a few moments on the rough stone which had then been taller than me and looked down at the flotsam and jetsam moving in the water below, the memories flooding my brain in a confusing montage of images and emotions which seemed more like half-remembered dreams, making my heart crash in my chest. Every direction I looked triggered more memories; the bridges, the buildings, the people. Every church spire seemed familiar, probably because I had been inside most of them at one time or another. Even the buses, which had been my first passport to the outside world, were parked in the same place on the embankment, or 'Quays', as they were known.

Now I might be able to stay in a hotel suite in the best hotel on the south side, but it was the north side that I came from; that was where my roots were, and that was where

Going Home

Patrick Dowling was waiting for me with whatever information he had managed to glean from the archives of half a century before. Breathing deeply, I steadied myself and continued on my way to my appointment at the old City Hall building where the children's courts used to be, checking the map at every turn.

I felt like a small boy again as I announced myself to the receptionist and told her I had an appointment with Patrick Dowling. She made a call but hung up without saying anything.

'He's on the phone,' she told me. 'Take a seat and I'll try again in a minute.'

As I sat staring at the sweeping metal staircase, not knowing what I was about to find out about my own past, my heart was thumping like it used to when I was a boy running wild around town in search of an adventure. It was like I was waiting for the curtain to rise on an eagerly anticipated new show. Every time someone came down I watched to see if they were likely to be looking for me, and after what seemed like an age a smartly dressed man with slightly wild grey hair descended and walked towards me with his hand extended.

'Would you be Gordon Lewis?' he asked with a friendly smile. 'I'm Patrick Dowling. Welcome to Ireland. I hope it wasn't too difficult to find us; we're a bit tucked away from the other buildings in this area.'

He was tall and slim and I guessed he was in his forties, dressed in a dark two-piece suit, white shirt and tie, carrying a file in his other hand. He kept pushing strands of hair out of his face as he guided me towards a door on the ground floor, making polite conversation as he went, putting me at ease with typical Dublin humour.

Once inside the small room he closed the door and indicated for me to sit across the desk as he opened the file in front of him.

'So, Gordon, you want to locate the home you lived in when you were a child?'

'Yes,' I nodded, hardly able to breathe in my anxiety to know what the file was going to reveal.

'You would be amazed how many people like you come here looking for information about their past in Ireland. We do our best to keep records, but sometimes there are details which may be lost, or just not recorded.'

What was he saying? I felt a twinge of anxiety. Was he preparing me for disappointment? I nodded my understanding but couldn't think of anything to say. After a moment he looked down at the file again.

'A home for single mothers in Dublin in the 1950s, you say?'

'Yes,' I said, clearing my throat to stop the emotions from choking me. 'My home, where my mother brought me up until the beginning of the sixties.'

'The most infamous one, of course, was the Magdalene Laundries, where we now know that the girls and women were treated very badly, worked like slaves until they were old in order to atone for their sins. But those mothers weren't allowed to keep their children. Usually the newborn babies were taken away for adoption or put into orphanages. But as I understand it, this didn't happen to you?'

'No.' I didn't trust my voice to say any more.

Going Home

'You were a lucky boy to have your mother to take care of you. Is there anything else you can remember about it?'

'There were a lot of single women there, lots of us children too. Boys and girls. It was on the north side of the river and it was run by nuns.' He was staring at me blankly as I racked my brains for more details. 'I distinctly remember there was a mental hospital next door.'

He looked back down at his file for a moment. 'There was a mental hospital in the area near this one.' He pushed a map across the table and pointed to an area on the north side. 'The institution was closed many years ago and the building is due for demolition. I don't know what you'll find if you go up there. The whole area is very run-down. It is bound to have changed a great deal since the fifties.'

He fell silent for a moment as I picked up the map and stared at it, trying to make sense of it, searching for names that might ring a bell, but to my confused eyes it just looked like a mess of lines and letters. Nothing made sense. I needed time to calm down and digest the information.

'Does the name Morning Star Avenue, mean anything to you?' he asked. I thought for a moment before shaking my head. 'How about the Morning Star Hostel for Men? Or the Regina Coeli Hostel for Women?'

Regina Coeli. Was that a bell ringing somewhere at the back of my most distant memories? Or was it just that I wanted so much for something to sound familiar?

'No,' I said, 'I don't think so.'

'I'm sorry we don't have more details. There should have been files for every woman and every child in all these homes, but we had a burst water pipe about ten years ago and many files were ruined. All the names from that period were lost. I'm sorry that I can only give you so little to go on after you've come so far.'

At that moment I pictured myself going back to the hotel, picking up my stuff and catching the next flight back to New York, and the feeling of disappointment was overwhelming. I could see that Patrick was genuinely sorry not to be able to be of more help as he said goodbye at the door. I stood for a few moments on the pavement outside, not sure what to do next. I was still holding Patrick's map. There didn't seem any harm in at least going to look at the area he was talking about. Something there just might trigger my memories. I found Morning Star Avenue amid the jumble of print, worked out which direction I should be going in and set off.

It wasn't long before the landscape began to change, all signs of the prosperity of the city centre gradually fading into areas of industrial wasteland. I don't know how long I had been walking before I felt some vague stirrings of recognition. None of the street names rang a bell (though I wouldn't have been able to read them when I was a boy anyway), but every now and then I saw a building or a view which I thought was familiar among the ruins and the occasional new developments. Then I would dismiss the idea again, telling myself I was imagining these things just because I wanted so much for them to be true.

Reaching the end of a long road I saw a large red-brick building, very different to everything that surrounded it. It looked imperial, like it had been a British headquarters of some sort. It seemed so familiar but no matter how hard I concentrated I couldn't quite bring the memory into focus.

Going Home

The sound of loud voices caught my attention and I saw a group of people gathered on a litter-strewn piece of land further down the street. There seemed to be something familiar about them as well. As I drew closer I could see that they were men and women of different ages, but they were all drinking from bottles and I realised they had the same shabby, shambling look of the destitute, people who have 'fallen through the net' in society and ended up at this desolate roadside. Despite the bleakness of the scene, however, it felt strangely like home.

None of them gave me a second look. It was like I was an invisible ghost passing them by. I crossed over the road to the corner of the imperial-looking building and found a street sign announcing that I was standing in Morning Star Avenue. So was this the mental institution that I remembered? The one that Patrick said was due for demolition? Another street sign told me that the road would lead to a dead end. As I walked further along I noticed there was a slight slope, just enough to make my leg muscles ache, bringing back a memory of walking up a steep hill when I was a boy. Was this the same hill, turned into little more than a slope now that my legs were longer? I stopped and looked around at every view, desperately trying to recall distant pictures from the past.

I noticed grey railings along an overgrown garden to my right and a picture flashed up in my head. The narrow front garden had a statue of Our Lady Mary, the Virgin Mother, and on the wall beside a drainpipe a blue plaque announcing 'Regina Coeli Hostel'. I felt a lurch of excitement in my chest. That was the name Patrick had given me which had rung a distant bell. Now that I was actually standing in front of it that bell was becoming clearer. This had to be the right place.

Behind the garden stood a long, two-storey, red-brick house. This was it – my first home! Regina Coeli was still standing after all these years. It was much smaller than the giant, rambling premises that I remembered as a small child, but now that I focused on it I could see details which reminded me of specific events. As I stared past the railings the memories came flooding back. I took my time looking around the garden at all the corners and spaces where I had played and hidden as a child, seeing them from a different perspective. Now the grounds which had seemed so enormous appeared quite modest. Something was missing. I concentrated hard and realised that next to the small house there should have been two huge wooden gates adjoining the building but they had gone. It didn't matter. I was that little boy again. I had found my childhood home, the place which had seemed to me to be paradise, and now I would be able to unravel the rest of the story.

Chapter Two
Divine Intervention

The steady drizzle had soaked through Cathleen's coat, making the bite of the cold wind even sharper as it stabbed at her fingers, which had locked painfully around the handle of the modest suitcase containing all the possessions she had in the world. Her feet were wet inside her shoes and the water was dripping down her face from her drenched headscarf and hair. The clouds had extinguished the last vestiges of light from the moon and no lights shone from any of the closed or abandoned buildings that loomed up around her.

Turning into Morning Star Avenue, every muscle in her body aching from the long walk and the heavy case, she saw a group of people huddling round a bonfire, swathed in layers of ragged clothes, their faces lit eerily by the flames licking up from the fiercely burning rubbish. They all seemed to be holding bottles in hands bandaged with layers of grubby mittens, swigging as they talked, trying to warm themselves from the inside as well as the outside. They all turned to stare at her as she walked towards them. Her heart was thumping in her ears. She had no experience of people like this, no way of gauging whether they would resent her straying into their area. Would they ask for money? She had none to give them. Would they attack her? There were too many of them and they would easily be able to overcome her. Should she turn and run? If she did that she would have to drop her case in order to stand any chance of escaping in her current state, and where would she run to anyway? This place was her last chance.

Holding her nerve she kept walking, trying not to look in their direction, trying not to look scared. She could hear the crackling of their fire as she drew closer, the sparks struggling up into the sky before being extinguished by the rain.

'You looking for someone?' a voice called out. It sounded angry.

'You lost?' another asked.

She turned and looked straight at them, facing up to her fear, telling herself that they were just people like her, currently down on their luck. 'I'm looking for Regina Coeli,' she replied.

They all laughed, as if they had guessed as much. They exchanged comments, which she couldn't hear but guessed were lewd from the way they cackled and jeered at their own wit, apparently enjoying her discomfort.

'Keep walking up the hill,' a woman's voice called out to her once the noise had subsided. 'It's the only house up there. You can't miss it.'

One of the men made another comment and they all cackled again, turning their faces back to the warm, orange glow of the flames and the comfort of their bottles. Cathleen walked on into the darkness until a glow of a single lamppost appeared ahead of her. As she drew closer she saw a lone figure standing stock still beneath the light. She glanced back to see if any of the down-and-outs were following her, but everything was silent and black and wet.

Moving the suitcase to her other hand she took a deep breath and kept going towards the still figure. As she drew closer she realised the figure was a statue of the Virgin Mary, standing behind some railings in the front garden of a red-brick house that she guessed must be her destination.

'You silly woman,' she muttered to herself, relieved to have arrived but now nervous about the reception that might await her inside. She paused for a second, putting down the case and stroking her stomach, stretching the muscles in her shoulders and back, raising her face to the rain for a few seconds as she composed herself for the giant step she was about to take into the unknown.

She spotted a small door set into high wooden gates, with a bell beside it. As she reached up to ring it the gate opened and a woman appeared, throwing a heavy overcoat over her shoulders, her head down in preparation for walking in the rain. She almost bowled Cathleen over in her hurry.

'Can I help you, ma'am?' the woman asked. 'Are you looking for somebody?'

'Is this the Regina Coeli Hostel?' Cathleen enquired.

'Yes, come in,' the woman said, retracing her steps through the doorway and leading her into the hallway of the house. 'I'm Sister Kelly. Let's get you out of that wet coat.'

Cathleen was aware that a puddle was forming around her on the stone floor as she shrugged off the coat and untied the scarf, attempting to mop some of the water from her blonde hair.

'Take a seat, my dear,' Sister Kelly said, glancing down at Cathleen's belly. 'I was just on the way home myself, so I will fetch Sister Peggy to take care of you.'

Cathleen sat on a wooden bench as Sister Kelly bustled out of the room, and took several deep breaths. The kindness of the older woman and the relief of taking the weight off her legs and back made her want to cry, but she held back the tears and composed herself for whatever was going to happen next.

A few minutes later a small woman in thick glasses and a big blue apron bustled into the room, carrying a worn piece of towel.

'Oh, you poor thing,' she exclaimed, 'you're wet through.' She handed Cathleen the thin towel. 'Dry your hair before you catch your death. I'm Sister Peggy.'

Sister Peggy watched for a moment as Cathleen attempted to dry her face and head a little. This was not the sort of girl she was used to seeing at the gates of Regina Coeli. To start with she was obviously older – Sister Peggy guessed she was probably in her mid thirties – whereas most of them were teenagers when they first arrived. Her clothes looked better than the others too. They were certainly not grand in any way, but even in their drenched state she could see that this was a woman who looked after herself and cared about her appearance.

'Let's get you through to the fire,' Sister Peggy said. 'What shall I call you?'

'My name's Cathleen Crea.'

Divine Intervention

When she stood up Sister Peggy could see that Cathleen was several inches taller than her and she guessed, from looking at her stomach, that she was about seven months pregnant. She led her through to a sitting room where a fire gave off a welcoming glow. Cathleen sat close to the grate and her wet feet began to steam gently in the warmth.

'How are you feeling, my dear? Nervous, I dare say.'

Cathleen smiled, not trusting herself to speak in case she started to cry, afraid that if she let even one tear out she would not be able to stop the torrent.

'You'll be fine; you have nothing to fear here. We're not going to be asking you any questions or making any judgements. You don't even have to use your real name if you would prefer not to. You will simply be "Cathleen" to us, if that is what you would prefer. Let's have a pot of tea.'

'I want to keep the baby,' Cathleen said once the tea had been brewed and she was beginning to thaw.

'Sure, you do,' Sister Peggy patted her hand reassuringly, 'and so you will. Let me tell you a little bit about who we are. We're all volunteers working here from the Legion of Mary. We like to be known as "Sisters", but we're not nuns. You won't find any of us walking about in black.' She gave a little chuckle at the thought. 'We all understand and respect the need for privacy and anonymity. If you want to keep your child a secret from the world, that is fine. You can live here while you prepare for the birth without anyone else knowing, and you and the child can stay afterwards as part of the community. If you have a boy you can stay until he is fourteen. If it is a girl then you can stay a little longer.'

'I have no money, Sister,' Cathleen confessed.

'I'm sure that's right, my dear. Everyone here is in the same boat. Once you have had the baby we would ask you to pay for your board and lodgings by going out to work. The child can be looked after here while you are out and provided with one free meal every day.'

'Who would take care of the child?' Cathleen asked, hardly able to believe her luck at finding such a refuge from the storm.

'Some of our single mothers do not go out to work, preferring to stay here during the day and look after their own children and those of the mothers who do go out to work. The working mothers pay the ones who care for their children from their wages.'

'I see,' Cathleen said, taking another sip of her tea and staring into the fire.

'We do have a few rules,' Sister Peggy went on. 'There can be no pets, no alcohol and no men in the hostel or in the grounds. There can be no exceptions to those rules.'

'I understand,' Cathleen replied.

'Shall I show you where you will be staying?' Sister Peggy asked, putting down her cup and saucer. 'Do you feel up to it?'

'Yes.' Cathleen stood up, despite her legs feeling a little wobbly, and followed Sister Peggy up a staircase.

'Until the baby is born you will be staying upstairs in this house,' Sister Peggy explained, opening a door into a large open dormitory. There were ten neatly made beds on each side of the room. Beside each of the twenty beds was a baby's cot. 'That is the only spare bed we have at the moment,' she said, pointing to the furthest bed, 'so that will be yours. The mothers are all having supper with their babies at the moment. In a few minutes they will all be coming up here and it won't be so peaceful. Let me show you the facilities.'

They went back downstairs and Sister Peggy showed her the open washrooms with three bathtubs and four toilet cubicles. 'All these walls could do with a lick of paint, for sure,' she said, seeing the expression on Cathleen's face as she looked around the shabby facilities, 'but everything is spotlessly clean.'

'It all looks just fine to me, Sister,' Cathleen said quickly. The whole of Regina Coeli felt to her like a sign from God, as if he had heard her prayers and decided to give her and her baby a second chance. She certainly didn't want to show even a hint of ingratitude in the face of such kindness.

'Over there,' Sister Peggy said, pointing through the window at a dark building across the grounds, 'is where the older children and their mothers live. I'll show you all around tomorrow, when it's light. We just have a little bit of paperwork to do now, so let's get that out of the way.'

Leading Cathleen into a tiny office space she handed her a form and a pen. 'If you can just register here, then we can get you settled in and introduce you to the others. You don't have to put your real name, just decide what you would like to be known as while you are with us.'

Cathleen stared at the form for a few moments before making a decision and carefully writing down the name 'Kay McCrea'. This was a new name for a new life. Cathleen Crea had disappeared from sight in this new world. Now it was just Kay McCrea and her unborn baby starting again, safe, secure, hidden from the outside world and the baby's existence a secret from everyone in her past life.

By the time she took her suitcase up to the dormitory all the other women were already there. Many of them seemed little more than children themselves as they chattered to one another, some of them bouncing babies on their hips while others were settling theirs down in their cots, trying to rock them to sleep despite the surrounding noise of voices and crying. Cathleen felt very grown up as she walked all the way down the middle of the room. None of them looked as if they had been taking care of themselves, their hair was lank and unwashed, and their pasty complexions in need of some healing rays of sunshine. Dark shadows ringed their tired eyes and none of them seemed to have the energy to smile. Cathleen felt almost maternal towards them. A few of them nodded to her as she made her way to her designated bed and she smiled in return, but none of them introduced themselves or spoke to her. She was happy with that, wanting nothing more than to lie down and sink into a deep, exhausted sleep.

She was pulled back to consciousness just before dawn by the cries of the first baby to stir and demand attention. One or two of the girls let out muffled curses as they tried to cling to sleep for as long as possible. Gradually they started up conversations as they lifted their babies out of their cots to feed them. Cathleen lay quiet, putting off the moment when she would have to talk to anyone.

'Good morning, ladies,' Sister Peggy said, moving through the dormitory to check that everyone was alright. 'Have you all met Kay, who joined us last night?'

Cathleen pulled herself up, her bump making it an awkward manoeuvre, aware that all the girls were now looking in her direction, still without smiles, or even much interest.

'I thought you might like a bit of a tour round the rest of the grounds this morning, Kay,' Sister Peggy said, 'to familiarise yourself with your new home.'

The other mothers were going about their business again, any vestige of curiosity they might have had about the newcomer apparently sated already. 'That would be nice,' Kay said. 'Thank you.'

After joining in the bustle of washing and having some breakfast, Cathleen and Sister Peggy ventured out into the bright winter sunshine. Many of the younger children had already burst out of the confines of the buildings and were running around the damp grass as happily as in any school playground anywhere in the world.

'This is Bridie,' Sister Peggy said, taking her to a woman with sad eyes. She was dressed all in traditional black, reminding Cathleen of her own mother and aunts. Cathleen guessed she was probably in her forties, her dark hair peppered with grey. She was watching over a group of about five children. It was a relief to see someone closer to her own age. 'She will be looking after your baby once you are ready to go out to work.'

'Do you have a child here yourself?' Cathleen asked, and the other woman's sad eyes lit up.

'My Joseph is five now,' she said proudly. 'He's just started going to school.'

'He's a lovely boy,' Sister Peggy said, 'a credit to you, Bridie. You can be sure your baby will be in safe hands, Kay.'

Without knowing any more about Bridie, Cathleen knew instinctively that that was true.

'Let me show you the chapel,' Sister Peggy said, leading Cathleen back into the house and up to a door next to the dormitory where she had slept. 'We have services on Sundays and Holy Days, which I hope you will join us for. The local priest leads them for us.'

Sister Peggy knelt down in front of the small altar, slowly crossed herself and whispered a prayer so quietly that Cathleen could not make out the words. After a few seconds she knelt down beside her, placed her palms together, lowered her head and closed her eyes. The two women remained there for several minutes, silently thanking the Lord for everything they had.

'Now,' Sister Peggy said, pulling herself to her feet, 'let me show you the rest of the hostel.'

The buildings, which had once been a British army barracks, were set in three acres of grounds. There were several blocks of forbidding, three-storey, grey stone buildings. Some parts were depressingly run-down, with broken windows and missing doors.

'It's enormous,' Cathleen said as they walked towards the first of the buildings.

'So it is,' Sister Peggy agreed. 'We don't fill every building, just a few of the more habitable floors. About a hundred and fifty women live here at any one time, usually with one child each. You will come across to one of these buildings once you are up and about after the birth.'

The wide open spaces on the inhabited floors had been turned into gigantic open dormitories, their stone walls and high ceilings blackened by smoke from the open fireplaces which burned Irish turf all day long and provided both warmth and basic cooking facilities, heating pans of water for washing and making tea. In these blocks there was only one toilet for every forty people, less if there was a blockage, and to make life easier many of the women kept their own enamel basins and chamber pots under their beds.

'Do they have no privacy?' Cathleen asked as she looked around.

'You soon get used to it, my dear.'

Sister Peggy introduced her to a few of the women, but none of them seemed particularly interested, doggedly carrying on with their daily chores.

'These are care mothers,' Sister Peggy explained, 'the ones like Bridie who are looking after the children for those who go out to work.'

Cathleen was relieved to think that it was going to be Bridie who was looking after her baby rather than any of these morose and silent girls.

'What happens on the other side of the perimeter walls?' Cathleen asked as they walked back to the red brick building.

'You mean outside our prison walls?' Sister Peggy said, her eyes twinkling mischievously. 'There's a wood mill over there. It's more like a warehouse for the timber. The Dublin bus depot is over there. That,' she said pointing to particularly dark and forbidding-looking building, 'is part of the Grange Gorman Mental Institution. We call them "the crazy ones", Lord bless their souls. The children are terrified of them. They think they're going to escape over the walls and attack them.'

'Oh,' Cathleen couldn't hide her own disquiet.

'Don't worry, my dear, they can't get out. They're locked up tight for their own good. Sometimes you will hear their screams in the night, poor creatures. You'll get used to the sounds. Would you like to go back to the dormitory now and rest? You look a little tired.'

Cathleen was grateful for a chance to lie down and think about everything she had seen. However sweet Sister Peggy had been to her, and however grateful she was to find a refuge from the cold, wet streets of Dublin, the idea of bringing her child into such a place brought a chill to her heart. She racked her brain to try to come up with a better solution to her predicament, but could think of nothing. There was one person who might help, of course, but she could never ask that of him. At least here she had a bed and food and they would let her keep the baby. She told herself she must be grateful for such mercies and that she would find a way to get out once the baby was born and she had regained her strength. If all these young girls could bear to live here, then surely to God she could manage it too.

Over the next two months she threw herself into the routine of the hostel, never leaving the premises and making herself as useful as possible with the other mothers in the kitchen or in the dormitories, gradually making some sort of contact with those who were willing to talk to her and spending as much time as she could with Bridie.

One evening, when the two of them were sharing a well-earned cigarette by the fireplace, Cathleen confided some of her fears about the impending birth.

Divine Intervention

'It'll be fine,' Bridie assured her. 'Before long you'll have a beautiful baby and that will make everything you've gone through worthwhile.'

'I'm not so worried about the birth, it's more the future that concerns me. I want so much more than this for my child and I don't know if I will be able to provide it.'

'Love the child, Kay, that's all you have to do. Material things don't matter. Children don't know the difference between expensive clothes and cheap ones.'

'In here they might not,' Cathleen agreed, 'but what about outside? There's a big heartless world out there where people will judge my child for not knowing who his father is.' Bridie reached over and squeezed her hand, not able to think of any words of comfort. 'Your Joseph is such a lovely boy,' Cathleen went on, 'so kind and considerate with the other children, and so helpful to you. You've brought him up well. Thank God it's going to be you looking after my child.' Bridie gave her friend's hand another squeeze, embarrassed by the praise.

Most of the other girls paid Cathleen little attention but there was one, Bridget Murphy, who seemed to have taken an instant dislike to her. Bridget was a big, fat bully of a woman who seemed to see Cathleen as some sort of challenge to her authority. Cathleen had seen her reducing one of the youngest girls to tears.

'Empty my piss pot,' Murphy had instructed the girl.

'Empty your own piss pot,' the girl retorted, her bravado undermined by the tremble in her voice.

'Empty my piss pot you fucking whore,' Murphy screamed as the girl scuttled tearfully from the room. Everyone else averted their eyes, not wanting to attract Murphy's vitriol onto them.

'And you …' Murphy screamed at Cathleen. 'You need to watch yourself around here with all your airs and graces. Who do you think you are? Think you're too good for the rest of us, you do.'

Cathleen didn't respond, and from then on Murphy referred to her as 'the Lady', a nickname that the others also started to use for her, but as a show of respect rather than a term of abuse.

On 25 February 1953, Cathleen gave birth to Francis Gordon – that's me – her secret child, and my life at Regina Coeli was under way.

Chapter Three

A New Start

In 1947, six years before I was born, Cathleen, my mother, was still living at home with her widowed mother and Mike, her unmarried older brother, in the village of Lucan. She was twenty-nine years old and unmarried and becoming increasingly fearful that if she didn't do something soon her situation was never going to change. She didn't necessarily feel the need to be married; she just didn't want to spend the rest of her life in Lucan, living exactly like her widowed mother before her.

Nothing had changed in those parts of rural Ireland in living memory. Farming was virtually the only industry, and poverty was considered normal for most of the population. Young people with any ambition were leaving the countryside and heading to Dublin or London, or even further afield, much as they had done for centuries. Cathleen's other brother, Christie, had left for work and marriage in Dublin. Her older sister, Lily, like most of her friends from school, had married and lived nearby, trapped in the same cycle of poverty as their parents and grandparents. Cathleen had a rare job in the village grocery store and what little money she earned she shared with her mother.

Christie wrote regularly to his sister from Dublin, regaling her with tales of the city and the wonders of fine restaurants, shops and theatres, as if hoping to tempt her to follow his example. Sometimes he would enclose money to help see them through the week. Cathleen devoured every detail that he wrote and talked often to her mother about following Christie to Dublin.

But her mother was always adamant. 'No, no, Cathleen, it wouldn't be right for a respectable single woman to live and work in Dublin. Your father would never have allowed it. You need to find a nice local man, like everyone else, and settle down here. You have no shortage of admirers and you know that.'

She did indeed know that, being proud of her long blonde hair and bright blue eyes, but none of the men who had shown an interest had been able to offer her the sort of life that she wanted. All they had to offer was more of the same. Then, in the late summer, she received an extra letter from Christie, addressed specifically to her.

Dear Cathleen,

Just a short letter to say I have a good friend who works in the Four Courts Hotel in the city centre. There is a job going for a chambermaid. The position comes with accommodation. You will need to come to Dublin next Thursday for an interview if you are interested. Take a chance …

All my love
Christie

A New Start

Cathleen felt her heart rate quicken at the thought of finally taking such a plunge into the unknown. Having Christie already living in the city meant that she wouldn't be completely alone, but it was still a giant step, and she knew exactly what her mother's reaction would be. She decided there was no point in telling her at this stage, since she might not even get the job and would then have worried her mother unnecessarily. So, for the first time in her life, she concocted a lie.

'Do you remember my friend, Mary?' she asked her mother casually that evening.

'Which Mary would that be then?' her mother asked.

'Oh, you remember,' she swept on, avoiding catching her mother's eyes in case she gave herself away. 'She's asked me to help her move house on Thursday, so I'll be taking the day off from work.'

She quickly changed the subject and spent the following few days rehearsing all the answers she would give to the questions that might come up at the job interview.

Although Lucan was less than fifteen kilometres from the centre of Dublin, it was a full day's walk along winding roads for most of the villagers, who couldn't afford to buy tickets on the bus or the train. With increasing excitement and a feeling that everything in her life was about to change, Cathleen bought herself a return ticket on the bus and made sure her best clothes were clean and pressed.

The Four Courts Hotel, which was attached to the city's court main buildings beside the mighty River Liffey, was the largest and best business hotel in Dublin. The grandeur of the old buildings took her breath away as she walked back and forth in the street outside until it was time to go in for her interview. She was committed now, and as good as a million miles away from everything that she was familiar with.

When the hotel manager looked up from his desk and was confronted with an attractive, personable 29-year-old woman with a dazzling smile, he didn't take long to make up his mind to offer her a job. Cathleen was considerably more mature and self-assured than the sort of girls who normally responded to advertisements for chambermaids.

'Can you start in a week?' he asked after a few formal questions.

'I can,' she heard herself reply, hardly able to believe that she had made such a momentous decision so quickly, and suddenly nervous about how she would break the news to her mother that not only was she moving to Dublin, but that she had also lied to her about what she was up to that day.

'Then I would be delighted to offer you the job,' the manager said.

As she walked out of the hotel Cathleen wanted to shout for joy. Despite her reservations about defying her mother, she felt she had suddenly been released from her past. It was as if a weight had been lifted from her shoulders and all the opportunities of the wider world had opened up to her. The decision to leave home had been made, and now all she had to do was go through with it. As she walked along the bustling streets, filled with prosperous, busy-looking people, she knew that she would never be able to go back to living in countryside, working in the same shop, marrying one of the men she had known all her life and bearing his children – ending up exactly like her poor mother.

Eager to share her excitement and in no hurry to go home, she met up with Christie, who was as overjoyed as she was at the thought of having his beloved little sister joining him in the big city.

'How are you going to tell Mammy?' Christie asked, once the initial euphoria had worn off.

'Lord knows, Christie,' she said,' she's never going to be happy about it.'

'You mustn't let her talk you out of it,' he said, 'otherwise you will never escape. There's a lot more to life than Lucan, Cathleen. This is a rare opportunity.'

'I know that,' she said, squeezing his hand, grateful to him for his support and understanding.' Don't worry. I won't let you down. I'm grateful to you for making me do this.'

She had every intention of confessing the whole story to her mother the following morning, but somehow there was never an appropriate moment, so she decided to wait till the next day, promising herself that she would sit her mother down and break the news gently. All the time she was practising how she would phrase it in order to make it sound like good news rather than bad. There would be the money that she would be able to send home for one thing, and better chances of meeting a good man in a big city. She found it increasingly hard to look her mother in the eyes and was obviously not behaving like herself.

'Is there something the matter, Cathleen?' her mother asked several times.

'No, Mammy,' she assured her, 'there's nothing the matter. Why should there be?'

She could tell that her mother was not convinced. Another day passed and she told herself that she really was going to have to come clean the next day.

'Mammy,' she said, when the moment finally arrived, 'there's something I need to tell you.'

'What would that be, Cathleen?' her mother asked, with a look in her eye which suggested she had been expecting something like this.

'I've got myself a job in Dublin,' Cathleen spoke quickly, as if jumping into cold water and wanting to get the shock over with quickly, 'starting next week.'

'What sort of job would that be?'

'In a hotel.'

'Oh no, Cathleen. If your father was alive today he would not allow such a thing to happen. You don't want to be going to a city all on your own. It's too dangerous. You wouldn't know a soul apart from Christie. Get that silly idea out of your head right now.'

'But it will mean that I will be able to send you more money,' Cathleen said. 'I'll be earning double what I earn in the shop.'

'You don't need to be doing a thing like that. We'll get by, just like we always do.'

'Mammy, this is my big chance to better myself. I'm not getting any younger and I have to do more with my life than just stay in the village. I want to be independent. I've never asked you for anything before, but I am asking this of you now. Let me work in Dublin. If things don't work out I promise to come straight back home.'

A New Start

Her mother fell silent. She knew her daughter well enough to know that she would not have taken such a decision lightly. The thought of losing her hurt terribly but she understood why she wanted to go. Deep inside she had known that this day would eventually come, and at least Christie would be in the city to watch over his little sister.

'I can see you've made your mind up,' she said eventually, 'and I don't want to be keeping you here against your will. I'll be praying for your safety.'

A week later Cathleen again put her best dress on and caught the early bus. This time she was carrying all her worldly possessions in a single case. As soon as she had arrived and left her case in the bedroom that she would be sharing with several other female employees, she was informed of her duties by the manager. Work would start at five in the morning with the preparation of breakfast for guests, followed by the making up and cleaning of the rooms. She would be expected to work long shifts, and the chores would sometimes be hard and demeaning but Cathleen didn't care. She felt so relieved to have finally escaped and to have been given a chance to better herself and her prospects for the future.

She found she had a lot in common with the other employees living in the hotel. All of them were single and when they talked about their pasts she learned that most came from small villages that sounded just like Lucan. On her days off she would visit her brother, who would show her the sights and take her home for tea with his wife, a local Dublin girl. They had already had a boy in the first year of their marriage and proceeded to have another child every year until they finally stopped at nine. Both inside the hotel and out in the streets, Cathleen was drinking in the possibilities of city life. She took in everything: the clothes that the women wore when they were out shopping or having lunch, the way the men behaved in the hotel restaurant, their manners and their clothes, their ready smiles and polished shoes. She gazed longingly into hairdressing salons and clothes shops, knowing that she couldn't afford any of it but dreaming that maybe one day it would be her turn. It was all a million miles from the simple lives led by the farming community she had grown up in, and she was happy that she had taken the plunge and opened herself up to the possibility of adventures.

Every few weeks she would purchase a return ticket to visit her mother or her sister, Lily, in order to share out her earnings and catch up on the local gossip.

'Have you met any fine Irish gentlemen at that hotel of yours, Cathleen?' her mother would inevitably enquire.

'No, Mammy,' she would reply. 'I told you; that's strictly against the rules.'

'Well,' her mother would sigh, 'sometimes you just have to bend the rules.'

'Would you like to come and watch some motorbike racing next week at Phoenix Park?' Christie asked over tea one day.

'I'm not really that interested in your motorbikes,' she laughed, 'you know that.'

'Oh, go on,' he said, 'it'll be a nice day out in the fresh air for you. It'll take your mind off work for a few hours. A friend of mine is racing.'

A New Start

'All right, then,' she said, knowing just how much her brother loved bikes, 'that would be lovely, thank you.'

The following week was a heat wave, and the racetrack was crowded with fans enjoying a day out. Cathleen managed to find Christie with the riders and the bikes, deep in conversation with his friend, who obviously knew even more about the subject than her brother. After a few moments Christie looked up from the bike he was studying and saw her standing there.

'Ah, you got here,' he said. 'This is Bill Lewis. Bill, this is my sister, Cathleen.'

Bill turned towards her and smiled. He was in his late thirties, she guessed, and had jet-black hair swept back from a handsome face. Slightly shorter than her, he wore a leather jacket and a cigarette dangled in the corner of his mouth. Something passed between them like a spark of electricity.

'So,' he said, taking the cigarette from his lips, 'you like bikes?'

'Not especially,' she mumbled shyly, 'it's my first time.'

'Well, maybe you should take a ride on one,' Bill grinned, a flirtatious glint in his eye. 'Maybe I should take you for a spin around the city one day. You could learn about bikes and see the sights at the same time.' He kept eye contact with her as he offered around his cigarettes.

The men then returned to talking about bikes and Cathleen listened and watched. She liked this polite, confident man. He was very different to the young men she had met in the village, more mature but reserved at the same time, a proper man. He looked a bit like Clark Gable, who she had fallen in love with as a girl when she was taken to see *Gone with the Wind*. He even had the same moustache.

Several times through the afternoon she caught him looking at her, and when he won a couple of races but still behaved so quietly and modestly she found herself genuinely excited for him. High on his success, Bill insisted that Christie and Cathleen joined him in the pub at the end of the day's racing.

'He likes you,' Christie told his sister as Bill went up to order another round of drinks.

'Don't be daft,' she said, digging a sharp elbow into her brother's ribs but unable to keep a blush of pleasure from rising into her cheeks.

'Seriously. He asked if I would mind if he asked you out.'

'And what did you say to that, Christie Crea?'

'I warned him you were an independent woman and wished him the best of luck!'

'Christie!' she said with mock anger, already knowing that if Bill did ask her out she would be saying yes.

Bill then embarked on a campaign to woo her, turning up at the hotel almost every day at times when he knew she might be free for a chat and a cigarette. He was always dapper in a suit and tie and every time he wanted to know when she would be free for him to take her on a spin round the city. She held out for a while, even though she wanted nothing more than to spend more time alone with this man, and eventually she gave in.

'All right then,' she said, 'how about next Wednesday afternoon?' She could see from his face that he was genuinely delighted, and surprised to have finally convinced her.

A New Start

'That's settled then,' he said, 'Wednesday it is. We'll go for a spin and then I'll take you to O'Brien's – my favourite pub.'

When he turned up on the dot of midday on the following Wednesday, several of Cathleen's colleagues made sure they were there to tease her as she climbed on the back of the bike for the first time, wearing her one and only best dress. The moment she was settled and had her arms around his waist, her face close to the soft, sweet-smelling leather of his biking jacket, Bill twisted the throttle and the bike roared off down the street. Cathleen would have preferred to slow down and enjoy the ride, and when they eventually pulled up outside O'Brien's and dismounted, her legs felt decidedly wobbly. Bill, it seemed, had literally swept her off her feet.

As they walked into the smoky bar the room fell silent, all heads turning towards them, and Cathleen realised she was the only woman there. This was not the sort of pub that respectable women would normally be seen in. There was a moment of awkwardness among the men, which Bill appeared not to notice, and some of the other drinkers nodded towards Bill as if they knew him well.

'What would you like to drink?' he asked as they made their way to bar.

'I'll have a gin and tonic,' she replied, surprising herself.

They sat at a corner table and chatted while Bill downed three pints of Guinness. Mostly he talked about motorbikes and his Alsatian, Trigger, which seemed to be the two main loves of his life. Cathleen could see that he was entirely at home and comfortable in the bar, and she liked the fact that he was willing to share his world with her. That didn't mean, however, that she wanted to spend the rest of the day in a drinking men's bar, which seemed to be the way things were going if she left them up to Bill.

'Shall we go and see a film?' Cathleen asked.

'A film?' Bill said, obviously surprised.

She was coming to realise that he was not a man who had been on many dates before, which she thought was charming. She could see that he had no idea what a girl might be wanting to do. From the little experience she had of men – mainly her brothers – she half expected him to say no.

'Why not?' he said after a moment's thought. 'Let's do that.'

She had noticed that there was a Clark Gable film on and teased Bill that she had chosen it because the star reminded her of him.

'Do you think so?' he said, staring closely at the poster outside, obviously pleased by the compliment. 'Do you think there's a resemblance?'

Cathleen laughed. 'Yes there is, but perhaps I shouldn't have told you. I think you're a bit of a vain man, Bill Lewis.'

'Oh no,' he grinned, steering her firmly inside the picture house, 'not at all.' But she noticed him examining his own reflection in the glass as they queued at the ticket booth.

She liked the way he had agreed so easily to do what she wanted, even though she could tell he was not particularly interested in films himself. He was gentle and mild-mannered and she liked that too. There was a fondness growing inside her which she had never experienced before, and she found herself looking forward more and more acutely to his visits to the hotel and to their days out together.

A New Start

She learned that he was actually fifteen years older than her, much more than she had imagined, although he didn't look it, but had never been married. She doubted if he had even had a serious girlfriend before, which she found charming. He was already something of a confirmed bachelor in his ways, but he was always eager to please her if she let him know how. As the weeks passed she had a feeling that he had started to model himself on Clark Gable in his clothes and hairstyle, and she hoped that he was doing that in order to impress her. She noticed that he couldn't pass a mirror or a piece of glass without glancing into it.

When he eventually kissed her, having had enough drinks to steel his courage, it was so gentle and right that she felt sure they would be together for ever.

They often went back to the picture house, and sometimes they would ride out into the Wicklow Mountains on the bike, posing as a married couple for the benefit of the managements in the small hotels and bed and breakfasts they stayed in. As they sat together in pubs or listened to the live ceilidh bands that played everywhere in those days, or gazed out over the beautiful hills and meadows of the Irish countryside they started to talk about what a future together might be like. The more they got to know about one another the more they felt they had in common, with a shared outlook on life in almost everything. Being together was just so easy. Now she understood why she had never been interested in the farm boys back home. She just knew she was meant to be with this man in every way.

Both, however, were aware that there was one major obstacle they were going to have to face up to sooner or later.

Bill was a Protestant and Cathleen was a Catholic – and this was Ireland, where such a difference mattered more than possibly anywhere else in the world. Between them lay a chasm of historical bitterness and division so wide and so deep that most ordinary people no longer even understood or questioned why it was there; they merely believed that those who lay on the other side were to be avoided at all costs.

These religious differences didn't seem like a problem to either Bill or Cathleen personally, who were both happy for the other to belong to a different faith since they believed in all the same fundamental things in life. But both of them also knew that it was going to be an enormous problem if they ever got to the stage of telling their families about their relationship.

'My mother won't like it,' Cathleen admitted as they lay in one another's arms during one of their outings into the mountains, 'but I'm sure we can win her round eventually. I'm sure we can win them all round when they see how we feel about each other.'

'You've not met my sisters,' he said with a sad shake of his head. 'They will be unmovable on something like this.'

But by that time it was too late, because both Bill and Cathleen had fallen deeply in love and knew that whatever their families might say about the religious differences, they wanted to spend their lives together.

Chapter Four
Decision Time

Bill was the second youngest in a family of four boys and four girls. Their father had set up a business delivering wood to factories in Dublin, using a horse and cart. He was proud of being his own boss and had done well enough to buy a house in the south side of Dublin. They had become close to being a middle-class family and aspired to continue their social rise, particularly the girls.

Bill had started out wanting to be a surgeon, but his father's finances did not stretch quite far enough to provide the sort of education needed for such a career and an alternative had to be found. Bill's father knew that his son was good with his hands and gifted at making things. During his rounds delivering wood to local factories he got to know many of the joinery companies. Eventually he recommended Bill to a well-known company as an apprentice joiner, and after five years of training and hard work Bill became a master-craftsman.

Although Cathleen and Bill's families were very different, there were similarities in the situations they eventually found themselves in. Bill was not entrepreneurial, and when his father died he felt he had a duty to stay at home with his mother and four sisters since his brothers had all joined the British Army to fight in the war and later stayed in England in search of work. Bill had wanted to join the air force but his mother, frightened that she might lose all her sons in battle, asked him to remain behind and he lacked the ambition to argue about it.

The two elder sisters, Susie and Annie, were more business-minded and assertive than their peaceful brother, and looked after the family business, believing Bill to be too young for such responsibilities. The two younger sisters, Jenny and Sara, also had considerable influence over Bill, insisting that he stay at his job and concentrate on his career as a joiner. Being the sort of man who liked a quiet and comfortable life, he had until then gone along with whatever they told him, allowing them to cater for all his everyday needs in return for bringing in good wages and living at home. Jenny was a seamstress and Sara worked in a doctor's surgery.

When Bill met Cathleen, however, at the age of forty-five, his sisters noticed that their brother had changed, although they had no idea why that might be. He went out more often and spent more time in front of the mirror checking his appearance. There seemed to be a new spring in his step. Cathleen had also encouraged him to set up his own business, something he had never got round to doing before. The workshop was an instant success but no one in his family realised that the idea had come from someone else.

Decision Time

'You got yourself a girlfriend, Bill?' they joked, but he just grinned and shook his head. He was not yet ready to face the anger that would inevitably erupt once they found out the truth.

Visitors to Ireland were often fooled by the apparent friendliness and hospitality of the people they met. They were lulled into an impression that it was a romantic land filled with a mellow people who knew how to enjoy themselves in the pub and how to tell a good story. What they didn't always see was the darker side, where religion played a crucial role in both uniting and dividing communities. Virtually everyone went to church, whether they personally believed in God or not, and most people still clung to a certainty that whatever they had been told when they were young by priests and teachers and parents was the absolute truth. The vast majority of the population in Southern Ireland were Catholic, making a minority like the Protestants all the more defensive of their faith. We lived alongside each other. We spoke the same language, but a surname could instantly reveal that someone came from the other side of the chasm formed by hundreds of years of hatred and suspicion.

Neither Cathleen nor Bill felt comfortable with the religions they had been born into. Cathleen went to church once a week because that was what she had always done, but she found Catholicism oppressive and riddled with rules about how to avoid going to hell. Everyone seemed obsessed with sin and guilt. Bill was from a Protestant family but had even less time for his Church, while Catholicism seemed ridiculous to him. Neither of them allowed their religions to stop them going away for romantic weekends together in the Wicklow Mountains. It was inevitable that such out-of-character behaviour would arouse Bill's sisters' suspicions.

'Where do you keep disappearing off to then?' they wanted to know.

'Just travelling around on the bike,' he lied.

'With who?'

'Other bikers, friends.'

Nothing the sisters could say would persuade him to give even the slightest clue as to what he got up to when he was outside the house.

There was no question in either Bill or Cathleen's minds when they were together that their relationship was serious, but they also both knew that it could not progress any further until they confessed to their respective families. For two years they managed to convince themselves that it was 'too early' to take such a drastic and potentially painful step and they continued their relationship in secret, meeting in pubs, going to the picture house and taking the bike up into the mountains for the occasional nights away.

The first person Bill confided in was his brother Eddie, who had moved to England and was working as a joiner on the film sets. 'I've met a wonderful woman,' Bill wrote, 'and she has encouraged me to set up my own workshop, which has turned out to be very successful. The problem is that she is from a Catholic family and I'm not sure how to break the news to our mother and sisters.'

Eddie wrote back immediately, delighted to hear that his brother had finally met someone but sharing his concerns. 'I can hardly imagine them welcoming a Catholic into the family with open arms. I fear that Susie and Annie may be particularly venomous when they find out. If I were you I would break the news to our mother first and the sisters later. Take it in stages to ease the pain. If you want a future with this lady then there is no escaping what you have to do.'

Bill knew that Eddie was right and he sat his mother down at her kitchen table the next day. She was a tiny slip of a woman who had lived all her life in Dublin and went on to reach the great age of ninety-five despite endless health scares. He started by opening up his heart to her.

'I've met the most wonderful woman,' he said and she clapped her labour-reddened hands together in excitement at the news.

'Oh, Bill, that is the best news possible. What is she like, this wonderful woman?'

'She is very beautiful, with blonde hair and blue eyes. We get on so well. We never argue. She's a hard worker. She has a job in a hotel. Her brother is a good friend of mine.'

'How long has this been going on?'

'Two years.'

'Two years, Bill? Why on earth have you kept her a secret all this time?'

'Well, you know me, Mammy,' he grinned. 'I didn't want everyone making a fuss.'

'I know you like your privacy, son, but two years is a little extreme, don't you think? Even for you.'

'Perhaps. But now I've gone and told you.'

'Ah, we all knew something was going on. We guessed it was a woman. I am so happy for your, darling Bill.' She placed her hands around his face and pulled him towards her, kissing him on the forehead. 'So, when can I meet this lovely woman?'

'Soon,' he said, 'but it has to be the right time …'

At that moment Susie and Annie entered the room and immediately saw from the expression on their mother's face that something momentous was going on.

'Bill has met a woman,' their mother blurted out, 'just as we suspected. They've been going out for two years.'

'Two years?' Susie said. 'She must be a very special girl for you to have wanted to keep her to yourself for so long.'

'She is very special,' Bill smiled shyly, 'that's for sure.'

'Who's the lucky lady?' Annie asked. 'Why haven't we met her before?'

Bill could see that as the news sunk in their suspicions were rising to the surface. He lowered his eyes to the table and wished he hadn't let the cat out of the bag. Things were now running out of control. This was not how he had planned it. All he wanted now was to escape to the pub where no one would ever ask you awkward personal questions.

'So,' Annie insisted, 'what's her name?'

Bill remained silent for a few moments and the tension in the room rose. 'Cathleen,' he mumbled eventually.

'Cathleen?' Susie said. 'Cathleen who? For goodness sake stop being so coy, Bill!'

'Cathleen Crae,' Bill growled, still not taking his eyes off the table.

It was like a bomb had gone off in the room. Everyone there knew that Crae could only be a Catholic name. No one spoke as they took in the enormity of what they were being told. Bill waited without raising his eyes, not wanting to see the expressions on their faces.

Annie eventually broke the silence. 'Surely you're not serious about a Catholic, Bill?'

Bill said nothing. He had known that they would disapprove, but deep inside he had allowed himself to hope that they would be pleased for him all the same, that they would wish him luck despite their reservations. From the continuing silence he knew that they were never going to come round to approving of a mixed relationship. They were making it perfectly clear that it was a matter of principle and once they had taken that stand there would be no going back. He dreaded having to go to Cathleen and confess that he was never going to be able to get his family to accept her. He knew she would be devastated by the news and the implications it carried for their future life together.

Without saying another word he stood up and left the house, walking to the pub to drown his sorrows among his male friends. As the Guinness started to give him renewed strength he felt his spirits rise. Maybe it was just a knee-jerk reaction. Maybe once they had thought about it his sisters would realise that Cathleen made him happy and that that was more important than the religion that she happened to be born into. He went on drinking until late; wanting to be sure everyone would be asleep by the time he got home.

The moment he woke up sober the next morning he knew that they had been false hopes. The atmosphere in the house was tense and heavy, as if there was an impending storm. His sisters kept on niggling at him in the following days, refusing to allow him to escape from the drama that he had created at the heart of the family. He ignored them for as long as he could, but eventually the storm broke and the shouting started in earnest. Things were said that could never be taken back and Bill was terrified that it would all lead to him losing Cathleen, the only person he now wanted in his life. If he had to choose between her and his family he had no doubt what his choice would be, but would Cathleen be willing to attach herself to a man who had alienated his whole family, including his mother? Would she be willing to spend her life with a man knowing that his family despised her and would never allow her over the threshold of their home?

The easiest way for him to avoid the pain and worry was to go to the pub and stand at a bar with his friends, buying round after round and allowing the difficulties of the world outside to drift on without him. He found visiting Cathleen at the hotel increasingly hard, because he could see that she wanted to talk about their future and about their family problems and he just didn't want to have to break the news that he was never going to win his mother and sisters over. He knew he should grasp the nettle and be honest and open with her, but he couldn't bear the thought of her telling him that there was no future for them. Instead he told Cathleen that the reason he wasn't getting to see her so much was because of pressures of work, but she wasn't fooled by such a transparent lie. When he hadn't shown up for a week she went out looking for him. It wasn't hard to find him, propping up the bar in O'Brien's.

'Hello, Bill,' she said, trying to pretend that it was the most natural thing in the world for a young woman to walk into a

Decision Time

bar like this on her own. 'I was worried about you. You haven't been around for a while.'

Recovering from the shock of seeing her, Bill tried to straighten up but was unable to stop himself from swaying. Cathleen pretended not to notice.

'Cathleen, my dear,' he said, her name slurring on his tongue, 'let me get you a drink.'

'I'll have a gin and tonic, Bill,' she said. 'Can we sit down?'

Once they were sitting at a table she stayed quiet and waited for him to start talking. Her patience paid off and bit by bit he told her what had happened when he had broken the news of the relationship at home. The more he talked about his sisters, the angrier and the more frustrated he became, banging his glass down on the table after every sip.

'Bill,' Cathleen said eventually, putting a cool hand on top of his and looking deep into his troubled eyes, 'do you truly want us to be together?'

'Yes, I do, Cathleen,' he said and she knew he was speaking from the heart.

'If you do, then we can make this work,' she went on, calmly, like a mother calming a fretful child. 'We'll work on them.'

Bill stared at her but said nothing. He knew that someone as sweet and reasonable as Cathleen would never be able to understand the depth of his sisters' prejudices and the strength of their bitterness. They could 'work on them' for a hundred years and they would never change their minds. Of that he was quite certain.

'And I have some good news,' she continued. 'My mammy has invited you over for lunch. She wants to meet this man that I speak so highly of.'

'Have you told her that I'm not a Catholic?' he asked.

'She guessed when I told her your surname was Lewis.'

'What did she say?'

'She thought from the name you must be Jewish.' They both laughed.

'So how did she react when she found out the truth?' he asked.

'She was shocked, I'm not going to lie to you, and she certainly didn't approve, but I told her she had to meet you. I told her you are an incredibly fine and good man. I told her how much she would like you. "I didn't set out to meet a Protestant." I told her. "It just happened that way." So, she said she would be willing to meet you, to give you a chance.'

Even through the haze of alcohol Bill was touched by Cathleen's words and by the fact that she had been willing to stand up for him and for their relationship. It seemed that there might be hope for them as a couple after all.

Even though he arrived in Lucan a little late, Bill's charm worked its magic on Cathleen's mother and her brother, Mike. The two men instantly fell to talking about motorbikes, while the lunch of bacon and cabbage was being prepared. Cathleen sat back and watched in wonder as Bill chatted and joked with her mother over the meal as if he had known her all his life, loving him all the more for his ability to make the old woman laugh out loud. After lunch the two of them continued to talk while they enjoyed a cigarette, sending Mike and Cathleen out for a walk in the garden.

'I like your Bill very much,' her mother whispered as they prepared to take their leave and Bill was revving up the bike, 'but there's still the problem of him not being a Catholic.'

Decision Time

Cathleen kissed her mother goodbye and ran to jump on the back of the motorbike without saying anything else. At least they had made some progress and she didn't want to say anything on the spur of the moment which might jeopardise the feeling of goodwill that enveloped them all as they waved and sped off down the road.

Bill came out to Lucan to visit a couple more times. Encouraged by the reception he received from all Cathleen's family members, he steeled himself to face his own family once and for all and formally announce that he intended to marry Cathleen and to ask them to give their blessing. He asked his brothers for advice, and all of them agreed that the women needed to meet Cathleen before things got completely out of hand and relationships broke down irrevocably. Both Susie and Annie had become preoccupied with their own wedding plans and Bill hoped that they would have mellowed since the first shock of the news. Once they were married they would both be moving out of the family home anyway and would be less affected by anything he might choose to do with his life. It did not take long for him to realise he had completely misjudged the situation.

'You mean you are still going out with this woman?' Annie demanded, obviously horrified.

'Yes, of course. We intend to marry.'

'Have you taken leave of your senses?' Susie said. 'We assumed you had seen the error of your ways and it had all cooled down.'

'No, no,' he assured them, 'quite the opposite. We intend to marry.'

'She'll only be after your money,' Annie said. 'That's all she'll be wanting.'

'I would like to bring Cathleen to meet you. I am sure that if you got to know her you would like her and it would put your mind at rest about her motives.'

'We don't want any Catholics in this house,' the sisters said, almost in unison. 'We have absolutely no intention of meeting this woman.'

Although Cathleen's family liked Bill immensely, they didn't want the couple to marry either.

They could see no way out of their predicament. Neither of them felt able to convert to the other's religion, knowing it would alienate them for ever from their families, and so they remained trapped in a sort of limbo, wanting to be together but not quite able to abandon their families completely. The strain inevitably took its toll on their relationship, making them argue even though both of them wanted the same things. Bill believed he had no future in Ireland without Cathleen at his side and began to lose interest in his business. It was as if he was deliberately cutting all his ties to his homeland. When, on top of all the ill-feeling with his sisters, his beloved dog, Trigger, died of old age, he couldn't see any point in staying.

Both aware that they had reached a point where a decision had to be made they took the bike for one last trip out into the Wicklow Mountains. Stopping at a favourite spot they sat in silence for a while, just staring at the view and listening to the birdsong, neither of them wanting to say the things that they both knew needed to be said. Eventually Bill broke the silence.

Decision Time

'It's not working, Cathleen,' he said. 'We're not working. The fighting and shouting – everything's going wrong.'

'I'm sorry, Bill,' she said, taking his hand. 'I don't know how it's got so bad. I just don't seem to be able to help it.'

He put his arm around her shoulders and pulled her to him, holding her so tightly she could hardly breathe.

'We have to leave Ireland, Cathleen,' he said. 'We have to leave now if we want to make this work.'

She buried her face in his chest, not wanting to look at him and not wanting to speak, torn in half by her desire to be with him and her fear of cutting herself off from her family and heading into the unknown. Moving fifteen kilometres from Lucan to Dublin had been a big enough step; she wasn't sure how her mother would cope if she announced she was planning to leave the country altogether, and with a Protestant.

Taking her silence to be agreement, Bill wrote to his brother Eddie about finding work in London. Eddie wrote back to tell him that he knew of a job as a joiner in the film company where he worked.

'It can be yours if you want it,' he wrote.

Bill felt a new surge of optimism about the future. He was happy to put all the feuding and arguing behind him. He was so angry with his sisters that he didn't care if he never saw them again. As long as he had Cathleen by his side he knew he would be happy. He would also have Eddie in London to help him get settled. He immediately wrote back, accepting the job, committing himself to making the break from Ireland, and went to see Cathleen to tell her what he had decided.

'Come to England with me,' he said, 'and then we can live together.'

'You mean live in sin?' she said, feeling overwhelmed at the prospect of defying everything she had ever been taught to believe in.

'We can get married,' he said, 'once we're settled.'

'Oh, I don't know, Bill,' she said. 'I don't know if I could just up and leave my family. Mammy is getting old now and frail. I don't think she will be with us that much longer.'

'Just forget about families,' Bill urged her, terrified that she was slipping away from him, 'let's just focus on ourselves for once. We've both waited long enough for this chance. The film company pays good money. We can make a new life in London. Please come with me.'

'I need time to think. You can't just spring this on me and expect me to decide there and then.'

'OK.' He held up his hands in surrender. 'Take as much time as you need. I'm not leaving for several days.'

Taking her in his arms he kissed her and held her tightly. There was a rumble of thunder and rain started to fall on them as they clung together, neither wanting to be the first to let go.

As Cathleen lay in bed that night she couldn't sleep. Bill's words kept going round and round in her head. She wanted so much to find the courage to just throw up everything and board the boat to England with him, but her mother's sad face kept haunting her. Would her mother ever forgive her if she did such a thing? The idea of embarking on an adventure into the unknown had seemed exciting when Bill first suggested it, but in the chilly small hours of the morning it

Decision Time

felt different. Not knowing where they would live, how she would find a job and whether Bill would be able to support her all seemed like insurmountable potential problems.

After several days with virtually no sleep the time had come to make the final decision. Bill came to see her.

'I've thought about it a lot,' she said. 'It isn't a decision I would ever take lightly because there are too many people involved, my family as well as you and me.'

'I understand,' he said. 'So, what have you decided?'

'I think you should travel to England first. It will be easier for you to get settled if you are on your own, not having to worry about me and whether I am happy.' He opened his mouth to protest but she placed her finger on his lips to stop him. 'Then, when you are settled and established I can follow.'

He looked stunned. She could see that he had been expecting her to say yes and his disappointment was obvious.

'We can write to one another every day,' she said.

'I think you're making a mistake,' he said once she had eventually fallen silent. 'I've got a job to go to. I will be perfectly able to support you. We can stay with my brother, Eddie, and his wife until we find a place of our own ...'

'I'm sorry,' she said. 'I just can't leave without my mother's approval. I know the guilt would eat away at me and I would start to resent you for it. And I am not as brave as you; I need the security of a job and knowing where I am going to be sleeping at night.'

Bill opened his mouth to protest again.

'I've decided, Bill. I'll not be changing my mind.'

On the day that the boat departed Cathleen went down to the port to see him off. Bill looked as smart as he always did in his suit and tie, carrying two suitcases, one containing the tools of his trade and the other all his clothes and possessions. She clung on to him, unable to speak for the sobs that wracked her whole body. 'I'll write every day,' he promised. 'I love you.'

Finally she was forced to let him go. As he joined the back of the crowd walking up the ramp he turned to wave. 'See you in London,' he called back before disappearing into the boat.

Chapter Five
Back to the Beginning

I stood outside the Regina Coeli Hostel with Patrick's map clutched in my hand for at least twenty minutes, maybe more, trying to work out what I wanted to do next. What was I hoping to achieve here? Was I going to be able to deal with the emotions which I could already feel welling up inside me?

Half of me wanted to run into the building like I used to when I was a small boy, and half of me could hear my mother's voice inside my head, telling me that we were *never* going to 'go back' and that I must put all such thoughts out of my mind. Had I betrayed her by even coming to look for the place?

The more I stared at the shabby buildings and the overgrown gardens, the more I remembered and the more torn I felt. Part of me was excited at the thought of going back to explore my distant childhood, but the other part was worried that I would be disappointed, disillusioned, or that my memories might prove to be false. Perhaps the past wasn't quite the paradise that I had believed it to be. There must have been a reason why Mammy forbade me to even think of coming back.

It was fifty years since I had stood on this spot, but it was beginning to feel like it was only yesterday. The difference was that now, looking through adult eyes, I could imagine just how frightening it must have been for my mother when she knocked on the door for the first time with her 'terrible secret' growing inside her.

I noticed that the front door was standing ajar but no one seemed to be coming in or out. A kind of silence hung over the place. It was certainly no longer the buzzing hive of activity that I remembered. Taking a deep breath, I pushed my doubts aside, walked up the path and pressed the bell. I couldn't hear any ringing but I waited a few more minutes, with my heart thumping in my ears, before sticking my head in and calling out, 'Hello? Anyone there?'

A woman who I guessed must be in her sixties appeared through an internal door which I remembered led to a small office. 'Good afternoon, sir,' she said politely. 'Can I help you at all?'

'Hello,' I replied, as nervous as a naughty small boy who had missed a curfew. 'Good afternoon. I'm looking for Regina Coeli ... Is this it?'

'Yes, sir,' she smiled at me kindly as if realising that I needed encouragement and gentle handling. 'My name is Mary, would you like to come in?'

I accepted the invitation and followed her into the office. Everything in the room looked so familiar; everywhere I looked another memory was triggered.

Back to the Beginning

'This was my childhood home,' I blurted. 'I've been searching for it for a long time, with no success at all. I feel a bit like I have just struck gold.'

She smiled at me, nodding her understanding and looking entirely unsurprised, as if she had heard this story a thousand times before.

'It's God's will that you are here now,' she said quietly, gesturing for me to sit down.

'I want to find out more about Regina Coeli and the mothers and children who lived here at the same time that I did,' I said. 'I'm trying to find details about the people here at that time.'

'When would we be talking about?' Mary asked.

'The 1950s. I left in 1962.'

'Ah, well then, I was here in the sixties, but I was very young, no more than a teenager myself.'

I did a quick mental calculation and realised that meant she must be in her seventies.

'But we kept no records of the women who came here,' she continued. 'That was the policy, to allow them to have a private life. They could go under whatever name they chose and we never asked any questions. It was a refuge for the poor girls who wanted to keep their babies, who didn't want to get taken into the Magdalene Laundries and have their babies taken away from them.'

This was the second time the subject of the Magdalene Laundries had come up that day. It seemed they still weighed heavily on the consciences of Dubliners.

'Tell me your name,' she said.

'Gordon Lewis.'

'Lewis,' she mused. 'Now, let me think …'

'My mammy's name was Kay McCrea, but she was originally Cathleen Crea …'

'McCrea.' She looked at me intently. 'Now that does sound familiar, but it was a very long time ago. I've just brewed a pot of tea, would you join me in a cup?'

'That would be very welcome, thank you.'

As she poured the tea she started to reminisce fondly about her early days. 'So many memories,' she said. 'Over the years I met some lovely women. But what do you want to know about Regina Coeli, Gordon? You must tell me what you remember about living here and I'll do my very best to fill in the gaps.'

'The earliest memory I have,' I said, taking the cup from her, 'is of pushing a pram around the grounds. I can't have been more than three years old. There were always prams to play with in the hostel because everyone had babies. We had no real toys but it never bothered us, we just played with whatever came to hand. We could be very inventive with sticks or paper bags, and occasionally there would be the highlight of a live mouse or rat, which we would hunt down with our sticks, the older boys in the lead and the rest of us following behind in a state of great excitement. We were like a pack of wild dogs. There was a constant supply of rats. I used to be frightened that if we managed to corner one it would attack me. The older boys loved to tell us stories about that sort of thing. The danger made it all the more exciting.'

Mary nodded her agreement, sitting down opposite and giving me her full attention as if she were just as eager to visit the past as I was.

Back to the Beginning

'Back then I was known as Francis, not Gordon,' I went on. 'I was blissfully ignorant about the outside world, not a care in the world. I remember everyone in the hostel was a woman or a child, although there was one man, just one, who would visit from time to time. He was a kind old gentleman called Frank. Everybody knew him.'

'Ah, that will have been Frank Duff,' Mary nodded. 'It was he who made it possible for Regina Coeli to exist at all. He founded the Legion of Mary. His idea was that Catholic men and women could help single mothers without judging them. He set up this hostel as a refuge for single mothers who wanted to keep their babies. He believed passionately that it was better for children to stay with their mothers rather than being adopted by strangers. You should be grateful to him. God was looking over you and your mother.'

'Then there were the priests who came to call. The "men in black", the women used to call them. They didn't like them so much; felt they were looking down their noses at them, judging them.' Mary didn't comment, merely sipping her tea, so I continued. 'I had two mammies, my own and my caretaker mammy. She was called Bridie and she would look after me when Mammy went to work. I always knew that both of them loved me dearly.'

'You were lucky to have two loving mothers,' Mary said, 'when so many in the world go through life without a mother at all.'

'Oh, I know that,' I assured her. 'I know just how lucky I was. My mammy got to know Bridie before I was even born, and from that moment onwards she would never allow any of the other mothers to care for me. She and Bridie were best friends.'

'You say her name was Bridie?' Mary asked, as if still trying to put the pieces of a jigsaw together in her head.

'Yes. I remember her as being a kind and gentle soul. She had a son called Joseph, who was like a big brother to me as well as a close friend. Bridie had her own tragic story to tell as to how she ended up here. I think she came from a remote part of the west of Ireland and fell pregnant after being raped by a distant relative.'

Mary tutted; it was more a sound of sympathy than of disapproval. No doubt she had heard many such stories in her years at the hostel.

'Her family did not believe her story and disowned her, throwing her out onto the streets, alone and pregnant. She was lucky to end up here.'

'She was indeed,' Mary agreed. 'In those days many of those poor girls ended up in brothels or died in the backstreet abortion clinics. It would have been a long journey for her to get here in those days.'

Bridie was a typical young girl from the country, only seventeen years old when she arrived in Dublin, lost and alone. With nowhere else to go, she went into a church to rest and to pray. There she met a nun who took pity on her and directed her to Regina Coeli. From the first day she crossed the hostel's threshold she never left, at least not in the years I knew her. She became virtually a recluse, dedicating her life to being a caretaker mother to children like me, while bringing up her own son at the same time.

Back to the Beginning

'I remember she never wore anything but black,' I said. 'To me my mammy always looked young and beautiful, but poor, lovable Bridie always looked old. She had a beautiful heart, though. Kind to everyone, especially to me, and she treated me like I was her own son.'

From the moment I was born my life revolved around Regina Coeli. It was my world. I was forbidden to go past the two big wooden gates or ever to try to leave the grounds. These golden rules were drummed into me from the moment I could speak and understand. All the children seemed to have been given the same rules by their mothers. As youngsters we just knew that whatever lay outside the walls was frightening, perhaps because that had been the experience of most of the mothers who had taken refuge there, and perhaps many of the helpers as well. It was a hard life for women in Ireland in those times, particularly women who had 'sinned'.

The restrictions didn't bother me in the least. The hostel grounds seemed like paradise. There was everything I could ever want; lots of attention from mothers, plenty of other children to play with and acres of danger-free space to run around in. There was regular food, although I always wanted more.

'More food again, Francis?' Bridie would tut as I tugged at her skirt in search of a second helping. 'You cheeky devil.'

To me it was just one big extended family, with people looking out for one another and sharing what little they had. They were my family.

At the weekends Mammy would always spoil me with sweets or biscuits, bought with her Friday wage packet from the restaurant where she worked as a waitress. I was known as 'the one with the sweets' and I was always happy to share my good luck around. I was also considered the best dressed child there. Mammy made sure that I never wore second-hand clothes unlike most of the other children, and she would pass them on the moment I grew out of them. I loved being told how 'cute' and 'adorable' I was by the other mothers, and I was fast becoming the most talkative child in the hostel.

'You have the sweetest of faces, Francis McCrea,' the women would say, unable to resist ruffling my fine, light mop of curly hair. 'Just the kind of beautiful child any mother would want.'

I think what they liked most about me was that I talked to them like another adult, almost from the start. I could be a difficult child as well; stubborn and single-minded when I wanted something.

In my early days the routine nearly always started the same way. I would always seem to be the last in the dormitory to wake up and I would start by sitting up and looking around to see who else was about. Mammy, and the other mothers who worked outside the hostel, would have gone hours before, and the ones who didn't share their beds with their small children would have left their beds neatly made. I could rely on Bridie always to be there, keeping an eye on me. The older children would be getting washed and ready for school. I would sit up in the bed, which I still shared with Mammy, watching everyone bustling around me. All of us small ones had to wait for permission to get up.

Back to the Beginning

Once the schoolchildren had all left we leaped out of bed, always brimming with energy, and made use of the enamel chamberpots, or 'poo-pots', as we called them, which lived under our beds, all of us sitting in a line doing our business and chattering away. There was no sense of embarrassment about anything to do with nudity or bodily functions; it all seemed normal. Some of the women didn't always empty the pots as quickly as they should have done and the dormitory could end up reeking as a result. Such matters were usually resolved by those who were slow to clean up their children being chivvied into action by the complaints of other, more fastidious mothers.

Bridie would then round us up in our pyjamas and march us, one at a time, to a white enamel basin which was filled with hot water from the big kettle they boiled in the fireplace. I was lucky enough to have my own wash bag, so she always knew which face towel and soap to use on me. Once we were clean she would help us dress, encouraging us to do it for ourselves as much as possible. Right from the start we were encouraged to be independent and self-reliant in all things.

Breakfast was usually a mug of tea, white bread and jam and an egg with black pudding. It would be served up at a long table in the dormitory with benches for us and some chairs for the mothers. The black puddings were my favourite, although I had no idea at the time that they were made from animals' blood. We had a constant supply of eggs from the chickens we reared, and all the jams were home-made. The plates and mugs were made of enamelled metal. Sometimes, if there was nothing else, we could be given potatoes to keep us going.

Once breakfast was over we would race outside to play, giving Bridie a well-earned rest until one of us inevitably came back inside in tears for some reason.

Mammy relied on Bridie totally. She knew that Bridie looked after me, day and night, seven days a week and she couldn't do without her. Mammy wanted so much for me, and much of the burden for providing everything I needed landed on Bridie's exhausted shoulders. In order to be able to afford the things she wanted me to have, Mammy had to work every shift in the restaurant that she could get, which meant that she hardly ever got to see me in those early years, except when I was fast asleep in the bed beside her. Bridie would fill her in on whatever I had been up to each day.

My days revolved around play and make-believe. There were no books from which to learn or read, and no writing to practise. Nothing was organised and there was no preparation done for the first day that we would be sent off to school. My best friends were Connor, who was the same age as me, and Bridie's son, Joseph, who was five years older but seemed more because of his serious nature. Joseph was often designated the task of looking after me and was as much like an older brother as a friend. We saw ourselves as the 'three amigos'.

Lunch and dinner were very similar. There was no real choice. One meal was pretty much guaranteed to be the same as the next. We always had cheap cuts of meat, things like pigs' trotters, liver, heart and kidney, all kinds of offal. Then there were potatoes at every meal, presented in every way from boiled to mashed, and, of course, cabbage. Meats like chicken, beef or pork were considered luxury items in those days, and having never had them I didn't miss them. Since I was always hungry, perhaps because I burned up so much nervous energy, I wasn't fussy about food and never complained about anything that I was given. I would quite happily chew on a whole pig's trotter and eat whatever offal was put in front of me. It would be many years before I learned to hate them.

After playing all day I would be tired and hungry again by about four in the afternoon, but Bridie would insist that I wash the mud and filth off me before I sat down to eat.

'Why are you always so much dirtier than all the others, Francis?' she would want to know.

'Because I was looking for leprechauns and their treasure,' I would inform her, wondering why she found what seemed to me to be perfectly valid excuses so funny.

The sisters and some of the mothers would prepare the early dinner, which was free for all the children in the hostel. We all gathered in the Meeting Room or common area, the only place in the hostel outside the dormitories where all the mothers and children would meet, and we ate whatever was put on our plates. The best part of the meal was the cocoa drink that was served at the end in an enamel cup. Sometimes they had extras left over and Connor and I would go up to ask the sisters for more, saying 'We've been good today.'

Just next door to the Meeting Room were the communal washrooms. Once a week, usually on Sundays, Mammy or Bridie would bathe me in a rough-edged metal bath. I hated the feel of it against my skin when I sat in it, but I never complained when it was Mammy, no matter how hard she scrubbed, because I just wanted to be close to her. She was strict about cleanliness and took no nonsense from me. I could be a little devil at times and would complain a lot given the slightest opportunity, but I looked forward to those bath times because it was a treat to be with her, even if it meant having to endure the uncomfortable metal scourge on my bottom. I didn't get to see much of her and I missed her.

Mammy worked at least six and a half long days a week in the restaurant in the city centre. Serving customers all day was hard on her feet. She always had a half-day off on Tuesday or Sunday afternoons, when she would visit her mother's home outside Dublin, although I didn't know that at the time. As far as the world outside the hostel was concerned she was a normal single lady, friendly and hard-working. No one had a clue that she had a child, not even her own mother. She never mentioned anything about me to anyone. I was her secret child.

Mammy had lots of secrets, but I think I was the biggest one. Her mother and family were completely oblivious to her real life, believing that she lived alone in a rented room somewhere in the city. She told me later that her mother would frequently ask her about her social life.

'Have you met any nice young men, Cathleen?' she would enquire.

'Oh, I will never marry,' Mammy would insist. 'I am quite content with my life as it is.'

When I was five years old Mammy said that I had to start going to the local school, which was just a few minutes away from the hostel, but illness interrupted her plans. Living in open dormitories, with a general lack of hygiene, sickness was common among the children. I always seemed to have something wrong with me, even if it was no more than a cough or a cold, but at five I became seriously ill and I was hospitalised for many months. I don't remember what it was that was wrong with me, but I do remember it was the first time I had been outside the walls of Regina Coeli since my birth.

Talking to Mary that day over a cup of tea was the first time I had ever talked about my mother's life like this. That, coupled with the familiar surroundings, which were bringing back so many memories, was stirring up emotions that I hadn't realised were lurking beneath the surface. I stopped talking for a moment and sipped the tea which had now grown cold, avoiding Mary's eyes as I struggled to regain my composure. I had finally shared the secret with someone. My mother had made me promise that I would never speak to anyone about our time at Regina Coeli. It was the way she wanted things to be, and I felt that I had betrayed her secret. I felt embarrassed but at the same time relieved.

'My goodness,' Mary said, kindly. 'You remember a lot about your childhood here. Let me top up your tea.'

She refilled my cup and I mumbled my thanks, finding it difficult to speak as I tried to stifle the tears.

'You know,' she said as she sat down again, 'I clearly remember the two big wooden gates next to this building that you mentioned. I was sorry to see the old buildings being taken down, or rather, falling down. We still only accommodate women here, but not just single mothers. We now have residents who have problems with drugs and alcohol. These are the new problems. Regina Coeli doesn't have as many people here as we used to, but it still operates on a charity basis.'

After a pause, which I still didn't fill, she carried on.

'Your memory serves you well. We did have caretaker mothers looking after the children. It was the only way the other mothers could go out and earn money to support themselves and their children in those days. All the women had to work. They were all afraid to reveal anything about their illegitimate children to the outside world. It was a complete taboo. The Catholic Church was very against the idea of women having children out of wedlock. Contraception for women and men was banned in Ireland, so naturally when a woman fell pregnant it had to be a secret. I believe this was the only hostel in Ireland where you could keep your baby. Very few people actually knew about it, because none of us wanted to draw attention to its existence, so a lot of the poor girls ended up going to the Magdalene Laundry and losing their children, never knowing that there was another option available to them.'

'How did mothers like my mammy find work without people knowing about their situations?' I asked, finding my voice once more.

'The hostel had a network of business people who helped place the women in work around the city. They were people who believed in and supported the work of the hostel, people who felt that mothers were entitled to a choice and that keeping the children with their mothers was better for them. You are right that a single mother looking for work in any other way would almost certainly have had to lie about her situation. There was a terrible stigma attached to the whole business all through the fifties and sixties.'

'My mammy worked in a restaurant in the city centre called Burns. She was a waitress there.'

'I remember the Burns family. They came from Germany after the Second World War and so they understood suffering. They were great supporters of the Regina Coeli network. They were one of a few small businesses that helped in their own discreet way. Tell me more about your mammy.'

I took a deep breath. 'My Mammy was thirty-five when she had me in 1953. It was very old to be having a first baby in those days and the doctors were very worried for her.'

Mary nodded. 'Most of the women here were very young. I do remember an older woman. Was she sometimes known by the others as "the Lady"?'

'Yes!' I could hardly contain my excitement. 'Yes, that's what they called her.'

'I didn't meet her personally,' Mary said, 'but I remember people talking about her. She was famous for being one of the very few who left to get married. As you say, most of the mothers had more than one name, and more often than not they were false names to help protect their anonymity. The common fear was that somebody would come looking for them. Because the hostel did not require them to reveal their true identities, neither did we have any records as to who these women really were.'

The excitement of hearing that my mother was remembered in this way after so many years added to the emotions which were threatening to overwhelm me.

'Would you like to have a look around the old place?' Mary asked.

'I would love that,' I said, although I had no idea what I was hoping to see.

Taking my tea from me she led me upstairs, where there were two dormitories. To my amazement they had barely changed in fifty years apart from the installation of some new washbasins. Mary then opened the door to the chapel. It was exactly as I remembered, only much, much smaller. She got down on her knees and blessed herself while I stood behind her a little awkwardly. In years gone by I would have done the same as her, but I didn't believe in religion any more. I had become a cynic. Mary didn't appear to notice, content in her own, quiet faith.

She then led me out into the grounds, the playing area where I remembered being so happy.

'There was an old tenement building over there,' I said, pointing towards some new-looking prefab buildings, 'three floors high, containing all the dormitories where we lived.'

'They were demolished, so they were,' Mary said.

There were single-storey prefabs crowded into virtually every inch of the grounds, making them look small and congested, a far cry from the wide open spaces I remembered. I stood still and stared around, remembering hordes of children screaming and running wild, chasing each other or pushing broken prams around, playing hopscotch or swinging on ropes. It seemed a sad, silent place now. The high stone walls that had marked the boundaries of my world for so long were still there, and I could even see the mental institution next door, still as menacing as ever with its broken windows and weeds sprouting through cracks and holes in the walls.

'The mothers told us so many scary stories about patients escaping over the walls at night,' I said. 'I guess they wanted to discourage us from climbing over the walls in the other direction.'

Mary laughed. 'You and your mother must have done well after you left for London?'

'Actually,' I said, 'it wasn't a bed of roses. But Mammy was happy and I did well with the opportunities that came my way.'

I couldn't believe I was opening up in this way to a woman I had only just met. I didn't elaborate any further about all the ups and downs Mammy and I had been through together. If I had, I would have been there all day, and I had already given away too many of my mammy's secrets for comfort. I thanked Mary for her kindness and for the tea and took my leave. As I walked down the hill, after waving goodbye to the small figure at the door, my mind was buzzing. It was as if I had opened a Pandora's box of memories, a box that my mother had firmly instructed me to keep closed for ever.

Chapter Six
So Long, Francis

By the time I was six I had spent five months in three different hospitals. I'm told that I nearly died due to a series of serious illnesses, but the thing I remember most was that it was very exciting just to be outside the walls of Regina Coeli for the first time. Mammy was my only visitor in hospital, as Bridie never left the hostel, having the other children to look after, and Mammy could only come when she could get time off work. I missed my friends but at the same time I was enthralled by the different kinds of people I saw coming and going on the wards where I was incarcerated, and all the different things they did and talked about.

There were doctors and nurses, and other patients and their visitors. Lying there, month after month, I was soaking up everything that went on around me. One of the things I noticed was that the men who wore white, the doctors and medical staff, were all much nicer to me than the men who wore black, the priests who haunted the hostel. The men in black never bothered to hide their low opinion of the women and children in Regina Coeli. As far as they were concerned the women were sinners and we were the products of that sin. The men in white, however, didn't seem to look down on me at all and seemed to want to help me in any way they could.

Mammy was obviously very worried about me, because I had never seen so much of her before. I was basking in her attention, and she kept promising that once I was out of the hospital things would be better and that she would spend more time with me. She must have felt so guilty and at the same time must have been so worried about the work she was missing and the money she was losing. It must have been tough not to have a partner to share the worries with, although I'm sure she poured it all out to Bridie once she got back to the dormitory.

I have no idea what was wrong with me during those months, or how close to death I actually came, but I do know that I thought it was all worthwhile for the interesting new experiences I was having.

'We have a surprise for you,' Mammy said when she was finally able to take me home from hospital.

'What is it?'

'You wait and see,' she said, refusing to respond to any of my excited questioning, just smiling mysteriously.

When we got back to Regina Coeli she took me upstairs, but not into the open dormitory where we lived. Instead, she opened a door into a smaller room. Inside, Bridie and Joseph were both waiting, unable to suppress their broad grins.

'Surprise!' they all shouted as I looked around the bedroom. It was no bigger than three metres by four and had four beds in it, two adult-sized ones and two child-sized ones.

'What is this?' I asked, unable to work out what was happening.

'We have our own bedroom,' Joseph said, jumping around the room with excitement, 'just the four of us. It's the only bedroom in the whole building.'

It was the best room I had ever been in, even though it was a bit cramped with so many beds and had no washing or toilet facilities in it. It was much better than the dormitories or even the hospital wards that I had experienced. Mammy, I discovered, was paying extra for us to have this room in the hope that I would catch fewer illnesses from the other children.

'Your mammy has got you a present too,' Joseph said, unable to contain himself.

'What?' I wanted to know, 'what have you got me, Mammy?'

She smiled and reached under her bed, bringing out a cowboy hat and a pair of toy guns in a holster. I couldn't believe my eyes. It was the start of a period during which I think it would be fair to say Mammy spoiled me. I guess nearly losing me had given her a terrible fright and she was just glad that she still had me.

Having our own room made Joseph and me feel really special, but I noticed that several people started to treat us differently, as if they thought we were putting on airs and graces – as if we thought we were better than the others. One or two of the women already resented Mammy because she was a bit older and took more care of her appearance. Most of those who called her 'the Lady' did so out of respect, but these ones meant it in a sneering, derogatory way. At the time, of course, all this went straight over the top of my head, because I thought she was wonderful and I knew Bridie did too. They were the only two adults whose opinions mattered to me at that stage.

When I was about six all the children from the hostel were invited to a charity Christmas party organised by the Dublin Bus Company.

'You are very lucky children,' the Sisters told us, 'there will be lots of nice food and presents.'

That was all I needed to hear to become intensely excited, and by the time the Sisters came to pick us up in a Dublin bus I was already flying. We were driven to a place that I had never been to before and shown into a building which was as smart as any of the places I had seen in films. I couldn't stop staring around me as we were led through a grand entrance hall, past a sweeping staircase into a large ground-floor room. There in front of us were tables and chairs all decorated with brightly coloured balloons and covered with different-sized boxes, all wrapped in Christmas paper.

The room was packed with children I had never seen before and there were smiling grown-ups everywhere, all wanting to give us a good time. I had never seen so much food laid out in one place in my life. There were sandwiches, jellies, ice-creams, cakes, cakes and more cakes. There were lots of things that I had never even heard of, and I was determined to try as much of everything as I possibly could, including my first ever taste of Coca-Cola in a bottle, a drink that was far too expensive for Mammy to ever buy for me. Everything tasted great, and on top of that it was all free. It was like I had arrived in Heaven. There was music and there were party hats, which even the usually sombre priests were wearing. Then there were sweets handed round with no restrictions on how many we could have. Connor was completely in awe of the whole thing. Being quite shy around strangers, he sat in the corner and kept to himself, but I couldn't believe my luck and scooped up handfuls of the things, cramming them into every pocket I could find in my jacket and my shorts. When every pocket was bulging to capacity I found an empty box and filled that too, with the intention of carrying it back to Regina Coeli with me at the end.

Finally we were corralled together and told to sit down. 'Now,' one of the organisers announced, 'we are going to ask you to sing for your supper.'

We didn't need telling twice and, starting with 'Old MacDonald had a Farm' and 'Davy Crocket, King of the Wild Frontier', we sang at the top of our voices. Then, to my complete surprise, one of the priests singled me out.

'Stand up please, Francis,' he said.

I thought for a moment I was going to be told off for being so greedy and filling my pockets with so many sweets. I quickly slid my box of extra goodies under a nearby table.

'Would you sing everyone a song on your own, Francis?' the priest asked. 'There would be a prize in it for you if you felt you were able to do that.'

The mention of a prize, combined with the fact that I was high from the excitement, and probably Coca-Cola, overcame any inhibitions I might have had at such a request. Taking a deep lung full of air I sang 'Wooden Heart',

So Long, Francis

Mammy's favourite Elvis Presley song. When I finished everyone was clapping and telling me how wonderful I was, sending me even further up on Cloud Nine.

Then another priest called my name. 'Would you come up on the stage now, please, Francis?'

Sure that this time it would be because of my overflowing pockets, I made my way nervously through the crowd and up the steps. I needn't have worried. When I reached the stage I was presented with my prize, an even bigger box, wrapped in fancy paper.

'Would you do us the honour of singing us another song, Francis?' the priest asked.

More than happy to keep the eyes of the room on me for as long as possible while things were going so well, I launched into a Mario Lanza song I used to hear Mammy listening to on the radio. Never having sung it before, I hadn't realised how hard it was to reach the high notes that Mario Lanza made sound so effortless, and everyone was laughing and clapping at my hopeless attempts to emulate the great tenor. I didn't care. I was on too much of a roll to care about a bit of mockery now.

As soon as I left the stage I tore the wrapping from the prize, revealing a bright red boat with white sails. I had no idea what they expected me to do with this stupid boat, since I certainly didn't have anywhere to sail it and there was no spare space in our bedroom for something that big. To make up for this disappointment I collected some more sweets and asked around to see if anyone would like to buy the boat off me, but nobody was any more interested in it than I was. I now had more sweets than I could possibly handle, so I sold some of them instead, going home with my pockets full of both sweets and money. I had learned a number of extremely valuable lessons that day, the main one being that there was a whole world of opportunities just waiting for me outside Regina Coeli.

Due to my stays in hospital I missed the first half of my first year at school, but eventually I was able to go in 1958 – and it felt as if another world had opened up for me. For the first time ever I was allowed out into the streets of Dublin with the big children with no adult supervision and no walls to contain me. It was a ten-minute walk to and from the school each day, and seeing life on the streets each morning and afternoon, even for that short period, was exhilarating beyond belief. It immediately made me want more of the same.

We would all leave the hostel together each morning, a group of about fifteen of us aged between six and fourteen. The big ones were supposed to look after the little ones, a responsibility which the girls took a great deal more seriously than the boys, needless to say. We must have been an intimidating sight for anyone who crossed our paths: shouting, running and chasing one another along the streets, high on life and intoxicated by this tiny slice of freedom. At the same time we were always aware that we were outsiders, different from people who lived in normal family homes, which made some of us a little more defensive, some a little more aggressive and loud.

Where the girls would try to keep us in order, the older boys would goad one another on to do more and more outrageous things. I watched in wonder as they ran after passing trucks, hanging off the back of them, sometimes as many as five at a time, whooping and cheering as they tried to see who could stay on the longest. I didn't have to be asked twice before joining in, and it wasn't long before I was one of the front runners in such games, never for a moment considering the dangers and never experiencing the slightest tremor of fear. I felt I was immortal.

The small school was housed in a two-storey Edwardian building of grey Irish stone. It always felt cold and had only basic facilities. We did all mix with the other pupils during school hours, but we always looked out for one another first. Our friendship with the other children, however, didn't extend beyond the school gates. We had no idea what their home lives were like and they certainly weren't allowed to come back inside the walls that made us invisible to the outside world.

Inside the classroom I found things harder. To begin with I had difficulty stopping myself from chattering all the time. I had barely drawn breath since I learned to talk and I did not realise that when teachers roared 'Quiet!' they really meant it. Disobedience was not tolerated, and I was constantly being hauled out to the front of the class because I couldn't shut up, receiving stinging blows from a cane on my hands, on the backs of my legs or my backside.

About forty children between six and eight were grouped into one form and the wooden desks and chairs were far too big for me, my feet dangling in mid-air when I sat down. There were no school fees, but the parents had to pay for everything we used in the classroom – books, ink, paper and pencils – and the teachers were constantly drilling into us the need to be careful with all the material we used, otherwise it would end up costing our parents money.

We learned only a few subjects, English, Gaelic and Religious Studies, but even so I struggled to follow what was going on. I was not an academically gifted child. In fact, if I was at school these days I think I would be classed as having 'special needs'. I certainly wasn't good with languages. My English was bad enough, but Gaelic, which was compulsory, was a complete disaster. The lessons seemed to drag on for hours, and I sometimes thought I might die of boredom and frustration before the end. They didn't even attempt to teach us mathematics.

My writing didn't go any better than my reading. I hated the pens we had to use, which were just nibs on the end of sticks that you constantly had to dip into a bottle of ink as you wrote. You then had to finish off by drying the writing with a piece of blotting paper so that it didn't smudge everywhere, but with me that never seemed to control the spread of the ink. By the end of the day my fingers were always black, and often the stains had managed to spread over my shirt and face as well. Religious Studies was the only thing I found interesting, because it was all about stories from the Bible, and I loved stories of all sorts.

For me the best part of the school day happened in the playground. The moment the school bell rang to signal playtime, we would all be up and charging out of the classroom with a clattering of seats and feet and happy, shouting voices. Unless we were being taught by the dreaded Mr Kelly, who would make us line up and leave in an orderly manner. If we rushed or were chaotic in any way when he was there, he would take great pleasure in keeping us confined to the classroom for the rest of the break, a fate worse than death for a small boy – sometimes I'd feel I was going to burst from a mixture of pent-up energy and boredom.

Once we exploded into the freedom of the playground it was either 'war games' or 'cowboys and Indians', and I had soon become one of the ringleaders. My games were mostly based on films which I had seen at Regina Coeli. Every six months someone from a charity would come to the hostel with a projector and a film. It was an eagerly anticipated event. We would watch, enthralled, despite the fact that frequently the film would break and the lights would have to go back on so that emergency repairs could be made. For weeks afterwards we would be acting out the story in the playground. Sometimes that meant that I got a little rough with my friends, and they were beginning to learn not to mess with me. I mean, whoever heard of a wimpy cowboy or soldier? But then I would be the 'good guy', cleaning up the town. I guess I was stretching my wings and learning where my boundaries might be.

Sometimes all of us from the hostel would get together in the playground, lining up in a long row and linking arms, then moving slowly around shouting, 'Join us and be in our gang!' Some of the other children then formed a rival gang and we would attack one another, sending children scattering in all directions. Occasionally things got a bit out of hand, and we were seen as bullies, which puzzled us because we were just doing what we always did. We did play gentler games too, like marbles and kicking empty tin cans around, but they were never as much fun.

There were no sports lessons at school and no equipment apart from hurling sticks and an old football. A hurling stick was a long piece of carved wood, curved at one end. You held it at the top and hit a small ball with the curved end. Hurling was a fast game that involved lots of running and dribbling the ball along with your stick, while other players tried to get it away from you.

The only time I saw live games of either hurling or soccer was at Phoenix Park in Dublin. Connor and I would join the older children on expeditions to watch the amateur teams play, marvelling at the speed at which they could move around the pitch. Both games were played in a very macho, aggressive, Irish way, with the players getting possession of the ball by any means possible. Fear did not seem to be an option, and there was often blood streaming from a player's head or someone would be sporting a black eye by the end. Both of us longed to have hurling sticks of our own, and heaven knows what damage we would have inflicted if we had had our wishes granted.

School finished at three o'clock sharp. The bell would ring and we would race out, clutching our satchels. To be honest, there wasn't much in mine apart from a stupid bottle of ink, a pen, pencils and few sheets of paper. We would roar onto the street like escaped convicts, spreading out in all directions as the girls desperately tried to keep some control.

'You'd better stay together!' they would shout after us, over and over again as we scattered out of control. 'Or we'll tell on you!'

So Long, Francis

We liked to explore different routes home, prolonging the moments of freedom, taking detours along the narrow embankments of the stinking River Liffey. Buses would be lined up along the riverside, drivers relaxing and chatting with one another as their passengers waited patiently on board for their journeys to start. We would be shouting and laughing and messing around. Some people watched us with pity in their eyes and we would hear them saying, 'Ah, bless 'em, those poor unfortunates'; but there were more who showed open disapproval of our rowdy behaviour and often scolded us, calling us 'brats'. They didn't like our loudness, our scruffy appearance or our colourful language. I guess they disapproved of our very existence in their city. We were never afraid to answer back, and what might start as good-natured banter could often become more abusive and foul-mouthed.

'Right,' someone would eventually say, 'I'm going for the police!'

That always made us run off. We all feared the police a great deal, a fear instilled by our mothers, who certainly didn't want them coming round Regina Coeli and stirring up trouble for them and for the Sisters. Everyone living there knew that they were lucky to have that sanctuary and no one wanted to do anything to jeopardise it.

Close to the hostel was a small shop selling newspapers, cigarettes and sweets. The couple who ran it were always very nice to me. Mammy gave them a little money each week so that I could choose sweets for treats. There were other local people who I came to recognise on the walks to and from school, but none of them ever spoke to us because they knew where we were from. I didn't know a single soul on those busy Dublin streets, apart from those who came from the hostel with me. There were two completely separate worlds, the secret world of Regina Coeli and the outside world. Inside our safe haven we were all the same, but in the outside world we felt very different. We were outsiders who had to stick together for protection and reassurance.

Living in the hostel made all of us seem older than our years, both mothers and children. When we were small we were surrounded and influenced by a lot of older companions and grew up quickly. We had to fend for ourselves in the dormitory, and while we were cut off from the outside world in one respect, we were worldly-wise in another. We all repeated the wisdoms we had heard from our mothers, and rumours spread like wildfire from dormitory to dormitory. I was insatiably inquisitive and absorbed every story and every ounce of gossip like a sponge, both the good and the bad.

Not everyone living inside the hostel was nice to me. Bridget Murphy was a big, fat slob of a woman who resented Mammy, believing that Mammy thought herself superior and was 'putting on airs and graces'. She took her venom out on me whenever possible. Most of her taunts I could shrug off, but then she discovered my Achilles heel – my name.

'Frances is a girl's name,' she sneered.

'No, it's not,' I shouted, glowing red with indignation at such a slight, both to me and to my mother for choosing my name. Seeing how wounded I was by the jibe, however, meant that she never let it go. I took to hiding whenever I saw her coming, but it was never going to be possible to stay out of her way all the time in such a close community.

One night Joseph and I had already gone to bed and we were talking with the lights out, as we always did, when we heard the sound of women's voices raised in anger outside the door. We were used to hearing arguments and confrontations erupting every now and again, but this one seemed to be escalating out of control. Most fights were over petty things like children squabbling or differences of opinion about discipline. Sometimes one of the mothers would become upset with one of the Sisters, but in most cases it was the Sisters who calmed things down if the mothers or children couldn't resolve them themselves. It didn't sound as if anyone was trying to stop this fight.

We could hear other women jeering and cheering the two shouting women on. There were the sounds of people punching and slapping and falling. Never one to let an interesting situation pass me by, I climbed out of bed and opened the door a crack, peering out.

To my amazement two of the mothers were actually physically fighting, surrounded by an excited, baying crowd who were egging them on. I opened the door a little wider and realised that one of the protagonists was my arch enemy, Bridget Murphy. Then, to my absolute horror, I realised that the other one was my normally calm, composed and serene mammy. I had never ever seen her like this. She had hold of Bridget's hair and was dragging her around, swearing with words I didn't even know she knew, and throwing punches like a bare-knuckle street fighter. Her normally perfect hair was dishevelled and falling over her face and her top was torn.

Horrified, I couldn't stop myself from bursting into tears. One of the on-lookers turned and spotted me and shouted for them to stop. By this stage Bridget was lying flat on the floor with Mammy on top of her. Mammy managed to squeeze in one final slap in the face and shouted a few more obscenities before pulling herself upright. Bridget was crying and seemed to be in genuine pain, but Mammy obviously had no sympathy and was itching to hit her again. Bridget had obviously tested her to her limits and she had finally flipped. I later found out that she had suggested that Mammy only had the money for things like the bedroom and nice clothes for me because she did a little 'extra work' on the side. Even if I had heard her say that at the time I would have had no idea what that 'extra work' might be.

Satisfied that she had won the battle, Mammy stood up, tried to push her wild hair back into place, and then scooped me up in her arms and took me back to bed.

The thrashing she had received at my mother's hand did not, however, crush Bridget's venomous spirit. On the contrary, it made her attacks on me all the more venomous and personal, and in the following months she increased the level of her teasing, although she was always careful only to do it during the hours when Mammy was out at work

'Just take no notice, Francis,' both Bridie and Joseph counselled me, 'and she'll soon grow tired of it.'

But she didn't seem to be tiring of it. In fact she seemed to be increasing in her enthusiasm for baiting me. Finally I'd had enough. Emboldened by my mother's spectacular cat-fighting display, I decided that I would not put up with it a moment longer. I devised a plan for the next time Bridget teased me for having a girl's name.

A few days later I was playing in the dormitory with Connor and Joseph when Bridget came over and started her usual taunting. I said nothing, simply waiting until she had said whatever she wanted to say and had turned to walk away. I then sprang to my feet, ran up behind her and jumped on her back, grabbing a handful of her greasy hair and pulling it with all my strength.

'Get down, you little devil,' she screamed, thrashing around wildly until she finally managed to dislodge me. I fell to the floor but instantly sprang back up and ran away. I could hear her furiously cursing and swearing behind me, but knew she was too fat to be able to catch me. I felt extremely satisfied that my plan had worked. I thought that now she realised I wasn't going to just lie down and take her abuse she would be more careful, but in fact the opposite happened.

The next day we were playing in the yard when she started on me yet again, humiliating me in front of everyone. Some of the others started to laugh as she chanted: 'Frances is a girl's name! Frances is a girl's name!'

Part of the problem was that I actually believed she was right and I felt ashamed and embarrassed as well as angry. Like Mammy, I flipped and ran up to her, kicking her big, fat legs as hard as I could. I kicked again and again, over and over as she howled and tried to swot me away like an annoying fly. Then I ran round behind her and kicked the back of her knees, bringing her screaming to the ground.

'You little devil,' she shrieked, 'I'm going to kill you!'

With surprising speed, no doubt fuelled by her anger, she got back on her feet and chased after me. I could see that she was now completely out of control and actually was likely to kill me, so I ran to find Bridie and Joseph, with Bridget thundering up behind me. She chased me round the yard and up into the dormitory. I couldn't find either of them and Bridget seemed to have found superhuman energy in her fury.

'What's going on?' Bridie said, appearing from nowhere, attracted by the mayhem. She and Joseph stood between me and my attacker.

'Now you listen to me, Bridget Murphy,' Bridie scolded, 'you're to stop teasing the boy all the time. It's gone on long enough and you had this coming.'

Bridget looked as if she was going to attack Bridie now, but as she looked around she saw other mothers gathering around and she must have known that they would all turn on her if she laid a finger on someone as well loved as Bridie. Snorting like a bull, she spun on her heel and limped away.

'You,' said Bridie, turning her attention to me, 'stay out of her way for a few days.'

No one ever teased me about my name again, but I had come to a decision about it all the same.

'From now on,' I announced to Mammy when I next saw her, 'I'm going to be known as Gordon. Goodbye, Francis!'

Chapter Seven

He Who Dares

Once a month, on a Tuesday afternoon, Mammy started treating me to a visit to a picture house in Dublin. It was like walking into a different world, a make-believe, fantasy universe where even the staff seemed to me as glamorous in their uniforms as the film stars depicted on the posters outside.

I was always on my best behaviour whenever I was out with Mammy. I knew that was what she expected of me and I was determined never to let her down. I wanted to make her as proud of me as we walked down the street, hand in hand, as I was of her. Before we left the hostel she would make sure that I looked like a smart, clean, polite little 'boy next door' and not like one of the 'unfortunates'. I would be wearing my best clothes; a smart white shirt and tie, shorts and a jacket. If there was even the faintest of marks on me or the clothes, out would come the white handkerchief and I would immediately be wiped clean. No passer-by would ever have suspected our secret. We looked exactly as Mammy wanted us to look: a mother and son from a nice Dublin family on an outing. What mattered most to me was being alone with her.

Once we reached the picture house, Mammy would buy our tickets and then I would make a beeline for the kiosk, where she would buy me an ice-cream and a selection of sweets, and a packet of cigarettes for herself. We would then make our way through to the auditorium, nearly always the first to arrive. It was exciting just to sink into my seat amid all the luscious drapes and rich, dark reds and sparkling golds, staring up at the ceiling lights which looked to me like the stars in the night sky, and watching the other people coming in to find their seats. The air of excitement and expectation and the sugary delights of the sweets combined to make the whole effect magical. Being together with my mammy in those moments made me the happiest boy in the world.

It must have taken a great deal of courage for her to walk hand in hand around the centre of Dublin with her secret child. What would have happened if she had bumped into someone she knew? How would she have explained me away?

Within ten minutes of the lights going down and the film starting, Mammy would have fallen asleep, exhausted by the never-ending grind of being on her feet, serving customers six and a half days a week. I would let her sleep, losing myself in the world unfolding on the big screen above me as I stuffed myself with sweets. Despite the fact that she would inevitably doze off and miss large parts of them, Mammy chose the films because they starred her favourite actors; people like Robert Taylor and Mario Lanza. She particularly liked Elvis Presley, who seemed to be producing new films every few months at that time, all set in the most exotic, colourful locations and full of beautiful women and songs that made me want to leap up and dance. My favourites were always the war films and Westerns – action films with heroes and villains.

Once the film was over and we emerged back out into the evening light I wouldn't be able to stop talking about whatever we had just seen. As we made our way to a restaurant for an inexpensive meal, Mammy would listen distractedly as I prattled on. I would just keep talking and talking, knowing I was completely the centre of her attention and wishing every day could be like this.

There were also the odd occasions when I would still be awake when she arrived home from work and she would be able to play with me before bedtime. My favourite game was to stand on her shoulders, holding on to her hands, trying to stay balanced for as long as possible as she walked around. On those occasions she would be the one to put me to bed instead of Bridie.

To me it felt like Mammy lived for her work. I never remembered a time when she hadn't worked hard in order to give us a better life. I knew that she was doing it for me, but I still missed her immensely when she wasn't there. If it hadn't been for my illnesses and my close shave with death I'm sure she would have worked even harder and been away for even longer hours. She was entirely selfless and she lived completely for me. I knew that too. She had no idea what the future might hold for us, but she had a strong conviction that things had to get better and we needed to be ready for any opportunities that might arise. I was clearly happy in the hostel and had fun nearly every day, but she must have known that it wouldn't be good for me in the long run. We had to find a way out, and I'm sure she was thinking about it every moment of the day as she waited on tables and came home to the hostel and climbed into bed beside her sleeping son.

To the outside world she appeared to be a hard-working, independent single woman. If anyone dared to ask if she had a boyfriend she would tell them her days of dating were over.

'I'm forty now,' she would say, 'and far too old for all that sort of thing.'

The friends and family who had known about Bill Lewis assumed that she had simply moved on with her own life, having accepted that they could not be together. No one in the hostel, including me, knew anything about Bill or anything else in Mammy's past before the day she arrived at the door of Regina Coeli with me inside her.

Mammy hadn't set eyes on Bill since the day she watched him boarding the boat for England. He had written frequently in the first few months after leaving Ireland, but gradually the gaps between the letters grew longer, until he was writing twice a year and sending the odd postcard from wherever he was working in Europe, building film and stage sets. The relationship seemed to have developed into more of a friendship than a romance. London was the perfect place for him to build a brand-new life, and as the months went by and Mammy didn't follow him, Bill must have started to fall into the ways of the many other unmarried Irishmen who left their homeland. He worked hard and he spent his earnings in the pub with his friends. If he'd met any other women he wouldn't have told Mammy about them. I'm inclined to think that he didn't, but she began to assume that he had.

His letters and postcards were sent to Mammy's mother's house and she would pick them up on her monthly visits there. She had stopped bothering to reply, since she didn't much like what she was reading, believing that he was deliberately avoiding talking about his private life and his feelings for her. But still they kept arriving.

'I see you have another letter from Bill,' her mother would say to her. 'How's he getting on over there in London?'

'I don't know,' Mammy would shrug. 'I haven't bothered to read it.'

That was not the truth, she read every one of them, but they never contained anything more than pleasantries, which she took to mean that he had something to hide from her. I think that during those years she actually believed she was now destined to be a single working woman all her life.

Her job was fifteen minutes away from Regina Coeli. Her basic salary was low, but she did very well from her tips because people always liked her, and that was what paid for our little treats like the picture house and the sweets. Never once did she ever take me to see the workplace where she spent so much of her time.

'Can we visit your restaurant?' I would ask whenever we were walking into town, but she would pretend not to have heard me and would change the subject.

That was how I grew to know that I was her big secret. Piece by piece I was coming to understand her double life. It

started with the 'special rules' that she instilled in me as soon
as I was old enough to grasp what she was saying.

'You are never to go outside the big gates of Regina Coeli,'
was the first one. As I got a little older she added some more.
'Always be polite and well-behaved. Never speak to strangers and under no circumstances ever tell anyone where we
live.' Right from the beginning I realised that there were
some secrets which had to be kept.

Living in the city of Dublin was like living in one great
gigantic church. There was a church everywhere you looked
and religion played a key part in everyday life, particularly at
Regina Coeli. Most people went to church two or three times
a week, and the Sisters were always reminding me how
important it was that I shouldn't just go on Sundays, but on
all the Holy Days and Saints' Days as well. To me it seemed
as if there was some reason why I had to go and pray every
day of the year.

'It's very important that you be a good Catholic boy,' they
were forever telling me, and it is hard not to end up brain-
washed in such circumstances.

The priests, those men in black, played a key role in Irish
society. When Southern Ireland became independent from
England they ensured that the Roman Catholic Church was
highly influential in the make-up of the Irish Constitution.
In school we spent a large part of the day learning about the
Church and what it stood for. We learned about the Pope,
the priests, the nuns and the teachings of the Bible, and we
were told that it was all part of God's way of making us
better Roman Catholics.

He Who Dares

Joseph was a good example to me. He was a lot like his mother, quietly spoken, small and skinny with straight black hair and sad eyes. He was a very caring boy who would do anything for Bridie and would help anyone in need. He always kept an eye on me, always patient and always laughing when I was messing around, which was most of the time. If I needed to go to the local sweet shop before I was allowed to go on my own, he would go with me as my chaperone. He made sure I got to bed on time and he even made my supper sometimes when I got home from school, if Bridie was busy. He always spoke quietly and slowly, in a sort of saintly manner, which contrasted with my loud, boisterous, headstrong manner. He talked a lot about becoming a priest himself when he grew up. He was infatuated with Catholicism and the Church. He actually enjoyed going to Mass and often took me with him, although for me it was more a way of getting out and about.

I would trail along behind, copying whatever Joseph did. He bowed his head outside the church, and so did I. He blessed himself before he went in, and so did I. Once he was inside he blessed himself again, and so did I, this time with holy water from a stone bowl by the door. Then I followed his lead in kneeling down and putting my hands together before we sat in a pew, knelt again, put our heads down and started to pray. He was such a good person that it was quite hard to argue with him and not be his friend, despite the fact that we were so different in so many ways. Our personalities were polar opposites, but he was my best friend and that made Mammy very happy. She knew that with Joseph around I was in safe hands.

The priests in the Church knew Joseph, just as they knew most of the mothers and children in the hostel. There was no escaping them. Joseph always made sure I was neat and tidy for church. He went to every service, whether it was daily Mass, a benediction or a confession. I was very much guided by what he did. I didn't really care about the ceremonial procedures but as well as enjoying just getting out of the hostel I got a great deal of comfort from tagging along with Joseph. I would change my behaviour completely to suit the occasion; happy-go-lucky Gordon one minute, then pious Francis the next. It was like having a split personality.

First Holy Communion was a rite of passage for every Catholic child, and mine was to take place in an imposing-looking big church near the Liffey. On the big day I made my way down to the church to meet the other children from school. We were all dressed in white, perfectly clean and tidy, our hair neatly combed into place. We held prayer books and had rosary beads hung around our necks. The nuns and priests were outside with all our families and friends, gathering us together before the big event. My family that day consisted of Mammy, Bridie, Joseph and Connor, and we talked in hushed voices to one another while we waited for the go-ahead to enter the church. Needless to say, the ceremony involved a lot of prayers, songs, kneeling and bowing before receiving communion from the priest.

I had received communion before, and had got into trouble for chewing the wafer like a sweet when it was placed in my mouth rather than letting it dissolve. Apparently that was a sin, and I was petrified that I might do the same thing again by mistake. So petrified was I that I almost choked when I tried to swallow it whole and it got stuck half-way down. The service continued around me as I struggled to breathe and to disguise that struggle from everyone sitting behind. After what seemed like an age, air finally made its way through to my lungs once more.

Once the service was over, all the families and friends gathered outside the church and, to my amazement and absolute delight, I discovered that the children taking Holy Communion all received gifts of money to celebrate their big day. Poor Mammy, however, was mortified, as she had no money to give to the other children. As parents of children who weren't even at Regina Coeli started putting money into my hands, she tried to persuade me not to accept it.

'We don't want anyone's pity,' she muttered to me. 'You must give it back, Gordon.'

She didn't stand a chance. As far as I was concerned it was a perk for me as much as for every other child, and once the coins and notes were in my hand or my pocket there was no way I was going to be giving them back. I knew that Mammy wouldn't want to make a big fuss in front of everyone, as that would only draw attention to her embarrassing situation, so I simply pretended not to hear her protestations.

By that stage I had already started to understand the importance of having money, mainly because I never had any of my own and I knew how much of life was unavailable to you when your pockets were empty. Money, I had realised, gave you freedom. It was money which had meant we could have a private bedroom for the four of us, and it was money which meant that I could buy more sweets at the shop than most of the other children from the hostel, and go to the picture house. Having a fixed amount to spend in the shop each week had also taught me about the need to save and budget if I wanted to make those sweets last all week. Mammy had always explained to me how lucky we were to be able to afford these things, but she had also pointed out how hard she had had to work to make it happen.

Slowly but surely I was given more freedom as I grew older. On Saturday afternoons Joseph and Connor and I were allowed to go to the local picture house. It was still the only time we were allowed out on our own apart from going to school. We had to promise to chaperone one another and we had to be back by seven in the evening, at which time the gates would be locked. If we missed the curfew we would then have to ring the bell, which meant we would be found out and would run the risk of not being allowed out the following week.

I could hardly contain my excitement each time we queued up outside the Tivoli, pushing and shoving our way through the crowd of eager children towards the box-office window. I always took just enough money to pay for one small ice-cream and a packet of Rolos – a tube of seven deliciously soft, caramel-filled chocolates. Sometimes I would decide to exercise immense self-control and save the money by not buying anything at the kiosk, but most of the time the agony of then having to watch other children in the audience eating their treats was too much to bear.

I was becoming aware of how different we 'unfortunates' looked from the children of the outside world. It wasn't just that they had more money for things like sweets; it was obvi-

He Who Dares

ous in everything from the clothes and shoes they wore to the haircuts they had. They were different.

The older we got, the closer Connor and I became. His mother worked most of the time, just like Mammy, but he didn't have a second mother like Bridie to look after him. In other ways his mammy was very different from mine. She had a problem with alcohol and was often drunk around the hostel. Connor was very different from Joseph too. He had a face full of freckles, fair skin and red hair. I particularly remember his freckled nose. He was much bigger than me, stocky and tough for his age. He was never as well dressed as I was and always looked in need of a good scrub down, but he had a permanent grin on his face and a glint in his eye. Nothing ever seemed to faze him. One day Connor got into a big fight with two older boys at school. They were part of our group but they were frightened of him. It was a bloody affair but none of the blood spilt was Connor's. Since I was the only one he ever listened to, it fell to me to try to calm him down and get him back to the hostel in time for curfew.

Of the two of us I was more streetwise and disciplined, while he was a typical Dublin boy, with a strong Irish brogue. He wouldn't think twice about hitting another child, and he could be impressively rude too. We got on incredibly well but he was not a good influence on me, and my language was gradually getting bluer and bluer.

We used to go to Phoenix Park to play with older children and I would follow wherever he led. If he climbed a tree, then I would climb a tree. If he picked up a big stick, then I would quickly go hunting for a stick of my own. If we had any problems with other children he never hesitated to tell them where to go, fearlessly holding his ground. I learned a lot from watching him in action.

One of the things he loved to do was go to the local baths. I had never swum anywhere and was eager to experience the pool that he kept telling me about. I had watched Tarzan swimming in jungle pools and rivers, and it looked simple enough to me. I didn't have any trunks, but I didn't let that deter me, I simply stripped down to my white underpants. The echoing noise of happy voices and splashing, coupled with the smell of chemicals from the water, was intoxicating. I stripped off at top speed and ran out of the changing rooms, jumping straight into the deep end, assuming I would bob back up to the surface just like I had seen Tarzan do so many times at the Tivoli.

The first surprise was that I went a lot further down than I had been expecting. It seemed like I would never reach the bottom as the water closed in above me, cutting out all the bustle and noise of the poolside and filling my nose and mouth. After what seemed like an age I did bob back up the surface, but I didn't stay there – despite a lot of mad thrashing around I was soon sinking again, gulping in more water. The other boys were pointing and roaring with laughter, assuming it was all an act I was putting on to entertain them. Fortunately one of the lifeguards was more adept at telling the difference between a little show-off and a drowning boy and dived in to save me.

He dumped me on the side, where I lay gasping for breath like a newly landed fish, as the others gathered around to tell me how brave I was to dive straight into the deep end on my first time and thank me for giving them such a good laugh and such a good story to tell. I was happy to bask in their admiration, once I could breathe again, but I decided it wasn't a story I would share with Mammy or Bridie, because they might well have banned me from coming to the pool again. The whole near-drowning experience had done nothing to lessen my enthusiasm for swimming.

At school, however, the story spread like wildfire and now some of the older boys wanted to test out how brave I really was. I knew very well that I was not actually brave, just extremely reckless.

'We're going down the canal,' they told Connor and me after school one day. 'Do you want to come?'

'Sure,' we said, pleased to be included and always eager for new experiences.

'Have you heard of a game called Chicken?' they asked as we made our way down the backstreets, me almost having to run in order to keep up with everyone else's long strides.

'Of course,' we said, not wanting to let on that we didn't know what they were talking about.

The rules of the game were simple: you just copied everything that the leader did, and anyone who opted out was labelled 'chicken'. We walked until we came to the edge of the canal, and the bigger boys climbed onto a wall from which a long, slippery wooden beam straddled the widest part of the water.

'You have to walk across that to the other side,' they told us.

When I looked at the narrow beam and then down at the deep, mucky water below, I remembered the feeling of plunging to the bottom of the swimming pool and felt a spasm of real fear passing through me like an electric shock.

'Easy,' Connor scoffed, fearless as ever, despite the fact that he couldn't swim any better than I could.

The older boys crossed the beam one by one, their arms out to balance them as they concentrated on keeping their feet on the partly rotted wood. Finally it was our turn and Connor happily went first. My heart was in my mouth as I watched him wobble across, knowing that the moment he reached the other side I would have no option other than to follow. Looking down, the dirty water seemed to be rushing past at a terrible rate and I was sure that should I slip I would be swept away long before any of them would be able to get in to save me. Still, there was no choice, because anything was preferable to being called 'chicken'.

Connor reached the other side, and now they were all shouting at me to follow. I stretched out my arms to balance myself, like a circus acrobat on a high wire. I looked down and immediately started to wobble. I quickly stared straight ahead, concentrating on the other side and took my first step out over the water. The boys were all cheering me on as I moved forward, inches at a time, feeling like I was going to fall with every step. By some miracle I reached the other side.

Excited to have found two small boys who would do whatever they were told, the bigger boys then suggested we go on to something even more dangerous.

'We have to get back to the hostel now,' I said, quite sure that I'd had more than enough adrenaline going through my system for one day.

'Chickens!' the boys roared hysterically. 'You little chicken boys! You go back to the hostel and kiss your mammies good night then!'

'Feck off!' Connor shouted, squaring up to them and making them laugh even harder, albeit slightly nervously.

'Come on,' I urged him, 'or we'll miss the curfew.'

Connor reluctantly decided to follow me rather than take on all the older boys at once, and we raced back to Regina Coeli filled with joy at having survived such a daring adventure.

When we arrived at the hostel the gates had been closed already and we had to knock on the office door to get in. Sister Peggy opened the door and looked us up and down disapprovingly.

'What time do you call this?' she enquired.

'Sister Peggy,' I panted, 'we've been for swimming lessons.'

'Oh, really? Swimming? You should both be shrivelled up like prunes after being so long in the water.'

Despite the fact that we were obviously lying, she let us through. I knew that I had taken too great a risk and that the consequences of playing games as dangerous as Chicken were going to catch up with me sooner or later. Mammy always said I was like a cat with nine lives, but I was afraid I was using them up too quickly.

Chapter Eight
Off the Rails

Connor and I were always on the look-out for money-making opportunities. We had seen the man going into the barber's shop after carefully leaning his ancient bicycle up against the wall outside. We sauntered over to inspect the machine more carefully.

'That bike,' I said, with all the authority of an eight-year-old who had never even ridden a bicycle, 'could do with a good sorting out.'

'You're right,' agreed Connor, who had also never ridden or owned such an expensive thing. 'The chain needs to be stripped down and put back together again properly.'

'We could do it for him while he's getting his hair cut,' I suggested, 'and then he'll be giving us a tip when he comes out and sees how helpful we've been.'

The simple genius of the idea pleased us both and we set speedily to work removing the chain and spreading the pieces out across the pavement, our hands, clothes and faces soon becoming blackened and smudged with a mixture of mud and oil. It was not long before we realised it was going to be a bigger job than we had anticipated.

Neither of us spoke as we worked feverishly to get everything back together before the haircut going on inside was complete. The more we did, however, the more pieces there seemed to be fanning out around us, and the less we could remember how they had fitted together in the first place.

I heard the 'ding' of the barber's shop door opening and looked up from where I was squatting into the face of the newly barbered bicycle owner as he stepped out of the shop, refreshed and no doubt looking forward to riding his bicycle home for tea. His jaw dropped in horror as he took in the scene of devastation on the pavement, and then his face contorted into a grimace of fury. He even started to cry with a mixture of rage and frustration. I had never seen a grown man cry before. We all shouted at once.

'Run,' I shouted at Connor as we sprang to our feet.

'What the fuck do you think you're doing, you little bastards?' shouted the man. 'I'm gonna kill you, so I am!'

'Who the fuck are you calling a bastard?' shouted Connor, fearless as ever, squaring up to the giant of a man as he bore down with his fist raised.

'Run,' I shouted again, grabbing Connor's arm and dragging him after me.

Realising my plan was probably the wiser of the two, Connor joined me as we flew down the street, dodging round corners and over walls without looking back to see if the victim of our good intentions was closing in on us. We didn't stop until we had arrived back at the hostel and were hammering on the little door which was set into the high wooden gates, gasping for breath and desperately looking over our shoulders, expecting our pursuer to pound round the corner at any moment. I had never been so pleased to see the stern face of Sister Peggy as she opened the door, telling us off as we exploded past her and closing the door behind us.

Sister Peggy always had an air of authority despite her diminutive size. She found me a continual source of irritation, peering at me like an owl through her thick spectacles every time she had to tell me off for some new offence. She was always wearing a wrap-around blue apron like all the helpers at the hostel. She had never married and was a constant presence in our lives, living on the premises and only ever taking half a day off a week, on Sunday afternoons, when she would go out for tea with her married sister.

Because Mammy never got home from work until late in the evenings after all the customers had left the restaurant where she worked, I had a lot of time to make mischief every day after school had finished. When I was tiny I was more than content to play within the Regina Coeli grounds, which were large and full of interesting outbuildings, having once been a barracks, but it wasn't long before I wanted to expand my boundaries and follow the older boys over the back walls in order to explore the wider world. We were as hard to contain as a pack of agile little rats as we swarmed over the walls into the neighbouring bus depot and wood mill, daring one another to climb into the buses and running up and down the stairs, taunting the workers as they tried to catch us, or skidding around the edges of the oil pit, inches away from slipping into the black morass below, which looked deep enough to drown us.

Off the Rails

We spent happy hours playing hide and seek among the vehicles and piles of tyres and spare parts, everything reeking of oil and fuel, including ourselves. The Sisters often received complaints from the bus company, but they could never identify the culprits because we were too fast for them. I loved the buzz of the adrenaline, always wanting to take more and bigger risks, to push my adventures further and further. My only fear was that someone would tell Mammy what I was up to, but it seemed no one wanted to worry 'the Lady' unnecessarily. If I was caught doing something, Sister Peggy might report me to Bridie, but she never seemed to worry about anything and would always cover for me if she could, egged on by Joseph and Connor.

The wood mill was an equally rich source of adventure. The timber, stacked perilously high, was perfect for danger-filled games of hide and seek. The place was overseen by a man we nicknamed 'Jack', after Jack the Ripper, fantasising about the terrible tortures he would inflict on us if he ever caught us trespassing. I dare say he knew very well that we were there, although he pretended not to see us as we scuttled around in the shadows or at the top of the woodpiles. Jack always wore a hat, the wide brim pulled down to cover his face, and his clothes were always ragged and dirty. He seemed to live in the mill all the time, never venturing into the outside world, and in this he was like Sister Peggy, Bridie and some of the other women and nuns in the hostel. Dublin was full of these hidden, private little worlds, populated by people who had chosen to make themselves invisible to the rest of society.

* * *

It wasn't long before I wanted to explore beyond the confines of Morning Star Avenue, stretching my wings further than the bus depot and wood mill. The doors at Regina Coeli would always be locked at seven in the evening, which meant that anyone coming back late would have to knock and be let in by Sister Peggy, who would then interrogate them on exactly what they had been up to. Mostly I would manage to sneak back into the grounds just before curfew and could pretend I had been there all along, but increasingly often I would push my luck too far and not be able to get back in time.

'Where on earth have you been, Gordon?' Sister Peggy would demand.

'I had extra-curricular activities,' I would say – or, 'I had swimming lessons.'

I'm sure she saw through all these lies and talked about me to Bridie, but I didn't care, as long as Mammy never found out. She was the one person I never wanted to displease or disappoint.

There was only so far that I could get around Dublin on foot, so I took to using the buses. I had no money for fares, so I would always be looking around for the quickest escape route, ready to jump off whenever I thought a conductor had spotted me and was about to ask to see my ticket. Sometimes they gave chase, and occasionally I would find myself stranded in some part of town I had never been to before, with absolutely no idea what direction to start walking in. I enjoyed the excitement, although sometimes even I had to admit I had bitten off more than I could chew. On one occasion I found myself in totally unfamiliar territory at eight o'clock at night. It was already pitch dark and I knew that the doors at the hostel would have been locked for an hour by then. I would already have been running around at full speed for the whole day, because that was the only speed I knew, and I must have looked as weary as I felt as I dragged my feet along the streets with no idea if I was heading in the right direction or not.

'Are you OK?' a voice with an unfamiliar accent enquired.

I spun round to find myself confronted with the concerned faces of what I discovered was an Irish-American family, all worried by the sight of a small boy wandering the streets alone in the dark.

'Actually,' I admitted reluctantly, 'I'm a bit lost.'

'You are so cute,' one of the daughters said, her accent as American as the ones I had heard in some of the films Mammy and I had been to on our outings into the city. 'Can we take you home to America with us?'

They all laughed, so I knew it was a joke, but it sounded like a pretty good idea to me, from what I had seen of America in the films. Then I thought about leaving Mammy and Bridie and everyone else at the hostel and remembered that what I wanted most right then was to get safely home.

'Let's just get him home,' the mother said, as if she had read my thoughts. 'Where do you live?'

'Regina Coeli in Morning Star Avenue,' I blurted, 'on the North Side.'

At that moment a Garda (policeman) appeared on the other side of the road and to my horror the father walked over to him.

'Excuse me, Officer,' he said, 'could you help this young man? He seems to be lost. He says he lives at a place called Regina Coeli in Morning Star Avenue.'

For a second I contemplated running. Bringing the Garda to the hostel was considered the worst possible crime. No one there wanted to draw the attention of any authorities to our existence. The one thing the nuns didn't want was for their charges to get a reputation for being troublemakers. If I hadn't been so exhausted I might well have made a dash for freedom and taken my chances in the dark backstreets, but I doubt I would have been able to outrun a Garda with a car.

'The policeman will take you home, Sonny,' the kindly father reassured me.

My horror at the thought of turning up at the hostel with the Garda was now tempered by the prospect of being given my first ever ride in a car – even if it was a police car. I decided to bow to my fate and climbed into the back seat, leaving my American Samaritans waving as we drove off at a speed I had never experienced before. I stared out the window as the scenery flashed by, wide-eyed with excitement – and trepidation about the reception I would get at Regina Coeli.

I was sad when the ride was all too quickly over and I had to step back out of the warm interior with my escort, and deeply nervous as the Garda rapped on the hostel door.

'Good evening, Sister,' he said when Sister Peggy's face peered out. 'Do you know this young man? He seemed to be lost in the docks area.'

'Yes, Officer, I know him,' she replied, her bespectacled eyes boring into mine as she spoke. 'His name is Gordon. Sorry to have troubled you. I can take it from here.'

Off the Rails

Gripping my wrist she yanked me inside and firmly shut the door behind me, leaving the policeman standing on the doorstep without another word.

'What do you think you are doing, Gordon, bringing the Garda to our door? And what time of night do you call this to be coming home?' She was so furious she wasn't even drawing breath long enough for me to start spinning one of my tales, which was lucky because I was having trouble thinking of anything that would convincingly explain the manner of my return home. 'I'm going to be having another word with Bridie about your behaviour.'

I was terrified that this time I had gone too far and Bridie would be telling Mammy what I had been getting up to. I slipped into bed early that night, pretending to be asleep when Mammy got back, and the next morning everything seemed to be calm. I had got away with it again and I was free to continue my explorations of the outside world for another day.

It wasn't always my fault that I got lost. One afternoon I went on the bus with some of my older friends to visit the old port district. Being younger and smaller than them I sometimes had difficulty keeping up, however determined I might be, and on this occasion I fell so deeply asleep on the bus that my friends were able to slip off, stifling their giggles so that they wouldn't wake me, leaving the conductor to shake me awake at the end of the line and inform me that I needed to buy a ticket for the return journey.

'But I don't have any money,' I pleaded, which was completely true but did not touch his heart-strings as effectively as I hoped.

'Off,' he said, hauling me to my feet and marching me to the door. He'd obviously met too many kids like me before to fall for what looked like an old trick. Yet again I was stranded in a largely deserted part of town, just as the light was fading, with no idea which direction to start walking in.

Taking an arbitrary decision, I started putting one foot in front of the other in the hope that fate would give me some clue as to what I should do next. After what seemed like an age, as my legs started to ache and I was beginning to wonder if I would be tramping the streets all night or sleeping rough in a doorway somewhere, a car drew up beside me. The window wound down and an English voice called out to me.

'Excuse me,' he said in an accent I had to strain to understand. 'Do you know the way to Trinity College?'

I had never heard of Trinity College, but I wasn't going to tell him that. I wished that he wasn't English, because everyone I knew hated the English, even though none of them had ever met any, so I assumed they must be very wicked people. It was a historical hatred, based on the crimes of the 'Black and Tans' (a force of temporary constables recruited after the First World War to fight the IRA, mostly made up of British ex-servicemen, who became infamous for their violence and for their persecution of the Irish and for their attacks on civilians and their property). I could see that he had his wife and children in the car, so I was pretty sure that even though he was English he probably wouldn't murder me. It was a better option than a night spent wandering the cold streets.

'If you want to give me a lift to the centre of the city I can direct you to Trinity College from there,' I said, with enough self-confidence to convince him that I knew what I was talk-ing about.

'That's very kind of you,' he said. 'Hop in.'

I climbed into the back seat with his daughters, relieved to be able to sink back into the seat and not to have to walk another step. This was my second ride in a car, and this time it wasn't a police car. I settled down to make the most of the experience, every so often issuing an instruction in what I hoped was a confident voice: 'Take the next left … turn right at the lights …' although nothing that I could see from the windows looked even remotely familiar.

'Would you like a sweet?' the mother asked, passing the bag over from the front. I never said 'no' to sweets and I was also starving hungry, so I took a handful. As I felt the sweet sugar flowing into my veins and relaxed into the comfortable seat I never wanted the ride to end. I hoped that if I just kept issuing instructions divine intervention would eventually show me the way. It didn't.

'Am I right in thinking,' the father eventually enquired, 'that you are as lost as we are?'

'I think we might have taken a wrong turning back there,' I admitted. 'I'm not quite sure where we are now.'

'So, where exactly do you live?' he asked.

'On the North Side,' I said, hoping this meant he was now planning to drive me all the way home, 'in a road called Morning Star Avenue.'

We drove on in silence for a while, and then to my horror I saw that he had spotted a police car and was driving up to it.

'Excuse me,' he called out to the Garda. 'This lad is lost. He says he lives in Morning Star Avenue. Can you help him to get home?'

So there I was, heading home in a police car once more. It was well past nine o'clock by then, which meant that Mammy would be back from work and would be wondering where I was. What possible excuse could I make up? How could I persuade Sister Peggy and Bridie to back up whatever story I told?

'Wait in my office,' Sister Peggy said when she opened the door to the Garda's knock and saw it was me again. I was racking my brains to come up with something convincing as I waited.

'Francis,' she said as she came in, having seen the Garda off, 'you are the only boy here who would dare to come in at this ungodly hour! And with the Garda! I'm going to have to talk very seriously to Bridie about you again.' She was the only person in the hostel who still called me by my first name.

'Do what you want, Sister,' I replied haughtily, confident that Bridie would back me up.

Believing I had got away with it yet again, I was strolling jauntily back to my dormitory when a long, high screech halted me in my tracks. 'Gordon!'

I spun round in time to see Mammy heading towards me with an expression that looked less than tranquil. Since there was no possible route of escape, there was no option other than to face up to my fate.

'Where have you been?' she screamed. 'I've been worrying myself sick.' As she grabbed me and held me tightly I thought I detected a flicker of relief in her eyes at my safe return. Maybe there was still a chance of getting away with my transgressions if I exploited her maternal instincts. I smiled up at her with my sweetest and most innocent face; a cherubic look which I had always found melted the very sternest of hearts. 'Don't give me any nonsense about swimming lessons or extra schoolwork,' she warned as I opened my mouth to try exactly those excuses for size. 'Bridie's told me all about the late nights and the run-ins with the Garda!'

Betrayal! I tried to smile a little more sweetly and hoped a tear might spring to my eye in time to save me.

'But Mammy, I did stay in school for extra lessons, and then I went to the pool. I just got lost on the way home.'

'That's it,' she said, 'no more lies. I know exactly what you've been up to. I've spoken to all your friends and their mammies. I know everything. I am so disappointed in you, Gordon.'

Now my tears were genuine. 'Well, you're never here anyway,' I spat back. 'What do you expect?'

Shocked and angry, she lashed out, smacking me hard on the bottom. 'What do you think I'm working day and night for, you silly boy? It's so you can have the best life you possibly can. And what do you do? Lie to your mammy and ignore everything I tell you.' Every sentence was punctuated with a painful smack across the backs of my legs as I hopped about, trying to escape from her, running around the dormitory with her close behind me.

'I'm sorry, Mammy,' I sobbed. 'I promise I'll be a good boy.'

Finally catching me, she held me with both hands, her face inches from mine, her eyes blazing with anger. 'And don't you dare be rude to Sister Peggy ever again, and don't even think about wandering about the city after school. From now on you come straight back here and stay within the grounds. Do you understand?'

'Yes, Mammy,' I snivelled, deeply shocked by the strength of her fury. That night as I lay in bed, the backs of my legs still smarting from her blows, I realised that I had pushed my luck too far. I had overreached myself and things were going to be different from now on, although I didn't know exactly how different.

In fact things didn't change immediately. For a month or so I behaved impeccably, despite the fact that I wanted to scream with boredom and longed to clamber over the confining walls and escape into the streets for more exploring and more adventures. I'm sure it would only have been a matter of time before I cracked under the strain and returned to my old ways, and I guess Mammy realised that too because, unbeknown to me, she was making plans that would mean everything in our lives would soon be very different.

With nothing better to do one evening I had gone to bed early and was fast asleep by the time Mammy got home from work, then woke to find her sitting on the edge of the bed, stroking my hair back from my forehead. She smiled sweetly as I opened my eyes.

'I've brought you something,' she whispered as I struggled to wake up. 'It's apple.'

She held up a slice of apple pie and I pulled myself into a sitting position, watching her face carefully as I ate, grateful for the pie but wary that there was some other reason for her waking me. Had someone told her something else I had done?

'I had some good news today,' she said, laughing at the speed with which I was devouring the pie. 'An old friend of mine is coming from England to visit.'

'What friend?' I asked, my mouth full of apple and pastry. 'I didn't know you had a friend in England.'

'There's plenty you don't know about your old mammy, young man,' she said, squeezing my knee affectionately. 'His name is Bill. We knew each other in Dublin many years ago, before you were even born. He's a nice man; you'll like him a lot.'

Once I had finished eating she bent down to kiss me goodnight, tucking me back under the blankets. 'Sleep tight.'

There was no chance of that happening any time soon, as a thousand thoughts raced around inside my head. How could my mother have a friend that I knew nothing about? Why had she thought it necessary to sweeten me up with a piece of pie? I had never even thought that she might have had a life before she had me, and I wasn't at all sure I liked the idea. Who was this man? Why had he decided to come to Dublin now? The idea of Mammy having a boyfriend made me want to snigger, but it made me uneasy at the same time. I didn't want to be sharing my mammy with anyone else, however 'nice' he might turn out to be. I liked my life exactly the way it was and I didn't want some stranger coming along and upsetting things.

We were due to meet him a few days later on O'Connell Bridge at nine in the morning, a place I knew well from our walks to the picture house. Mammy was awake long before that, and I lay in bed watching as she dressed herself with extra care, wearing a flared floral skirt and a spotless white cardigan, fussing with her beautifully cut blonde hair and powder compact, even applying a layer of startlingly red lipstick, all the time talking nervously as she worked.

'You'll like Bill, Gordon, I know you will.'

'What does he look like?'

'I wish I had a photo to show you. He's a handsome man, dark hair and a moustache, a little like that film star, Clark Gable.' I had no idea who she was talking about, but I didn't interrupt her. 'He's always very smartly turned out. You'll like him, I know you will.'

Her nerves were making her gabble nonsensically and I tuned out. It didn't matter how many times she assured me I would like him – I was not so sure.

'You look very pretty, Mammy,' I said eventually and the smile she beamed in my direction gave me a warm feeling in my stomach. I just wished she wasn't going to all this trouble for a man I hadn't even met.

Despite me dragging my feet we arrived on the bridge well before the appointed time. The sun was shining and the sky was blue, but from where I was standing it just seemed like a mass of people hurrying past above me as we stood and waited. The minutes passed by agonisingly slowly. Mammy stared towards the south side of the bridge, her fingers constantly fiddling with her handbag. By ten past nine I could hardly contain myself, every muscle in my body aching to move. I wanted to watch the rubbish passing under the bridge, but I couldn't see much between the balustrades. I tried to jump up and see over the top.

Off the Rails

'For goodness sake, Gordon,' Mammy said, 'stop fidgeting. You'll get dirt all over your clothes.' She always took pride in turning me out as well as she could afford and I was dressed in my best shorts and white shirt, with a tie all but strangling me.

By twenty past she was starting to look truly worried and I was feeling hungry as well as bored. 'He's not coming,' I said, tugging at her skirt, 'is he?'

'He'll be here soon. Just be patient, for goodness sake.' At that moment she spotted him and smiled and waved with an excitement I had never seen before. I stood, rooted to the spot, staring at my mother as she jumped around like a joyful young girl. 'Do you see him, Gordon? I told you he would come!'

I peered into the crowd, trying to work out which man she was talking about, but there were too many people, too many legs rushing past me. Then the crowds seemed to part in front of us and I saw a smartly dressed man waving a newspaper in the air. He had dark hair and a moustache and the same wide smile as my mother. Only later would I discover that Mammy was right, he did look like Clark Gable.

Both of them seemed to have forgotten my existence as I looked up at them embracing and kissing. My jaw must have dropped because I had never seen anyone kiss my mother before, or hold her in their arms the way this stranger was holding her. After what seemed like an age of gazing into one another's eyes, grinning like kids who had just been given an ice cream, they remembered me and both looked down.

'Hello,' Bill said, 'you must be Francis.'

'My name is Gordon,' I replied, without a hint of a smile, 'not Francis!'

'OK,' he grinned, 'Gordon it is, then.' He then produced a long, strangely shaped tube of chocolate from his jacket pocket. 'This is for you, Gordon. It's Toblerone – chocolate from Switzerland.'

I couldn't believe my eyes. It was the most beautiful looking chocolate bar I had ever seen – in a long triangular wrapper – and it came all the way from Switzerland! Not that I had the faintest idea where Switzerland was, but just the sound of it was exotic enough. Having succeeded in temporarily placating me he returned his attention to Mammy.

'So,' he said, 'is there anywhere you would both like to go?'

'Can we go to the zoo?' I piped up. It was somewhere I had been nagging Mammy to take me for ages, but she had always told me it would cost too much money.

'Certainly,' Bill laughed. Pushing his paper into his pocket he took Mum's hand in one of his and mine in the other. This was a step too far for me. I still didn't feel I knew enough about this man and his relationship with my mother. I dropped his hand and scurried round to take Mammy's other hand, making them both laugh. I don't think there was anything that I could have said or done that would have pricked their bubble of happiness that day.

The moment Bill had paid for the tickets I rushed in through the gates, straight up to the first cage. Bill produced a camera from another of his coat pockets and took pictures of us, despite Mammy making some feeble protests about her hair not being straight. I dragged them round a few more cages before Mammy told me they were going to sit on the bench.

'You go off and explore,' she said. 'We'll just be waiting here.'

My disappointment at being deprived of my mother's full attention was compensated for by the excitement of having an entire zoo laid out around me and nobody telling me what I could or couldn't do. Although I wanted to see every animal in the place before the visit was over, I found myself constantly glancing back towards the bench to check what was happening. Neither of them seemed to be giving me a second thought. To start with they were holding hands; then Bill put his arm around her. I couldn't understand why they needed to sit so close when they had the whole bench to themselves, but I decided to think about it all later and make the most of enjoying the zoo for as long as they had forgotten me.

By the middle of the afternoon I was exhausted and very hungry. Bill beckoned me over. 'Shall we go and get some afternoon tea,' he asked, 'with sandwiches and cakes?'

'Yes, please,' I said.

'No, Bill,' Mammy said, 'you've spent quite enough on us already.'

My face must have shown my disappointment because Bill laughed. 'No,' he said, 'I insist. Come on.'

He didn't tell us where we were going until we were standing outside the doors of the grand Shelbourne Hotel and Mammy was staring at the menu which was displayed in a shiny mahogany box, looking aghast.

'No, Bill,' she said, 'this is far too expensive.'

'Nonsense,' he replied, steering us both inside.

For the first time in my life I was overawed and fell silent as I looked around at the grandeur of the best hotel in the city. I had never seen such luxury and beauty, from the sparkling chandeliers and rich wallpapers to the antique clocks and giant porcelain vases; it seemed like a king's palace. I had never even realised that such places existed or that people like us could just walk in through such exclusive doors. Bill must have been able to see how impressed both Mammy and I were as we were ushered into the main lounge area and shown to huge chairs with cushions that were softer and more comfortable than anything I had ever experienced. How was it possible for anything to be so soft? At the centre of the room a fire crackled in an ornate fireplace.

Everyone around us was so elegantly dressed and their clothes looked so new and expensive, I was suddenly aware of just how shabby and down-at-heel I must look, so obviously one of the 'unfortunates' from the North Side. I became self-conscious and didn't raise my voice above a whisper whenever Mammy or Bill addressed a comment or question in my direction.

When the waiter came to take our order Mammy asked for the high tea for herself and me.

'That would be fine,' Bill said, 'but I'll start with a pint of Guinness.'

'Really, Bill,' Mammy scolded the moment the waiter was out of earshot, 'it's a little early in the day for Guinness, don't you think?'

'It's never too early for a pint of Guinness,' Bill grinned, entirely unabashed. I was impressed at the way he didn't back down. I had never seen Mammy telling off someone else in the tone she usually reserved for me, particularly a grown man.

As we settled down he started to talk about his life in England and I found a thousand questions bubbling up in my head, overcoming my self-consciousness at being in such grand, hushed surroundings.

'What's London like?' I asked.

'It's better than you can ever imagine, Gordon,' he smiled. 'There's opportunities round every corner for a lad like yourself.'

'Where do you live?'

'I live in the north of the city, in an area called Finsbury Park.'

'Do you have a car?'

'No,' he laughed, 'I don't have a car. There's no need. There's buses and tube trains to take you every place you could ever want to go.'

'Do you have a dog?'

'No, I don't have a dog. Maybe I should get one.'

I was a little disappointed by both these bits of news, but then he dropped his bombshell.

'Would you like to come and visit some time, Gordon,' he asked, 'if I could persuade your mammy to bring you over?'

While I was still taking in the enormity of this casual invitation, our tea arrived, a succession of waiters bearing silver cake stands with several tiers of food on each. There were cakes as colourful and beautifully made as tiny works of art, sandwiches with their crusts neatly sliced off and a pile of warm scones with individual bowls of jam and thick cream. It was impossible to work out what to eat first. I wanted to try everything immediately, and then I wanted more of everything I tried. I did my best not to stuff my mouth so full I couldn't speak, but I failed. So all I could do as Bill laid out his plans for inviting us to London was nod vigorously as I chewed, swallowed and grabbed more, ignoring Mammy's disapproving looks.

Eventually we had demolished every scrap of food and I was sitting back in the cushions feeling bloated and contented.

'So, what are your plans for the evening, Bill?' Mammy asked.

'I'll be looking up some old friends and going to the pub,' he said.

'You go easy on the drink, now,' Mammy warned him. 'I know what you're like, Bill Lewis.'

Bill grinned like a naughty schoolboy and signalled to the waiter for the bill. Pulling his wallet from his jacket pocket he opened it up and I wasn't able to suppress a gasp at the sight of so much money. Bill laughed. 'That's just Irish money, lad,' he said, pulling a wad of English notes from his back trouser pocket. 'English money has much more value.'

'Will you stop flashing your money around in front of the boy,' Mammy scolded. 'You'll be putting all sorts of ideas into his head.'

Bill winked at me and put his English money away, pulling out a handful of Irish notes from his wallet and dropping them casually on the table with the bill. It seemed to me that Bill must be a very rich man indeed.

As we came out of the hotel into the cool of the evening air I felt the full impact of everything I had eaten. 'I don't think I can walk all the way home, Mammy,' I moaned. 'I'm too full.'

'Do you want to ride on my shoulders?' Bill asked.

'Absolutely not,' Mammy interrupted before I could accept the offer, 'he needs to walk off all that lovely food he's pushed down his throat. He'll soon feel better.' Bill looked at me and shrugged, as if we both knew better than to contradict Mammy. 'You go on and meet your friends,' she said. 'We'll get back home just fine.'

Bill crouched down to my level. 'Goodbye, Gordon, it's been a pleasure meeting you,' he said, 'And I very much look forward to seeing you again in London.'

'Give Bill a kiss,' Mammy instructed, but I really didn't want to kiss him or any other grown man for that matter. 'Come on Gordon, give Bill a kiss!' I gave him a darting peck on the cheek. He smelled pleasant; a mixture of soap and pipe smoke.

'Goodbye,' I said and he straightened up to say goodbye to Mammy, who also proffered a chaste cheek, although I'm sure he was hoping for something a little more passionate at the end of their first romantic day together in nearly ten years. Bill made a couple more offers to walk us home, but she was adamant. Now I realise that she had no intention of allowing Bill to see the sort of place where we were living and maybe he realised that too, because he didn't insist too hard.

I didn't see Bill again before he sailed back to London a few days later, although I'm sure Mammy did because they must have had so much to talk about, so many plans to lay. The events of that day kept buzzing around in my head. I wanted to remember every detail, every animal at the zoo, every cake at the Shelbourne. I wanted to ask Mammy a thousand questions about Bill and about why he had said he looked forward to seeing me in London, but I was always asleep by the time she got in at night and still sleeping when she left in the morning. It was four days before I finally managed to pin her down and start firing questions. At first she was evasive, as if wanting to keep the details to herself, but I was relentless.

'Bill and I have been corresponding for a month or two,' she eventually admitted, 'and he has asked if we would join him in London.'

That was all the information I needed. 'Yes,' I shouted, leaping up off the bed and dancing round the room. 'Yes! We're going to London!'

'Calm down, Gordon, will you?' Mammy said, catching hold of me before I could escape from the room and broadcast my news to the whole world. 'You must keep this to yourself for the time being. No one else knows apart from Bridie, and I've not told her every detail.'

'What have you not told Bridie?'

Mammy looked at me for a few moments, as if weighing up whether I would be able to handle a secret as momentous as the one she was about to tell me.

'Well,' she said eventually, holding my hand tightly as if to ensure that she kept me firmly tethered to the ground, 'Bill has asked me to marry him.'

Chapter Nine
Moving On

'We're going to visit my mother,' Mammy announced one evening. 'Your Granny.'

I was stunned. She had only recently started to talk about her mother in the vaguest of terms, and it had never really occurred to me that I would get to meet her myself. Her family seemed like a part of Mammy's life that had never had anything to do with me. I wasn't sure how I felt about this meeting.

'When?' I asked.

'Next Tuesday, after you finish school.'

'Where does she live?' I asked, trying to muster my thoughts.

'She has a house in a village called Lucan, outside Dublin,' Mammy said, making it all sound very casual. 'We'll need to take a bus.'

I was beginning to think this might be a grand adventure after all. The thought of going on a long bus ride with Mammy was exciting, but also a little scary. What if the conductor was one of the ones who had thrown me off buses for not paying in the past? Mammy would be horrified to know that I had been doing such things, although I'm pretty sure she suspected, which was why she was planning to get me away to London with her and Bill. At least I hoped that was the plan. I certainly hoped that she wasn't planning on going to London without me.

'She has a house?' I said, trying to imagine what it must be like to live in a proper house. 'A whole house?'

'Yes,' Mammy laughed at my astonishment. 'You'll see.'

Now I was really excited at the prospect of the trip. I had never actually been in a house before and couldn't imagine what it might be like. When the big day finally arrived I raced home from school and Mammy was waiting for me with all my best clothes laid out. I changed as fast as I could and Mammy made sure there was not a mark on me before we set off for the bus stop.

The buses only went every two hours and we had to hurry not to miss the next service. We made it with only seconds to spare. I climbed onto the bus after her, trying to be as inconspicuous as possible behind her skirts. My heart sank when I saw the conductor and recognised his face. I immediately averted my eyes and avoiding looking at him for the rest of the journey, although several times I glanced up and caught him staring at me with a puzzled look on his face, as if he knew that I was familiar but couldn't work out why.

'Why are we going to meet Granny now?' I asked as the bus rumbled out through the suburbs and into the countryside.

'You're nine years old now, Gordon,' she said. 'The time is right for you to meet her.'

Moving On

This didn't seem like a convincing argument to me but I didn't say anything more. Mammy was not someone who I could ever question too closely about anything; she had an air of privacy and dignity about her which made any cheekiness seem entirely out of the question, even for me. It seemed likely to me, however, that this meeting had more to do with Bill and the impending trip to London. I had noticed that ever since Bill had turned up Mammy had been acting differently and this bus ride seemed like part of the same thing. I changed the subject and continued to chatter happily until the bus eventually ground into Lucan and stopped at the bottom of a steep hill.

'Come on, Gordon,' Mammy said as she started to stride up the hill, 'keep up!'

As we neared the top I could make out a row of six small houses and Mammy pointed to one of the front doors.

'That's the house,' she said. 'Nearly there now.'

I had no idea what to expect as we made our way up to the door and knocked. There were some shuffling noises inside and it creaked open, very slowly. Whatever it was I was expecting, it wasn't the tiny, bent old lady who peered out at us. I was shocked by how old she was, with a hunched back which bent her head sharply to the right. She reminded me of the wolf who dressed up as the grandmother in *Little Red Riding Hood* and I felt slightly alarmed. She wore a long blue apron wrapped around her middle. Seeing who we were, she welcomed us with a soft voice and Mammy bent down to peck her on the cheek.

Once we were inside Granny looked me up and down. 'So, this is Francis,' she said. 'How are you?'

'I'm not Francis,' I replied firmly, 'I'm Gordon.'

'He prefers to be called Gordon,' Mammy explained with a nervous smile.

'OK,' Granny nodded, 'Gordon it is, then. Would you like a cup of tea, Gordon? And a piece of cake?'

She moved slowly to the fireplace where lumps of turf were burning, giving off clouds of black smoke, and sat down in what was obviously her favourite chair by the fire. An unpleasant smell hung over the room. I looked at Mammy and pulled a face.

'Minnie,' Granny called out, 'can you help me make the tea? And take the cakes and biscuits from the cupboard for Gordon.'

'Who's Minnie?' I enquired, not wanting any more mysteries.

'Minnie is my pet name for your mammy,' Granny explained.

'My mammy's name is Cathleen,' I corrected her, 'definitely not Minnie.'

'When she was young,' Granny said, with a smile, 'she had a cat called Minnie. She adored the cat so much that we started to call her Minnie too. The pair of them were inseparable.'

Mammy had a distant look in her eyes as she listened to her mother's story and watched me hearing it for the first time.

'I think it's a silly name,' I said.

I was not at all sure how I felt about this wizened old lady in the foul-smelling house. Because of the angle that her head was bent to I couldn't see her face clearly. There were just so many new emotions and sensations to be taken in at once.

Moving On

Mammy took a big kettle of water to the fireplace and put it on to boil. I could see this was going to take some time and wanted to explore the first house I had ever been in.

'Can I look around the house?' I asked.

'Of course,' Granny said. 'You go wherever you like.'

Feeling like I was setting out on an expedition into the unknown, I started in the kitchen where I found a cooker, a sink and a wooden dresser covered in cups and plates. The whole house was full of dark corners, and the smoke from the open fire seemed to have permeated and blackened every room.

Making my way up the narrow stairs I passed a window that was so caked in dust and mud that I couldn't see out, and came upon three doors, each leading to a bedroom. Each bedroom contained a single bed, a little table and a chair. In all the rooms there were small crucifixes and pictures of Jesus Christ. It felt a little like being inside a tiny church. I tried to imagine Mammy sleeping in one of these rooms as a girl.

The house obviously hadn't been decorated for years and the wallpaper was peeling off in places. As I stared at the pattern, trying to make sense of the design, I could hear Mammy and Granny talking downstairs. I moved quietly to the top of the stairs and paused to listen more carefully.

'I can't go on living at Regina Coeli,' Mammy was saying. 'It's not a good place for Gordon to grow up. Recently the Garda have been bringing him back after finding him in the city centre, up to no good.'

'And have you heard from Bill?' Granny asked.

'He came to Dublin for a visit about a month ago,' Mammy said. 'He says he wants to marry me in London.'

'What about the boy?' Granny asked and I held my breath as I waited to hear her answer.

'Bill is willing to look after the both of us,' Mammy replied. 'I would never leave Gordon. I'd never go to London without him. Since meeting Gordon, Bill has really taken to him and I think Gordon quite likes Bill too.'

I let my breath go and felt a wave of relief. Mammy wasn't going to leave me behind. The moment I went back into the room they changed the subject. Mammy made the tea and offered me a piece of cake.

'So,' Granny said as I tucked in, 'have you seen the whole house?'

'I have,' I said, 'but I couldn't find where the toilet is.'

'It's just out the back,' Granny said, 'in the garden.'

'In the garden?' I couldn't hide my surprise. 'At Regina Coeli we only have four toilets between us all, but they're not in the garden!'

The women both laughed at my amazement and Granny changed the subject again, firing off questions. How many times did I go to church each week? Did I like school? Did I have a dog?

'We're not allowed pets,' I said, sadly. 'I would love a dog.'

I looked at Mammy longingly, hoping that she was taking in this fact in case there was any chance that she would think of asking Bill to get me one once we reached London. She appeared not to have heard, and for the rest of the visit she and Granny talked about Bill and the trip to London.

'Will Bill be converting to Catholicism?' Granny asked.

'No,' Mammy said firmly, 'he will not. And I will not be becoming a Protestant either.' Her tone made it clear

Moving On

that as far as she was concerned that was the end of the matter.

I was shocked. Bill was a Protestant? How could that be possible? All I had ever heard was how evil all Protestants were and how we could never have anything to do with them, but Bill hadn't seemed evil at all. It was so puzzling and I had lots of questions, but I couldn't even think where to start, so I remained quiet and kept eating.

When it was time to leave for the last bus back into Dublin I put on my coat and went to the front door with Mammy, who gave her mother a kiss goodbye. Granny then turned towards me, obviously expecting me to kiss her too. I held back, horrified at the thought.

'Give your granny a kiss goodbye, Gordon,' Mammy instructed.

I closed my eyes so that I didn't have to look at her wizened old face from close up and pecked her quickly on the cheek.

'Would you like to come back and visit again?' Granny asked me, but I didn't reply.

'Why did Granny's house smell like that?' I enquired as we walked back down the hill to the bus stop.

'That poor old cat of hers is incontinent and messing all over the house, I'm afraid,' Mammy explained.

By the time we were back on the bus I was feeling overwhelmingly tired.

'How long has Granny known Bill?' I asked.

'About twelve years,' Mammy said and then I fell asleep before I could think of any more questions.

* * *

I would imagine that Mammy had a lot to think about. It must have been the most enormous thing for her to admit to her mother that she had a son who she had kept secret for nearly ten years, and that she was no longer going to allow anyone to come between her and Bill. She knew that Bill was our best chance of a good life and she was going to take it, no matter what both their families might have to say about it. That day she had finally taken a stand and openly rebelled in her own quiet and dignified way. I imagine it must have been an extraordinary feeling of relief for her after so many years of having to hide the truth.

After that everyone at the hostel knew about our plans because Mammy had to give her notice in at the restaurant. Those who liked us were as excited as we were that Mammy was going to get married and we were going to have a home of our own. Those who already resented Mammy for what they perceived to be her 'airs and graces', like Bridget Murphy, became even more envious. I could see that she was almost as excited as I was about the prospect of going to England and marrying Bill. She bought our tickets for the boat to Holyhead and the train on to London, and spent as much time as she could with her brother, Christie, and her sister, Lily, in the days before we left, knowing that it would probably be some time before she saw them again.

Best of all, I was given a letter to pass to the head teacher at school, to notify him of my departure. I was over the moon – this must mean I could put school behind me once and for all. I really didn't like it. I found it boring, and because of my extremely short attention span I never seemed to be able to follow what was being taught. I could never sit still for long, and I couldn't understand why I saw letters and words differently to other children. I was overjoyed at the thought that I would never have to sit in a classroom again.

I would lie awake at night imagining what London was going to be like. I couldn't wait to see all the cars and the bright lights and the exciting shops – especially the sweet-shops! Oh, what a choice of goodies there was going to be. And the picture houses that Mammy and I would be able to go to. A week before we left, Sister Peggy stopped me at the door as I returned from school one day.

'Francis,' she said, 'could I have a word with you?'

I wondered what I had done wrong now. I wasn't aware that I had been misbehaving. I waited for the inevitable telling off.

'I hear you are about to leave us, Francis.'

'Yes, Sister, that's right. We're off to London to live with Bill.' I really wanted to impress her with our stroke of luck. 'He has a car and a dog and Mammy won't need to work any more and will stay home with me all the time. Bill says I can have a room of my own and there will be a garden for me to play in and we'll have our own television …'

'That's just wonderful,' she said. 'We're all so pleased for you and your mammy. I'll always remember you both and keep you in my prayers. I wish you much happiness in London.'

With that she patted me on the shoulder and went back into her office, leaving me dumbfounded and touched. I had always assumed that she hated me because I was such a nuisance, and yet in those few words she had seemed to be genuinely fond of both of us, and genuinely hoping for our happiness.

The next day at school Connor came up to me in the playground while there was no one else around. He looked very sad.

'I hear you're leaving Regina Coeli,' he said. 'I'll miss all our adventures and hanging out with you.'

'Me too,' I said, 'but it won't be for ever. I'm sure we'll be back soon.'

He nodded but continued to look uncomfortable, as if there was something else on his mind but he didn't know how to say it. I waited for him to speak again.

'I'd really like to come with you to England,' he said eventually, staring down at his feet.

'That's a brilliant idea,' I said, wondering why I hadn't thought of it for myself. I knew that his mammy was always drunk and was pretty sure she wouldn't miss him. They never really appeared to talk to one another as it was. I was the only person Connor ever seemed to confide in. I was touched that he trusted me enough to show this vulnerable side of his character and thrilled at the thought of us having adventures together in the streets of London, just as we had been doing in Dublin. 'I'll ask my Mammy tonight.'

'Mammy,' I said when I next had her on my own, 'can Connor come with us and live in London?'

'Of course he can't, Gordon,' she said, stifling a laugh when she saw how serious I was about the idea.

'Why not?'

'What would his mammy say? I wouldn't like it if you suddenly disappeared off with someone else's mammy, would I? Besides, Bill only has just enough room for the two of us.'

This last piece of news was a disappointment since I had been imagining that everyone in London had houses big enough to fit an extra person into. I didn't say any more, because I could see she wasn't even going to consider the idea, and the next day I had to break the bad news to Connor, who stared at me intently as if drinking in every word I was saying.

'I thought she'd say that,' he said eventually with a sad little sigh, 'but thanks for trying.' I could see how hard he was struggling to hide his disappointment. 'I'll make my own way to England as soon as I can and I'll come and visit you.'

'That would be great,' I said, feeling sure that we would be back together again in no time.

Mammy went to visit her sister, Lily, one last time before we left. They had always stayed in touch, although until then I had been as unaware of Lily's existence as she still was of mine. They used to meet up once every couple of months on Mammy's afternoon off. Lily was five years older than Mammy, a widow with four children. Her husband had passed away when the children were still young. There was Terry, then seventeen, who was bright and had been awarded a scholarship to further his education in college. Lily was immensely proud of his achievement, but also relieved to have one less mouth to feed at home. Tony was sixteen and wanted to work in a garage as a mechanic. Dennis was the third boy, who hadn't been as lucky as his brothers and always seemed to be getting himself into trouble. He was something of a black sheep of the family but fervently believed that he would do better if he were able to get himself to England.

Dennis loved Mammy, perhaps because he was the youngest boy and saw the most of her. Mammy always had time for him and seemed to pay him more attention than his own mother did. Finally there was Dola, who was twelve. There had been one other baby a year or so after Dola, a boy called Francis, who had been born blind and mute and had died a year before I was born.

Mammy would always bring cakes and biscuits with her on her visits and they would sit and talk for hours about life and family. During all that time, however, despite her closeness to her sister, Mammy never let on that I existed.

'Bill has proposed to me,' Mammy told her this time, 'and I am going to be starting a new life with him in England.'

'That's wonderful news,' Lily said, giving her little sister a hug, 'I always said you should have married him years ago.'

At that moment Dola came in from school and the three of them sat together in the little kitchen laying plans for the wedding, discussing everything from the dress to the flowers, opening a bottle of sherry so that they could celebrate and toast the happy couple.

'What will you be wearing?' Lily asked.

'I've seen the outfit I like,' Mammy said. 'It's a blue two-piece with a nice cream hat.'

'That's great,' Lily enthused. 'Blue was always your colour.'

As she prepared to leave, Mammy found herself alone with Lily for a few moments.

Moving On

'There's something else I'd like to tell you, Lily,' she said. 'I have a son. He's nearly nine years old now.'

Lily's jaw hung open and absolutely no words would come to her. After what seemed like an age she found her voice.

'Why have you never told me this before? You've been carrying this burden all on your own all this time?'

'I didn't tell anyone,' Mammy admitted. 'I was afraid of being judged. I've never been able to find the courage until now.'

'Oh you poor thing,' Lily said, tears welling up into her eyes. 'What hardships you must have endured. What is the lad's name?'

'I called him Francis,' Mammy said, 'in memory of your Francis.'

Lily just stood, staring at her with her hand over her mouth and tears rolling down her cheeks.

'Please, Lily,' Mammy begged, 'don't tell this secret to anyone.'

'Of course I won't, Cathleen,' she said and the two sisters hugged each other tightly.

Mammy had planned to work right up to our last day in Dublin, knowing that we needed as much money as possible so that we could go shopping before we left. She wanted us both to have new clothes for the journey, not wanting to have to ask Bill for money before we had even arrived. She had been independent for far too long to be able to give up the habit at this late stage.

The other mothers at the hostel all wanted to come down to Dun Laoghaire Port with us to see us off, but the thought horrified Mammy, who didn't want any fuss. On our last night in the hostel I was in the grounds with Joseph and Connor when we heard that the mothers from our old dormitory were planning to throw a small farewell party. We sat on the wall overlooking the wood mill and made jokes and laughed like we always did, staying to watch the sun going down and not wanting the evening to end because we knew it would be our last together before things inevitably changed.

'When do you think you'll be back to see us?' Joseph asked.

'Oh, within a year,' I said, confidently, 'I'm sure of that. England will just be my second home. This will always be my first home.'

'Can I come and visit you in London?' Joseph asked. 'I'll be fourteen next year and my time here will be over.'

'Of course,' I said. 'That would be great.' I knew that Bridie really wanted him to become a priest and they were already looking for a new place to live together. It was never going to be easy to find a landlord willing to take on a single mother and her child, however grown-up that child might seem. The Sisters did their best to help find places when the children grew too old to stay there, but they had such limited resources it was really up to the mothers themselves.

'We should swear to remain friends for ever,' I said, 'and stay in touch no matter where we end up.'

The sunset seemed to glow particularly red that night and the beautiful twilight became eerie.

'This must be some kind of sign from God,' Joseph said. 'It's not normal. We should pray together.'

Moving On

The three amigos got down on our knees and prayed together for a couple of minutes. Being more of an optimist than Joseph, I saw this unusual display of light as a good omen for the trip that was now just a few hours away.

As the light finally faded we made our way up to the dormitory to join the party, which was already in full swing. There were about ten mothers, all talking at once, and some small children who had been allowed to stay up especially for the occasion. To my amazement I saw that Bridie was serving up alcohol in teacups – something that was strictly forbidden. It was not the first time I had seen her do it, since she was quite partial to a drop of the Guinness herself, but it was the first time I had ever seen anyone be this blatant about it inside the hostel. I glanced at Joseph, worried as to what the Sisters would say if they came in and saw what was happening, but he just grinned, grabbed my hand and ran with me to join the fun.

There was food laid out on the table and the gramophone was playing jaunty Irish music which the children were all dancing to. More people were arriving from the other dormitories, wanting to wish us farewell and a safe journey. Soon there were at least twenty mothers and their children in the room, with others coming and going. Several of them were crying, which puzzled me. I could see no reason for anyone to be sad, as I was convinced that we would be coming back often to see them all.

Suddenly the chatter stopped as Sister Peggy and two more of the older Sisters appeared in the doorway and walked into the middle of the room. As the music continued in the background, everyone froze and you could have cut the atmosphere with a knife.

'Will you join us for something to eat and a cup of tea, Sisters?' Bridie asked, proffering a cup of Irish whiskey.

The Sisters all continued with the pretence that it was tea in the cups and politely declined.

'We are just here to wish Kay and Francis the very best of luck in London,' Sister Peggy announced to the room, 'and bon voyage!'

'You've all been so kind to us over the last nine years,' Mammy replied, 'and I am eternally grateful for everything you have done for us.'

Everyone cheered and clapped and Sister Peggy had to dab her eyes for fear of the whole room seeing her overcome with emotion. So moved were the Sisters that they eventually gave in to Bridie's blandishments and indulged in a little celebratory tipple themselves. Before they left, Bridie climbed on a chair and made a short speech.

'I want to say a few words about the Lady,' she said. 'I have never in my life met anyone nicer or kinder and I just know I am going to miss her so much. And Kay, I would like to present you with this gift from all your friends in the dormitory.'

I could see that Mammy was taken by surprise, not having expected anything like this, and a little overwhelmed. She thanked everybody but did not trust herself to say any more, so she set about opening the beautifully wrapped present. She was completely stunned to find that they had bought her a set of soft, white Egyptian cotton sheets with a light green stripe around the edge. As I watched her opening the gift, I was hoping that they might be about to surprise me in the same way, but no such luck!

Moving On

One of the women broke into song with 'Take Me Home, Kathleen', a famous Irish folk song, and the others fell quiet for a while before joining in, by which time there was not a dry eye in the room.

I'll take you home again, Kathleen
Across the ocean wild and wide
To where your heart has ever been
Since you were first my bonnie bride.
The roses all have left your cheek
I've watched them fade away and die,
Your voice is sad when e'er you speak
And tears bedim your loving eyes.
Oh! I will take you back, Kathleen
To where your heart will feel no pain
And when the fields are fresh and green
I'll take you to your home again!

The party went on until late in the night, until eventually I had to surrender to exhaustion and go to bed. I fell asleep a very tired and happy boy, knowing that the following day our great adventure would begin in earnest.

When I woke up on my final morning at Regina Coeli I discovered that all the other children had already gone to school and Mammy had popped out to the shops for a few last-minute provisions. After a breakfast of bread and jam, washed down with tea, I went out to the playground in search of something to do, but there was no one there; the whole place was deserted. As I wandered aimlessly around all my old haunts I began to feel nostalgic about the happy years I had spent there. In search of some distraction I made my way up the stairs to the first floor, past the dormitory for expectant mothers, and entered the chapel. I blessed myself in the usual way and took a seat before kneeling and saying a prayer.

Dear God, thank you for looking after Mammy and me. Thank you for sending Bill to Dublin to visit us. Can you also look after Joseph and Bridie? They need to find a safe new home. Please help them. Please also help Connor and his mother to get to London. Don't let Connor get into trouble ... Please help Bill, the Protestant, to become a good Catholic like us.

Can I also ask for some more chocolate bars? I quite like the one in the triangular, cream coloured box – I think it's called Toblerone. Please make sure we have a nice house in London. Can I also have a dog in London? Sorry to ask for so much today, God, but I have been a very good boy lately, and I have been saying my prayers every day. God bless my mammy. God bless Bridie. God bless Joseph and God bless Connor. Hail Mary full of grace.

Wandering back to the dormitory I bumped into one of the older boys who wasn't going to school that day.

'Hello Gordon,' he said cheerfully. 'Fancy going down to the city centre? Or shall we play a game of dare in the bus garage?'

'Best not,' I said, 'it's my last day here and Mammy would murder me if I got into trouble.'

Moving On

When Mammy returned from the shop she set about packing our clothes into the two suitcases we would be taking with us. I was now utterly bored. Even being trapped in the classroom at school hadn't been as bad as this. I sat at the table, staring at the dead flies on the fly papers that dangled from the ceiling. I started trying to catch live ones that were moving about the table with the paper, pulling off their wings when they got stuck. Suddenly the room burst back into life as the other children returned home from school.

It was approaching four o'clock and we were ready to leave for the port. I tried to pick up my suitcase and Joseph came over to help. Connor helped Mammy with hers and we made our way awkwardly towards the front door. To my amazement I saw that Bridie had put on her coat. She had never left the hostel during my lifetime, but today she was going to come down to the port to see us off. I think Mammy would have quite liked for us to slip away on our own, but she was relieved to find that only Bridie and Joseph, Connor and his mammy were coming. We said our farewells to the others and made our way out into the street.

'It's great to know we have two homes,' I said, 'isn't it, Mammy? We have the hostel and Bill's house in London.'

She didn't seem to have heard me, or at least she didn't reply. She just took one last look at Regina Coeli and then walked away without turning back. I glanced over my shoulder once more as we made our way down the street and saw Sister Peggy standing at the door, waving and wiping a tear from her eye. I gave her one last cheerful wave before we disappeared round the corner.

We took turns with the suitcases because they were a lot heavier than we had expected as we hauled them on and off three different buses to get to the port. All the way there I bombarded Mammy with questions. How big would the boat be? What kind of bed would I have? Would the train from Holyhead to London go really fast? I'm not sure I was even listing to the answers, just wanting to vocalise the thousands of excited thoughts that were racing through my little head.

Nothing Mammy said prepared me for just how big the boat turned out to be when we arrived at the port and saw it towering above us at the dockside. I was by then completely beside myself with excitement and dying to go on board, but Mammy and the others wanted us all to wait together for as long as possible before we had to embark.

As the loudspeakers announced that the boat would be departing in fifteen minutes, Bridie and Connor's mammy were both wiping tears from their eyes. I couldn't understand why everyone was being so emotional. Even Connor was starting to cry now, which I had never seen him do before. I was just desperate to get going on the adventure and I was sure we would all be seeing each other again soon. I shared none of their fears or sadness. I was just brimming with hope and excitement for whatever the future might hold.

Finally Mammy managed to tear us away from their embraces, by which time she too was in floods of tears, and we made our way up the gangway with the cases, me still waving like a maniac.

'Can I help you with those cases?' a crew member asked as we entered the ship. The engines were already humming so loudly they cut out all sounds from the world we were leaving outside.

'Thank you,' Mammy replied, showing him our tickets.

'Follow me, please,' he said, setting off down a staircase.

We went down and down towards the cheapest cabins at the bottom. The throb of the engines grew louder as he led us along seemingly endless, airless passages and finally opened a door and showed us into a tiny cabin with four bunks. I felt a bit claustrophobic as I poked my nose in.

'Why aren't there any windows?' I asked

The man grinned. 'We're below the water level down here,' he explained. 'You wouldn't want windows this low in a boat.'

'I thought we should reserve a berth,' Mammy said as the man put our cases down and left. 'I'm told it can be a rough crossing sometimes.'

'Can we go back upstairs and explore now?' I asked. 'I'm not feeling at all seasick.'

As soon as we reached the decks I let go of her hand and started running in every direction, ignoring her worried calls behind me as I peered through doors and over the side and ran up and down every set of steps I could find. I made my way into a bar and Mammy followed behind, beginning to be extremely irritated that I wasn't taking any notice of her. There were a lot of men standing round the bar, drinking. Some of them turned as we came in and, seeing Mammy, called out to her, offering to buy us drinks. They seemed very friendly to me but Mammy just smiled and politely refused.

She spotted a couple of chairs at a table next to an older woman and we sat down. The woman winked at me and started talking to Mammy. She told us she had been back and forth to England three times on the boat.

'It takes about six hours to Holyhead,' she informed us, 'and the train from Wales to London takes about another seven hours.'

The men at the bar were still looking at Mammy, laughing among themselves and raising their glasses in toasts.

'They all drink to calm their nerves,' the woman said. 'They're terrified the boat might sink because none of them can swim. They'll all start turning green and running to the toilet once we get into the open seas, you'll see.'

Sure enough, over the next hour or two, as the boat started to rock from side to side and plunge up and down over the waves, virtually every one of them turned a funny colour and started falling over and being sick. I watched, wide-eyed, as they tottered about the place, thinking the whole scene was hilarious.

'I think we've seen enough now,' Mammy said, standing up, taking me firmly by the hand and saying goodbye to the woman. By the time we got back down to our berth I was beginning to feel a little queasy myself and was glad to lie down on one of the bunks and fall asleep for a few hours as I prepared myself for the next stage of our great adventure.

Chapter Ten

Brave New World

Wwe were woken at three in the morning by the sound of loud knocking on the cabin door and shouting voices in the corridors. We had been on the boat for six hours.

'Holyhead! Holyhead! Prepare to disembark in twenty minutes.'

Feeling dazed from so few hours' sleep, I pulled myself off the bunk and was shocked to see that Mammy had been sick during the night. Her hair was dishevelled and she looked very rough. She spent a few minutes trying to tidy herself up as best she could without the help of water or a mirror, and then we opened the cabin door and prepared to face the world. The hot corridor was filled with people charging towards the staircases with their luggage, and there was a strong smell of vomit everywhere, making me feel sick all over again.

'We'll wait till it has calmed down a little,' Mammy said, retreating back into the cabin and sitting gingerly on the edge of the bunk. I sat beside her, itching to get on with the adventure but also pleased not to be stuck among the legs of a crowd of grown-ups as they shuffled up endless staircases, banging into me with their suitcases. Eventually the last of the line could be seen and Mammy took a deep breath and stood up.

'All right,' she said, bracing herself, 'let's go.'

It was a relief to find ourselves stepping onto dry land and breathing fresh night air once more. A man in a black uniform put his hand up to stop us. 'Can you tell me what you have in your suitcases?'

'Just our clothes,' Mammy said. 'Nothing else.'

'Would you mind opening the cases for me, Madam?' the customs officer said without the slightest flicker of a smile crossing his stern face. He started by going through mine, but soon saw that there was nothing unusual. He scratched a white chalk cross on it and moved on to Mammy's case.

'What are these?' he asked, lifting out the sheets which the other mothers had given Mammy the night before we left. 'They look brand-new to me, in which case you need to pay tax on them if you want to bring them into England.'

'They were a wedding present from some friends,' Mammy said nervously, 'I am getting married in London, you see.'

The man looked hard at me. 'And who might he be, then?' he asked.

'He's my son,' she said, flushing a deep shade of red. The official delved further into the case and lifted out a couple of wedding cards wishing Mammy and Bill good luck. He stared at the cards, then back into the case. Then he stared at me and back to Mammy. After what seemed like an age he made a chalk mark on the case.

'You won't be charged this time,' he said.

Relieved, we carried on walking along the platform towards the train bound for Euston. The air was filled with hissing clouds of steam from the engine and I felt my excitement levels rising again. The platform was packed with people and their cases as they tried to find their carriages or waited to board. Luckily Mammy had had the foresight to reserve our seats; otherwise we would have been standing all the way to London. We found our carriage, which had six seats and a set of sliding doors separating it from the corridor, just like the trains I had seen in the films. It wasn't long before every seat was filled and we started to move out of the station. As we picked up speed and the sounds of the wheels on the rails took on a regular rhythm, I found my eyelids beginning to droop. I fought the tiredness for a while, not wanting to miss even a minute of the journey, but eventually I was overcome by sleep and drifted off.

I must have slept for four or five hours before my eyes popped open once more and I saw that Mammy had managed to repair the damage of the boat trip and was looking her usual refreshed and beautiful self.

'Are you OK?' she asked.

'Yes,' I nodded, noticing that it was now light outside and I could see fields and buildings and stations through the window as we sped towards London. I thought England looked lovely as I glued my nose to the glass, drinking in every detail. I loved the motion of the train and the clackety-clack of the wheels.

The sliding door opened and a train inspector stuck his head into the compartment. 'Breakfast is now being served in the restaurant carriage,' he announced, breaking into my trance-like state, and I realised that I was incredibly hungry.

'Can we have breakfast on the train?' I asked Mammy.

'I think we could stretch to that,' she said with a smile, and I was immediately out in the corridor, staggering on ahead of her as the movement of the train threw me from side to side, laughing delightedly as Mammy did her best to keep up. We had to pick our way through passengers sitting on their suitcases or on the floor, many of them asleep and leaning on one another for support.

The restaurant carriage looked like a proper restaurant, only narrower, the tables laid up with thick white linen cloths and proper, heavy cutlery.

'Can we sit beside that last window?' I asked the waiter and he showed us both to our seats. I immediately glued my nose back to the glass.

As we both watched the countryside speeding by, a man appeared from nowhere. 'Do you mind if I join you?' he asked.

'Of course,' Mammy said politely. 'Please do.'

I was annoyed that we weren't going to have the table exclusively to ourselves but cheered up as I listened to Mammy ordering a full English breakfast for both of us. I could hardly contain my impatience as we waited for the food to arrive. The train seemed to have picked up even more speed and everything on the table was moving around, which made me giggle. When the breakfast arrived it was as huge as I had hoped. There was toast, eggs, bacon, baked beans and sausages. If this was what English food was like I was going to like living here very much indeed.

The man who had joined us had a Dublin accent and started to talk to us as I got stuck into the pile of food.

'What part of Dublin are you from?' he asked.

'Central Dublin,' Mammy replied, making no attempt to go into any more detail.

'Oh, I live in the centre too,' he said, not taking the hint. 'Whereabouts do you live?'

Mammy hesitated before answering and before she could think of something to say I butted in with a mouthful of egg and sausage. 'We live at Regina Coeli,' I said, 'Morning Star Avenue.'

'Oh yes,' the man said without giving any indication of what he was thinking, 'I know the area well.'

Looking across I saw that Mammy had frozen and the expression on her face was painful to behold. I immediately knew that I had made a mistake and that she didn't like the idea of this man knowing our business. She kept her eyes firmly on her plate as he continued to try to make small talk. Eventually he gave up and, having finished eating, he excused himself.

'Don't you ever tell anyone where we lived in Dublin again,' Mammy spat at me the moment he was out of earshot. 'Do you understand?'

I had never seen her so angry with me before, although she didn't raise her voice for fear of being overheard by passengers at the other tables.

'Don't interrupt adults when they are talking,' she continued, 'and don't ever mention Regina Coeli again, do you hear? Our new life starts here in London and the past is in the past and forgotten. Regina Coeli is our secret.'

I had no idea why she had exploded so violently, and I didn't like the idea that I was never to talk about Bridie and Joseph and Connor again, but I understood that this was now a golden rule. I must never mention Regina Coeli to her again. Mammy was clearly upset, because she had lost her appetite and pushed her unfinished plate aside as I went back to work on mine.

It was a beautiful, sunny summer's day in 1962 as the train approached Euston Station and everyone started to get their things together in preparation for our arrival. People were opening the doors even before the train had stopped moving. Some dashed straight to the ticket barrier the moment the train stopped, where a crowd of friends and relatives were waiting for them.

'We're not rushing,' Mammy said firmly, 'the queue is already huge and we need help with our cases.'

It wasn't long before a porter spotted our predicament and came over to ask if we needed any assistance. Mammy accepted politely and the three of us set off towards the barrier together. I kept jumping up and down to see if I could see Bill over the heads of the crowd, but I didn't stand a chance. I was a little bit anxious that he might have changed his mind and that we would find ourselves stranded in a strange city, but I kept that thought to myself, not wanting to upset Mammy twice in one day.

As we passed through the gate Mammy handed over our tickets and then I saw him, waving his newspaper just as he had on O'Connell Bridge, only this time the silly newspaper came in useful because it meant I could see him above the other heads. As we reached him he and Mammy hugged and kissed each other for what seemed like forever. Eventually Bill looked down at me as I waited patiently for them to finish, with his arms still round Mammy, holding her tightly to him as if frightened to let her go.

'Did you enjoy your journey to London, Gordon?' he asked.

'It was great,' I said, and did not draw breath again all the way to the taxi rank as I told him every detail of the journey. Bill kept nodding to show that he was listening, but I could tell from the way he looked at me that he was a lot more interested in Mammy than in me and my endless babbling.

The porter opened the door of the black London cab and put the cases into the section beside the driver. This was another new experience that I had only ever seen in the films before.

'Where to?' the driver asked, although I could barely make out what he was saying because of his accent. At that stage I had no idea how impenetrable my Irish brogue was going to be for Londoners.

'Finsbury Park,' Bill said as we all clambered into the back and I pulled down one of the jump seats behind the driver so that I could sit facing Mammy and Bill who, I noticed, were holding hands as the cab wound its way through the streets. I was happy to let them talk as I stared out the window at the passing streets.

'I've got no food in the house,' Bill said, 'so it might be an idea to stop for something to eat before we go there.'

'All right,' Mammy agreed, although we were both still pretty full from our breakfast on the train.

'I know a good café just five minutes from the house,' he said, and Mammy seemed happy with the suggestion.

Finsbury Park is a suburb to the north of the city and was then well known for providing cheap rented properties and bedsits to a mixed community of Irish, Caribbean, Jewish and Greek people. Bill got the taxi driver to drop us and our luggage outside the café. It was obvious as we pushed our way through the door that the owner was not too pleased to see such large cases taking up valuable space. He seemed very unfriendly generally, and I could see that Mammy was unsettled by the frosty reception.

'Have you eaten here before?' she asked Bill as we sat down with the menus.

'Oh, yes, I eat here all the time,' Bill replied. 'The all-day breakfast is very good.'

'Not very friendly here, are they?' she said, 'considering you eat here all the time.' I could tell she was already making unfavourable comparisons between London and Dublin.

Bill ordered the breakfast and I did the same, having enjoyed the one on the train so much. Mammy ordered an omelette. When the food arrived it was nothing like the meal we had just eaten. Everything was swimming in grease and looked very unappetising. Mammy picked at her omelette but got nowhere near finishing it, and I had the same trouble with mine. Bill, however, tucked in with gusto, leaving a shiny, greasy, empty plate.

'The full English is my favourite dish in this city,' he told me, apparently oblivious to the fact that Mammy was extremely uncomfortable in the café and obviously wanted to leave as quickly as possible.

'Are there any other children living in our house?' I asked.

'No,' Bill said. 'You'll be the only one. But you'll soon make friends in the area.'

'Can we go now?' Mammy asked, standing up to leave.

Bill tucked his newspaper into his pocket, picked up our cases and we headed to 103 St Thomas Road, which was in a row of three-storey, semi-detached houses. We walked up a short front path, past hedges and flower-beds, and Bill rang the bell at the red front door.

'Don't you have your own key?' Mammy asked.

'Tenants aren't allowed a key to the main door,' Bill explained. 'If you know you'll be coming in late, then the landlord will lend you one for the occasion. It's more secure that way.'

I could see from the look on her face that Mammy was not impressed, but she was biting back whatever it was she was thinking of saying. A nondescript, middle-aged woman answered the door.

'This is Mrs Alexandra,' Bill said. 'This is Cathleen and young Gordon.'

'How do you do?' she squeaked in a voice so high I had to stifle a giggle.

She led us into the house, giving us a guided tour as we went. The first room we came to was a front room with a television in it. I couldn't believe my luck. I was going to be able to watch my favourite programmes without having to share with any other children.

'My kitchen and bedroom are through there,' Mrs Alexandra said, gesturing at the two other doors. We made our way upstairs to the first floor. 'This is where Old George lives.' She continued up to the floor above and showed us a bathroom. 'This is the bathroom, which you share with Old George, and this is your front door.'

She opened the final door straight into a bedroom with a large double bed. There was a window overlooking the road. I couldn't believe it – a room with a view! Bill dropped my bag on the bed and put Mammy's bag on the floor, straightening up and stretching his back muscles. This, I assumed, must be my room then.

Mammy opened another door and I peered into a kitchen with a little table and four chairs. We had our own kitchen! This was like a palace compared to our bedroom at Regina Coeli.

'The back garden is out there,' Mrs Alexandra said, pointing through another window. 'You can hang your washing out there on weekdays, but not on Saturdays and Sundays, as Mr Alexandra likes to read his newspaper in the garden at the weekends. The rent is due every Friday night.'

She handed over the rent book, which showed that two weeks' rent had been paid in advance. I gazed out at the garden, which was extremely small compared to Regina Coeli, imagining all the games I could play there, as the adults continued to talk about housekeeping matters, none of which were of any interest to me. I could see two boys of my age playing in the garden next door. Could they be my first new friends in London?

'They are the Green boys,' Mrs Alexandra said, seeing where I was looking, 'I'll introduce you to them in due course. They're from Ireland too.'

I couldn't believe my luck. It was all coming together so well.

'So, where will Gordon sleep?' Mammy asked Bill, startling me out of my reverie. What did she mean? Wasn't the first room my bedroom, then?

Bill looked uncomfortable, as if he hadn't fully thought this one through. Had he not been expecting me to come with Mammy after all? Had he imagined I would be sleeping on the floor? He had definitely promised me my own room.

'You'll be sharing with us then, Gordon,' Mammy said quickly.

'Bill said I would have my own bedroom,' I protested. 'He promised!'

'You'll need to be warned,' Mammy said, staring Bill directly in the eye, 'he kicks out like a horse in his sleep.'

They both laughed, but I didn't. I absolutely did not like the idea of sharing the same bed as Bill. I decided to say nothing at the moment, since Mammy was obviously so happy to be there and everything else about London seemed great. Later that evening Mammy made up the bed with her new sheets. We had so few clothes that unpacking took no time at all. I was beginning to get bored. There was no radio or television in the room, so I decided to go downstairs and watch the one in the front room.

I turned it on and found a channel that I liked the look of. I had just made myself comfortable in an armchair when Mrs Alexandra came storming in from the kitchen. She walked straight up to the television and firmly switched it off.

'Oh, no you don't, Gordon,' she squeaked indignantly. 'You don't go making yourself at home in my front room. You're not to be in here on your own watching television.'

Blushing crimson at the embarrassment and humiliation of having misunderstood the situation, I leaped out of the armchair and ran full pelt back upstairs to our room in the roof. I couldn't understand what had just happened. At the hostel we had always shared everything.

'Things are a bit different here,' Mammy explained as I exploded in and blurted out what had just happened. 'The front room is not a communal area. That is Mrs Alexandra's room, and her television. We have to be invited in to watch something, just like it was someone else's house. Maybe if you want to watch something and you go and ask her very nicely for permission she won't mind, once she gets used to having us here.'

This was a huge disappointment, after I had got it in my mind that I virtually had my own television, and I turned on Bill.

'You promised we would have our own television when we came to London.'

'Stop being a nuisance, Gordon,' my mother said sharply. 'Go and get washed and ready for bed. You're over-tired after the long journey and you need a good night's sleep.'

I could tell from her tone that there was no point arguing and I did as I was told. I got into bed, stretching myself out and enjoying the feel of the new sheets. I dozed off pretty quickly, and at about midnight Mammy whispered for me to move over to the side so that she and Bill could get in too. It was pitch dark by then and I couldn't see what was happening so I did what I was told and drifted back to sleep. A few minutes later I woke up again to hear Bill whispering to Mammy and I heard him kissing her.

'What are you doing?' I demanded.

'Go back to sleep,' Bill said firmly.

I closed my eyes tight shut and tried to do what I was told, but it was no good, I was now fully awake.

'I can't sleep,' I said. 'It's your fault, Bill.'

'Just try,' Mammy said.

'Bill,' I said after a few moments, 'when can we go to the picture house?'

He gave a non-committal reply, but I kept going. 'When can we get our own television? When can I try some English sweets?'

'Just go to sleep and stop with the questions,' Bill said, his voice starting to grow angry. I could hear him moving around Mammy.

'Stop bothering Mammy,' I said. 'Leave her alone.'

Mammy laughed. 'You go in the middle, Gordon,' she said, lifting me between them. 'Now go to sleep, the pair of you.'

Now I really was in the way.

The next morning Bill and Mammy managed to get up without waking me. Bill had to leave early for work. I eventually woke to find myself alone in the middle of the bed in the big room. I could hear no sounds of life in the kitchen. Compared to the morning noise and activity at Regina Coeli it felt as quiet and still as the grave. I pulled myself out of bed and went through to the kitchen to look for Mammy, but she wasn't there. The silence was overwhelming and I felt totally alone and abandoned. Had I been such a nuisance that she had decided to go off alone with Bill? She had seemed very different since we arrived, and I could tell that they wanted to spend time together on their own. I hardly ever cried but I felt the tears bubbling up into my eyes.

'Gordon, whatever is the matter?' she asked, coming in just as I started to sniffle.

'Where were you?' I asked. 'I thought you'd gone.'

'I just popped down to the local shop to buy a few groceries and pick up some bread and eggs for your breakfast,' she said, putting down her shopping and giving me a big cuddle.

After a few minutes I calmed down and Mammy started making breakfast while I stared out the window. An old man with a stick was taking clothes down from the washing line, and I wondered if that was Old George.

'You go and get washed and dressed and I'll have breakfast ready when you get back,' Mammy said, and I went off the bathroom happy once more. Mammy was never usually around at breakfast time when she had a job, and I loved the idea of just the two of us being together every morning like this.

When I came back in she was busy with the white oven. I had never seen one before because at Regina Coeli we had done all our cooking in the fireplaces. The table was set out with blue-and-white china provided by Mrs Alexandra. Until that point in my life I had only ever eaten off enamel plates and drunk from enamel mugs. It was all they had at Regina Coeli, partly because it was cheap and partly because sometimes fights would break out between the women and they would start hurling the crockery at one another. Now we'd left all that behind. No more miserable enamel plates and cups for us. There were two eggs on my plate.

'The eggs look different,' I said.

'They're poached,' Mammy said. 'Try them.'

I couldn't believe how delicious they were. This was just one new experience after another. By the time Mammy was washing up I was already getting itchy feet again, wanting to go outside and explore. From the window I could now see three boys playing in the garden next door. I wanted to meet them, so I went downstairs and let myself out into the garden. I found I could just see over the wall.

'Hello,' I said.

The three boys stopped playing and came over to take a look at the newcomer. Mrs Alexandra appeared from the house, wiping her hands on her apron.

'What are you up to, Gordon?' she asked.

'I'm just admiring your garden, Mrs Alexandra,' I said, 'and introducing myself to your neighbours.'

'Whereabouts in Dublin do you come from?' she asked.

'Mammy and I lived in the city centre,' I said cautiously.

'Where in the centre, exactly?'

'I don't know where exactly.'

'Did you have a garden there?'

'Yes, we did,' I said, 'but it wasn't as beautiful as your garden here.'

I hoped that my flattery would stop her asking any more questions, and it seemed to work.

'This is Gerard Green,' she said, indicating the tallest of the boys, who looked about the same age as me. 'That's

Brian, who's about a year younger, and Kevin, who's just four. This garden is not for you to play in, Gordon. You don't come out here unless you are hanging out clothes on the line, or collecting them in for your mother. Do you understand?'

She was beginning to remind me of the Sisters at the hostel with all their petty rules. All I could think was that Bill had promised me a garden to play in. It seemed this was another broken promise, along with the bed and the television. Bill, it seemed to me, was turning out not to be a man of his word.

'You can stay out here for now,' Mrs Alexandra graciously offered, 'and get to know your new friends.'

'What's your garden like?' I asked Gerard, once Mrs Alexandra had disappeared back into the house. 'Is it as big as this one?'

'Pretty much,' Gerard said. 'Why don't you climb over and take a look for yourself.'

This sounded like an excellent idea. To get over the wall, however, I had to step on Mrs Alexandra's flower-bed and one of her plants got crushed in the process. She must have been watching my every move from the window because she was back out of the house like a shot, shouting as loud as her little voice could manage.

'Get off that wall, Gordon! Look what you've done to my poor plant! If you want to go round next door, use the front door like everyone else.'

I leaped off the wall, ran back through the house and out through the front door. I ran to the Green's front door and rang the bell. To my relief Gerard opened the door and let me in. He introduced me to their mother, who told me I could call her Kit. I liked the Green boys a lot and they made me feel very welcome. They told me that they went to a local Catholic school in Highbury.

'It's called St Joan of Arc,' Gerard said. 'It's about twenty-five minutes' walk. If you go there we'll probably be in the same class. You'll need to get a uniform too.'

'Why do you need uniforms?' I asked. 'We never had them in Dublin. I don't think I have to go to school now I'm in London anyway. I'm finished with all that.'

The brothers all laughed at my naïvety. 'Everyone has to go to school until they are fifteen,' Gerard explained. 'It's the law.'

Funnily enough I wasn't too upset by this piece of news, since I had already made my first friends, and I remembered how bored I had been on the last day in Dublin when everyone else was at school and I was left on my own. When I got back home to Mammy I told her everything the boys had told me about the school and the uniform.

'You need a uniform?' she seemed surprised. 'Well if you do then we'll make sure you have one before you start.'

For the next couple of weeks I spent all my time with Mammy, only seeing Bill late at night after he had finished work and been to the pub. He and Mammy would then sit up into the early hours talking, and if I was awake I would listen for as long as I could before sleep overwhelmed me. During the day she and I walked all round the local area, finding out where all the shops were. One day as we left the house Kit Green was just coming out of her front door and I introduced them. They chatted for ages about the best shops and about school and where to get the uniform I would need.

'Would you like me to come down to the school with the two of you?' Kit asked. 'So you can register before term. It starts next week.'

Mammy took her up on her offer and the following week I started at the new school, but without a uniform. Bill had promised to make time to go shopping with us before term started, but he had let us down. For the first time ever Mammy actually took me to school herself on the first morning. By the time we got there the schoolyard was already full of children and parents. Going inside, the first thing I saw was the PE room. I couldn't believe how much equipment they had. A lady called Mrs McNamara introduced herself.

'I'll be your teacher for the next two years,' she said. 'Shall we go and meet the rest of the class?'

I waved goodbye to Mammy and set off with Mrs McNamara. As we came into the classroom she clapped her hands to quieten everyone down.

'Children,' she said, 'this is Gordon McCrea. He is going to be joining us this term and I hope you will all help him to settle in.'

She had called me Gordon and not Francis, and I could not have been happier. Actually I would have been a bit happier if I hadn't been the only one in the whole class not in the school uniform of white shirt, tie and jumper, grey trousers and maroon jacket. I was determined to make Bill come shopping by the weekend, no matter what.

'There's a seat for you in the back row, Gordon,' Mrs McNamara said, and I made my way down the aisle, exchanging grins with Gerard, relieved to see a familiar face.

The first thing I told Mammy when I found her waiting for me at the school gates at the end of the day was how unhappy I was about not having a uniform.

'I felt like the odd one out,' I complained. 'I just want to look like everyone else.'

'But do you like the school?' she asked.

'It's a lot nicer than my old school in Dublin,' I said, 'and Gerard is in my class so I already have a friend.'

'We'll talk to Bill about the uniform this evening,' she promised.

That night I went on and on at Bill until he finally gave in and agreed to go shopping for a uniform on Saturday. He and Mammy seemed very happy to be together, but Bill didn't really seem to know what to do with me. I guess he had never had anything to do with children before. He had imagined I was this sweet, angelic-looking little boy who knew nothing about life. I might have been academically weak, but the reality was that I already knew more about street life and people than he could ever have known.

For the previous ten years Bill's life in London had revolved around dreary bed sits, meals in dreadful cafés and drinking sessions in pubs. He worked five and half days a week and if he wanted some extra money he worked more hours and sometimes on Sundays as well. After work he liked to go to the pub and drink with his friends. He spent very little time in his bed sits, so the pubs, which were on every street corner in those days, had become his homes.

He usually had lunch with Mick, his best friend and work-mate, in a pub near where they worked in the city centre. Mick had come to England from Ireland twenty years before and loved to drink just like Bill. He also loved to gamble, which meant that he often had to borrow money from Bill. Listening to Bill and Mammy talking at night I learned that Mick had been married but the marriage only lasted a few months because of the drinking and gambling.

'From then on he gave up on women,' Bill was saying. 'He's very bitter about them.'

I decided I didn't like the sound of Mick at all.

When the first week of school was over on Friday I was relieved to have found that it wasn't a bad experience at all. I had made several new friends and most of the other children were from Irish backgrounds, which helped since I spoke with a thick Dublin accent. At a school church service the teachers had been impressed with my religious knowledge, which had made me feel good about myself.

'Bill's bringing a present home for you later,' Mammy told me that evening as she prepared supper for us all.

'What is it?' I wanted to know.

'You're going to have to wait for him,' she said with a smile. 'He wants to give it to you himself.'

I was so excited I could hardly contain my impatience as we waited for him. Would it be a school uniform? Or would it be a bicycle? I had been going on at him about both things for a fortnight, having given up my campaign for a television.

'All television programmes are rubbish anyway,' Bill had said and that had been the end of the conversation.

He hadn't arrived by 6.30, so Mammy and I ate dinner without him.

'Can I stay up until he gets home, then?' I pleaded.

'You may,' Mammy said.

The hours passed painfully slowly until finally, at 11.30, I heard him making his way up the stairs. He slowly opened the kitchen door. I was so pleased to see him at last, but I could also see that he was decidedly unstable on his feet, swaying back and forth as Mammy stared at him angrily. I had seen enough men staggering out of pubs in Dublin to know where he'd been. He had a box clutched under the arm and he smiled at me sheepishly.

'What time do you call this?' Mammy demanded. 'Your dinner has been in the oven five hours now.'

Bill gave a giggle like a naughty schoolboy. 'That's what Mr Alexandra wanted to know – what time did I call this? I had to wake him up to get in.'

'Oh, Bill, it's not right,' Mammy scolded. 'You have to get him to give us a set of keys.'

'I will organise it,' he assured her, forcing himself to put on a serious face.

'You're drunk and you're irresponsible,' Mammy snapped.

'Don't be like that, Cathleen,' he said. 'I had to stay. There was this little get-together in the pub to celebrate my big day.'

I didn't understand what he was talking about. All I knew was that Mammy kept on berating him and he appeared to have forgotten the box wedged under his arm.

'You have no consideration for either of us,' she was saying. 'All you care about is enjoying yourself with your friends and spending money at the pub. You can sort your own dinner out!'

With that she stormed out of the kitchen. I could tell she was really upset with him, but I didn't follow her. I was curious to see what he would do next, plus I still wanted to know what was in the box.

'I love your Mammy very much,' he slurred, thumping his body down in the chair next to me. 'I've waited a long time to be able to marry her. She's the only woman I've ever loved.' He gave a long sigh and then stared at me for an uncomfortably long time, as if trying to refocus his thoughts. 'You're a lovely boy, Gordon. You know that? You're a lovely boy. Your mother is so proud of you.' He leaned forward as if about to impart a profound secret. 'I promise I will always be here to look after you, Gordon.'

Gathering his thoughts, he remembered his dinner and rescued what was left of it from the oven. Taking off his tie after a bit of a struggle he started to eat with his eyes half closed. I waited, staring at the present which he had placed on the table.

'Open your present, lad,' he said. 'Go on, open it.'

At last! I tore off the paper and opened up the box to reveal a pair of roller skates.

'Sorry it's not a bicycle, Gordon,' he said, 'but your Mammy wouldn't hear of it. Said you would be bound to have an accident on the road.'

'It's fine, Bill,' I assured him. 'Skates are great. Thanks.'

By now I was exhausted and it looked as if Bill was about to fall asleep at the table too, so I slipped next door to join Mammy, who was in bed, still looking furious. I showed her the skates and grinned.

'Bill's given me skates,' I said. 'They're great.'

I felt strangely elated, partly by the prospect of being able to tear around the streets on skates, and partly by the words that Bill had said. I knew he would never have been so emotional if he hadn't been drunk, but it was still nice to hear how much he loved Mammy and how proud she was of me.

I woke up feeling excited that today was the day we were finally going to buy my school uniform. I jumped out of bed and went into the kitchen, where Bill and Mammy were sitting together at the table. I was relieved to see that they were talking and smiling after what I assumed was their first ever big row. Clearly Mammy had forgiven him.

'Have your breakfast,' she told me, 'and then get washed up.'

After I'd freshened up I went back into the bedroom and saw that Mammy had laid out on the bed a blue two-piece suit and a cream-coloured blouse and matching hat.

'Do you think I should wear these with it?' she asked, holding up a string of pearls.

'Yes, definitely,' I said. I knew these were her best clothes.

'Did Bill tell you what's happening today?' she asked.

'Bill's told me lots of things,' I said with a grin, 'but he did say that I was going to be getting my school uniform this morning. He also told me how much he loves you.'

Mammy beamed happily. 'That's all he told you? He didn't mention that we are getting married today? So I don't think we'll have time to go to the school shop.'

I was furious and bitterly disappointed. I was so angry I wanted to hit something, but I burst into tears instead and refused to get dressed.

'You already live together,' I shouted. 'Why do you need to get married?'

Bill came in to see what the noise was about. It was the first time he had seen me cry and he was obviously taken aback. It was one of my finest performances, getting louder and louder as I stoked myself up into a major rage, letting out all the emotions that must have been building up over the previous few weeks.

'What's up with him?' Bill wanted to know.

'You told him he would get his school uniform today,' Mammy said, 'and he's built his hopes up. You shouldn't make promises you can't keep, Bill.'

'I'm sorry, lad,' he said, trying to reason with me, 'I wasn't thinking straight. We'll get it next week.'

'I don't care,' I screamed. 'You promised me that you would buy it today!'

Bill raised his hands in surrender and looked at Mammy for help, having no idea what to do next. She took me firmly by the shoulders.

'Stop crying now,' she said firmly, 'or no uniform. Get dressed. If there's time we'll go to the shop after the wedding ceremony, but only if there's time. I promise if we don't have time today we will definitely get it before next Saturday.'

Taking a deep, shaky breath I pulled myself together and within the hour we all left the house together in our best clothes.

'You look beautiful,' Bill told Mammy, and I couldn't have agreed more. I had never seen her looking lovelier than on that day. 'Let's get a cab,' Bill suggested, 'since it's a special occasion.'

'Oh, don't go wasting your money,' Mammy said, as usual. 'It's only a short distance, we can easily walk.'

I was surprised to hear her say that, knowing that the Catholic church in Highbury was at least twenty-five minutes away, but I kept quiet this time. I knew I had been a nuisance earlier and I didn't want to jeopardise getting my uniform. As we walked down St Thomas Road I noticed a small group of people gathered outside the Protestant church at the end of the road. They started to wave to us as we approached, which was puzzling. They greeted Bill when we reached them and introduced themselves to Mammy. They all stood chatting for a few minutes, and then a man who had introduced himself as Eddie, Bill's brother, reached out to shake my hand.

'Hello, Gordon.'

No one had ever done that before and it made me feel very grown-up. Then Bill's best friend – the Mick I had heard them talking about – did the same. I liked the fact that they both used the name Gordon rather than Francis.

I stood politely watching as they all chattered, and I couldn't help thinking that they were wasting valuable time when we could have been getting my school uniform.

'Young Gordon needs a carnation for his lapel,' Eddie said, 'to celebrate his mammy and daddy's big day.'

I was shocked to hear Bill described as my daddy. I hadn't thought of him like that. At that moment Bill came over and took my hand, leading me in towards the church with Mammy at his side. I was simultaneously shocked and horri-fied when I realised that they intended to walk in through the door.

'No! No! No!' I shouted, pulling my hand away from his. 'No! No! No! I'm not going in there. I can't go in.'

In my head I knew that to even step inside a Protestant church was a mortal sin, for which I would be bound to go to hell.

Mammy grabbed my hand and quickly led me away from the others into the church grounds. 'Stop shouting,' she commanded, 'and be a good boy.'

'What's the problem this time?' Bill asked, coming up behind her and obviously exasperated.

'It's a mortal sin to go into such a place,' I said, 'We'd be going straight to hell if we stepped inside that door.'

'But that's where your Mammy and I are getting married,' he explained.

I couldn't believe that I was hearing such a thing. I just kept shaking my head furiously and crying. Having no idea what else to say, Bill lit himself a cigarette and offered one to Mammy. She shook her head. By this time all the guests had disappeared inside and were waiting patiently for the bride and groom. Mammy was obviously making a supreme effort to remain calm and not make things worse.

'We can only get married if we do it in a Protestant church,' she explained.

'No,' I shouted. 'You could get married in a Catholic church if Bill was a Catholic. It's obvious that he has to do that first.' I must have sounded just like all their other disapproving family members.

'I can't believe the priests have got such a grip on him,' Bill said, and to my horror I saw tears rolling down Mammy's cheeks.

'Please, Gordon,' she said. 'Please don't ruin my special day. We are all God's children, whether we are in a Protestant or a Catholic church. Please don't make Mammy's happiest day a sad one.'

I felt like I was being torn in half, but after what must have seemed like an age to them I nodded my head reluctantly. Mammy wiped both our tears away with her white handkerchief. I realised that going inside was going to make her happy so I composed myself, took a deep breath and walked in, gripping her hand tightly, half expecting to be struck down immediately.

My biggest fear at that moment was that Mammy would eventually become a Protestant and be damned to go to hell for ever. I was surprised as I came into the church to see that it didn't look or feel very different from a Catholic one. I looked around slowly, drinking in every detail and beginning to calm down. Old English and Scottish flags hung on the walls, but I didn't know what they were for. I could see no confession box and no Virgin Mary statues. My Catholic guilt reminded me that I didn't belong there and I started to pray hard, begging for God's forgiveness for me and for Mammy.

'Mammy is a good woman,' I told him, 'she would have married in a Catholic church if she could have done.' I prayed that Bill would become a Catholic one day so that I'd never find myself in a place like this ever again. I was so engrossed in my prayers I completely missed the marriage ceremony and the proclamation of vows. All of a sudden they had exchanged rings, kissed and were married! Mammy looked at me and smiled radiantly, and I was really pleased to see her looking so happy, but even happier to be getting out of the church.

As we came out, the guests threw confetti over the happy couple and then they all stood around chatting, which seemed to be another frustrating waste of time to me.

'Shall we walk or take a taxi to the restaurant?' someone asked. 'There's only six of us so we should be able to squeeze into one cab.'

'Why don't we just walk back up St Thomas Road,' Eddie suggested.

Everyone seemed to go along with that idea, and after we had gone a few hundred yards Eddie and Mick suggested that we stop off at the local pub for a quick celebratory drink.

'We have a table booked at the White House,' Mammy said firmly. 'And aren't there a couple more of your friends meeting us there, Bill? We don't have time to stop for one of your "quick drinks".'

I could see that Bill was torn between Mammy and his best friends, but Mammy stood her ground.

'You can have your drink later,' she said, and the men laughed and carried on walking out of respect for her on her wedding day.

The White House was a Chinese restaurant that Bill had been to before, although he had never eaten Chinese food in his life, always ordering English dishes from the menu instead. I stared around me in amazement. In the few weeks in London I had seen more racial diversity than I had seen in my entire life in Dublin, from African and Asian to orthodox Jews and now Chinese.

'Is that real food?' I asked Mammy as I watched some strange-looking dishes being brought out of the kitchen.

'Don't worry,' she said, patting my hand, 'they serve English food as well.'

The lunch seemed to go on for hours as they ordered more and more drinks and it wasn't long before I realised I had no hope of getting to the school shop that day. I decided not to make a fuss in front of so many strangers. Eventually Bill asked for the bill and the waiter brought one for the food and another for the drink. I looked over his shoulder and saw that the one for the drink was three times as big as the one for food.

'Have they made a mistake?' I asked Bill. 'That is so expensive.'

He appeared not to hear me as he reached into his pocket and pulled out a wad of cash, turning away from me so that I couldn't see him counting it out. It wasn't the first time I had noticed how furtive he was whenever he got his money out.

On the way back home from the restaurant the men wanted to stop at the pub for a few more drinks.

'Oh, go on then,' Mammy said, 'we'll go back to the flat for a cup of tea.'

Eddie's wife came with us and the men disappeared happily into the pub. Mammy knew this was Bill's way of having a good time and she didn't want to spoil his fun. I went to bed that night knowing that Mammy was happy to be married to Bill, and that made me feel happy too. Early the next morning I got up while they were still in bed and announced I wanted to go out with my roller skates, partly because I couldn't wait to try them out and partly because I knew the newly-weds would want some time on their own for the first time since we had arrived in London.

'You enjoy yourself,' Bill said, 'but take care not to skate in the road.'

On Monday morning I set off to school looking forward to my second week. Bill had promised that we would go to buy the uniform after school, and Mammy had given me a note to give to my teacher explaining that my name was now Lewis. Mrs McNamara smiled as she read it and said she would inform the class of my new name.

By morning break time my class-mates were itching to find out what had happened.

'My Mammy has known Bill for a long time,' I explained, 'and they married at the weekend.'

They all seemed to share my opinion that this was good news and immediately lost interest in the whole subject, apart from one pretty, red-haired girl who had a deep scar running down the side of her face.

'Which church did they get married in?' she asked.

'Just one down the road from where we live in Finsbury Park,' I said, hoping I sounded casual enough for her to lose interest too, although from the look in her eyes it seemed she wanted to know more.

'I live in Finsbury Park,' she said. 'Which church are you talking about?'

'It's in St Thomas Road,' I said, and saw her eyes widen in a mixture of shock and glee as she realised that it wasn't a Catholic church. She could see that I was trying to hide something and continued to bombard me with questions.

'Your Mammy can't be married,' she concluded, 'if she got married in a Protestant church, because you are Catholics.'

I knew exactly what she was getting at because I felt much the same. The other children were now listening again and I could tell that my face was turning red with a mixture of anger and embarrassment. I wanted to punch the freckles off this girl's face. I bunched my fists just as the school bell rang and saved me from further humiliation.

My tormentor, however, was not finished yet. During the lunch break I was kicking a ball around with the other boys when she materialised beside me again, getting in the way and wanting to discuss the wedding once more. This time I ignored her and kept kicking the ball around her. By the final break time that day, however, she had grown more determined and managed to catch me on my own.

'I don't understand,' she wheedled, 'why your mammy got married in that Protestant church. My two uncles in Ireland are priests and my older brother is going to be a priest, and my daddy helps out at the church service every weekend.'

I knew that there was no point in trying to bamboozle her since she obviously knew far too much about the church, so I tried to ignore her again. But she wasn't going to give up that easily.

'What happened to your father? Is Bill your father? Why did Bill not marry your mother before you were born?'

I was not equipped with any of the answers for these questions. At Regina Coeli none of us had fathers, which was precisely why people labelled us 'the unfortunates', and why none of us ever discussed our situation. I didn't know what to say or how to shut her up.

'Piss off,' I spat, pushing her so hard that she tripped and fell onto the hard ground. 'Don't you know what the other children call you?' I continued, determined to become the attacker rather than the defender. 'Scarface!' I screamed, feeling guilty even as the word came out of my mouth.

'You are a nasty boy,' she screamed back. 'You don't have a real father and you never had one. That's why your mother got married in the Protestant church to a Protestant man!'

Now I was really angry and out of control. I pointed to her private parts and shouted. 'You are a cunt, you know. Yes, a horrible cunt!'

I had no idea if she knew the word, but I guessed that the pointing would have helped her to understand. I knew plenty more words like that; swearing was one of the things that living in the hostel had taught me well. She gave a little shriek of horror and ran off into the school building. I was relieved to have got rid of her but knew that I had stepped way over the mark. She was right; I had behaved like a nasty boy.

A few minutes later she emerged from the building with the school supervisor, her face streaked with tears, and pointed to me.

'Gordon,' the supervisor said, beckoning me over, 'have you been mean to her? Did you call her rude names?'

'She wouldn't leave me alone, Miss,' I said in the cutest, calmest voice I could manage. It was not the first time I had ever had to lie myself out of trouble. I was well practised in the art. 'She wants to be my girlfriend.'

'He's a liar,' the girl shouted, starting to cry again.

The supervisor obviously didn't know which of us to believe. 'Just play nicely, the pair of you,' she said, 'and be on your way.'

It was probably just as well that I was so skilled at lying and using verbal abuse as a weapon, otherwise I might well have ended up punching the little redhead, and then I really would have been in trouble.

Mammy was waiting for me at the school gates, and it should have been a happy day because we were going to buy my uniform, but the little redhead's words were going round and round in my brain. I knew I had been horrible and cruel, but I still didn't know how else I could have shut her up. It made me feel very sad, and I didn't want to confide in Mammy because she might have felt it was her fault.

'Bill's going to meet us at the shop,' she said as we climbed the hill together.

It was a small shop but it had a range of different school uniforms for sale. Mammy started to search for a jacket in my size while I admired the sports clothes. This was a whole new experience for me. Not only did we not wear school uniforms in Dublin, we hadn't had any sports lessons either. I was getting increasingly nervous that Bill wasn't going to show up and we would have to leave empty-handed. Eventually he arrived, by which time Mammy was able to show him the pile of things I needed. If shopping for clothes was a new experience for me, it seemed even more unfamiliar to Bill. I could see that he was shocked by the size of the pile.

'Is all this stuff necessary?' he asked, looking at some of the price tags and starting to put things back on the rails.

Furious, and determined not to be cheated out of my uniform again, I angrily grabbed them back off the rail and put them onto the pile.

'They are things he needs for school,' Mammy said firmly, 'no more and no less.'

'But how much is all this going to cost?' he asked. When the assistant passed him a bill he actually seemed to jump in the air with shock.

'What sort of shop is this?' he said, panic-stricken. 'This stuff is terribly expensive. Does he really need all this?'

I was beginning to become worried as to how this would end, and I could see that Mammy was deeply embarrassed by his behaviour. Then he turned his back on both of us and pulled money out of his back pocket, angrily counting out what he needed.

'I'll have virtually nothing left for the rest of the week now,' he grumbled as he stuffed the remaining notes back in his pocket, his face as sour as it could be.

'If you didn't go drinking every evening, Bill,' Mammy hissed, 'we'd have more than enough to buy the boy what he needs for school!'

We left the shop with our purchases in silence, but inside I felt enormously relieved to finally have the clothes I needed in order to look like everyone else at school. The atmosphere between Mammy and Bill was heavier than lead. I had never seen him in such a foul mood before. He didn't speak all the way home.

'I'm going to the pub for a drink before dinner,' he announced when we got there. Mammy said nothing as he left the house. The silence between them continued for two days and Bill came home late each evening after drinking with his friends.

As the weeks went by I started to find school difficult. The teachers expected more of me than they had in Dublin, where they prepared me for nothing except religion. I felt very backward in the class now and looked forward to physical education and religion. Some of the children took the piss out of me because I still spoke with such a strong Irish accent. Having a uniform wasn't enough to ensure you blended in; you needed to be part of a group as well.

Many of the Irish parents pushed hard for their children to do well at school, which created a rivalry between the children themselves. I fitted in with Gerard Green and his friends, but I found there were other children who didn't like them. I was very uncomfortable with the rivalries, but staying neutral was hard. Before I knew it, I found that I was caught up in the middle of a playground gang war. I participated in the physical pushing and sometimes in the fights that broke out. I began to get a reputation for being one of those boys who constantly got into trouble and I had to work hard to make sure Mammy didn't find out what was going on.

Chapter Eleven

Happy Families

It took me a while to find my balance on the roller skates, but once I got the hang of it I loved them. I loved the freedom, the speed and the danger. To begin with I did as I was told and stayed on the pavements and the paths in the park, but as I became faster it became more difficult to avoid people and so I inevitably started to use the roads. There were a few near misses with vehicles but I didn't care. I loved living life at full pelt, no matter what the risks might be.

Mr and Mrs Alexandra finally relented and gave us our own key to the front door, so I could come and go as I pleased without having to ring the bell all the time, but I was definitely not allowed to wear my skates indoors. They had never rented rooms to families before and I was constantly in trouble for making noise, particularly for running up and down the stairs. Mrs Alexandra was also worried about my potential for damaging her home. From the first day when I trod on her flowers, she lived in fear of what I would do next. I knew this because I had overheard her talking to her husband about me.

Happy Families

'That boy is wild,' she said, 'and the father has no control over him. He could set fire to the house. We can't trust him. We should get them out of the house.'

Coming back after racing around the streets I never wanted to take the time to stop and laboriously unlace the skates on the doorstep, so I would try to get upstairs in them before Mrs Alexandra noticed. She knew exactly what I was up to – she would listen out for the thumping and come rushing out to tell me off. It became like a game of dare for me.

Bill still refused to buy a television and Mrs Alexandra would occasionally let me watch hers, just to keep me quiet, but never for more than half an hour at a time, and only programmes for very young children, so I preferred to go round to the Greens' house to fuel my growing fascination with the flickering screen.

It was all a big adjustment for me. Back in Dublin I'd grown up surrounded by friends and able to run around freely in the open spaces of Regina Coeli. It had been like being part of an enormous extended family, and I was never alone. But in London I only had the Green boys for friends and I didn't get to see them all the time because their mother, Kit, was quite strict with them about the times when they could play and the times when I could come round to visit. I didn't have the freedom to run and play in wide-open spaces. and in comparison to the grounds at the hostel the Greens' garden seemed very small. I was having to get used to being alone for a lot of the time. I was trying to make more friends but I was finding it hard, partly because of my thick Irish accent, which meant that other kids had trouble understanding me and made fun of me. I got to spend a lot of time with

Mammy, which I loved, but I missed having friends my own age to gallivant around the streets with.

'Do you want to come in for a cup of tea?' Old George asked one day when I met him on the stairs as I was clumping my way home. He was always very friendly to me whenever our paths crossed and I looked forward to bumping into him. Apart from the Green brothers he was my only friend in London.

'I like having a nipper like you around the house,' he said as we went into his room. 'You make the place lively again. I like your spirit.'

He had photographs of himself as a young man, many of them in uniform. He had fought in both world wars and when we got to know each other better he showed me his medals, thirteen of them, all for acts of bravery.

'I'd like you to have them,' he said when he saw how impressed I was by the collection. I would have loved to own them, but Mammy put her foot down and wouldn't allow it. He was proud of his war record and loved to talk about it once he realised how interested I was. He was obviously still sad about friends he had lost over the years.

'How long have you lived here?' I asked.

'Forty years,' he said. 'I used to own the whole house, but as I got older it was too much for me to look after so I sold it to the Alexandras on the condition that I could stay here till I died. That's why I like it when I hear you running about the place. It reminds me of the old days when there were young people in the house.'

I was beginning to learn more about people, and men in particular. At Regina Coeli there had been virtually no men, but with Bill and Old George around I was making up for lost time. To me Old George seemed like one of the heroes in the war films that I loved so much. He made me realise that the older generation were fascinating because they had so much experience and could teach me so much about life. He never seemed to mind how much of his time I took up or how many questions I asked.

Three months after we moved in I came home from school to see Old George being wheeled out of the house by paramedics towards a waiting ambulance. He was obviously in a lot of pain and the sight of his suffering affected me deeply.

'What happened?' I asked one of the paramedics.

'He had a bad fall,' he said.

'Are you all right, George?' I asked.

He nodded and gently patted my head before they lifted him in, but he never came back to the house.

'He was getting too old and poorly to be able to look after himself any more,' Mammy explained, 'so he's gone to live in an old people's home.'

I missed him badly and thought about him every time I passed his door on the way up and down the stairs.

Mammy missed her family in Ireland as well, and she wrote home all the time to her mother, Lily and Bridie, updating them on all our news, telling them about family life with Bill and me. She never complained about Bill and never mentioned any of her problems, and she was always telling them how proud she was of me and how smart I looked in my new school uniform. They all wrote back to her as well and she would read the letters out loud to me. Granny would always be wanting to know if I was going to church and saying my prayers. She told Mammy how happy she was for her, but she also complained a lot about her own aches and pains.

'She's not been well for a long time,' Mammy would tell me, and I could see that it worried her to be so far away from her mother.

The letters I wanted to hear the most were the ones from Bridie, because I was hungry for news about Joseph and our other friends at the hostel. Bridie was always asking if I was behaving myself and seemed concerned about us. I think perhaps she was living her life through Mammy's letters. I suspect a lot of the women there dreamed of one day having a 'Bill' come into their lives, sweeping them off to a home of their own, but very few of them ever did.

Joseph had turned fourteen and Bridie was finding it hard to find a place they could move to now that they had to leave the hostel. Joseph was still set on becoming a priest. Mammy tried to keep Bridie's spirits up, encouraging her to believe that things would get better once she was outside the hostel, but she knew just how hard a struggle it was going to be for a single mother who had grown so unused to the ways of the outside world.

Not long after Old George had been taken away from the house, we received a letter from Connor's mammy with the most shocking news that I could imagine. Bridie had passed away suddenly from a suspected heart attack. Mammy and I were both devastated and couldn't stop crying.

'What about Joseph?' I asked, imagining what it must be like to lose your mother when you were so young and had no father. 'What will happen to him?'

'Apparently,' Mammy said, struggling to read on through her tears, 'he has been placed as an apprentice with a jeweller in the city, where he has been given board and lodging in exchange for his work.'

'Can we go back to Regina Coeli before they bury her?' I wanted to know. 'Then we can make sure Joseph is all right.'

'It's impossible, I'm afraid, Gordon,' she said. 'We've barely arrived in London and we have no money at all for the fare.'

'Can't Joseph come over here and live with us?' I persisted.

'He needs to stay in Dublin now he's fixed with a position as an apprentice,' she explained, but none of it seemed right to me.

I felt weighed down by worries and contradictions. I still hadn't come to terms with the Protestant wedding or Old George's sudden departure, and hearing that Bridie had gone as well was deeply unsettling. School was difficult and I was becoming increasingly aware that I was a 'bastard child'. God, I hated the word 'bastard'. It seemed to follow me around wherever I went. It made me realise that I was different. I looked at the other boys and girls at school and they all had mothers and fathers. I was beginning to wonder who my father actually was, but I knew it was not a subject I could ever bring up with Mammy or Bill. Just as Mammy had led a secret life back in Dublin, I was now leading a secret life in London, keeping my past to myself, not even able to fully understand it. Even the Greens believed that Mammy was a widow from Ireland and Bill was her second husband. Anxiety and anguish were becoming entangled inside me, and I was finding it hard to cope with so many things at once.

Mammy kept telling Bill that I was too big to be sleeping with them any more and I needed a bed of my own, but he didn't want to spend the time or the money on buying one, even though he had seriously underestimated how often, and how hard, I kicked out in my sleep. He was the one who bore the brunt of it and he clearly didn't understand me at all. He had been a bachelor for so long, only really mixing with other grown men, that he had no concept of what children were like, particularly a menace like me.

He wanted a simple life. He followed the same routine every day, always dressing in a suit and tie to go off to work, removing his jacket when he got there, rolling up his sleeves and tucking his tie into his shirt. He was always neatly shaved, with a trim moustache, and he kept his greying hair touched up so that it would remain jet black. After a hard day's work he just wanted to unwind with a few drinks, and he certainly didn't want to be having his peace of mind disturbed by the emotional problems of his wife, however much he might love her, and her complicated little boy. I knew exactly how to get around him when I wanted to, smiling and pretending to be a charming, innocent little boy. It took him a surprisingly long time to discover the real Gordon, and he still never worked out what to do when I played up – and, boy, did I play up!

One night I was jolted awake by Bill suddenly leaping out of bed with an anguished shout. For a second I assumed I had kicked him in my sleep, but he didn't usually make as much fuss as this. He turned the light on and started ranting and raving at me.

Happy Families

'Look what you've done!' he shouted, holding his sodden pyjamas away from his skin. 'I can't believe you've done this. I'm drenched.'

'What's going on?' Mammy asked, squinting in the sudden blaze of light.

'He's wet himself!' Bill shouted, 'and I'm absolutely drenched. You'll have to change the sheets.'

I was mortified and couldn't think of anything to say in my defence. I just had to sit there and listen to him going on and on. It was something that hadn't happened for years. Bill was making such a fuss that Mammy started to giggle. 'Well, I'm dry,' she chuckled. 'Are you sure it was Gordon and not you? Lord knows how many pints you drink every night.'

'It's not bloody funny, woman,' Bill roared.

Mummy eventually had to give in and re-make the bed just to shut him up, and all I could do was stand there shivering with embarrassment until she had sorted everything out. Every night for the next week the same thing happened, and by Saturday Bill had bought me my own bed. I continued to wet it every night and became so distressed about it that I would stop drinking half-way through the afternoon, and I prayed regularly to God and Pope John for help. I became paranoid about going to the toilet before falling asleep, but it didn't seem to make any difference.

I had also become very worried that there might be another World War. Whereas the news in Ireland always seemed to be about the Pope and the Church, in England it seemed to be all about Russia, the Berlin Wall, nuclear bombs and global destruction.

On top of the bed-wetting I was having nightmares and even started sleep-walking around the house when Mammy and Bill were fast asleep. Once or twice I went downstairs and tried to open the front door. Luckily it was locked and I couldn't get out. One time Mr Alexandra was woken up by the noise and came out to find me. After that Mrs Alexandra was frightened that I might walk into her bedroom. She was particularly worried if her husband was away or working nights. I always knew when Mr Alexandra was out in the evening, because Mrs Alexandra would play 'Moon River' by Henry Mancini, over and over again. It was a haunting, slightly spooky sound as it drifted up the stairs.

'She's a nervous woman,' Bill explained. 'The music probably helps her relax.'

To me it seemed likely she put the music on to try to block me out of her mind.

Mammy was also finding it a struggle to adjust to living in London. The main problem was lack of money. It was a far more expensive city to live in than Dublin, and she could scarcely afford the food and everyday items we needed on the money that Bill was giving her. Ever since leaving school she had been used to earning her own keep and being an independent woman. She knew the real value of money and always worked hard for it. For so many years she had scraped by, living her double life, and she had come to London with such high hopes that things would improve for both of us – and in some ways of course, they had.

The main problem was that she was having to rely on Bill for money. He had told her that she wouldn't have to work if she came to London, and she had liked the idea of having more time to be with me, probably hoping to keep me a bit more under control. Bill certainly wanted to have us there and wanted us to enjoy our new life, but he certainly hadn't anticipated how much more it would cost to support three people on one wage. Whether it was for my school uniform or the weekly shopping, Mammy was always having to ask him for more money, and she found it harder and harder each week. Every day I saw her carefully counting the change in her purse and doing sums to work out what we could and couldn't afford. Back in Dublin she had loved having her hair done each week – 'My special treat', she called it – but she didn't feel she could ask Bill to pay for that, so she went without.

The fact that Bill always turned his back to us whenever he counted out his money made it obvious that he didn't want anyone to know how much he had in his back pocket. He didn't want Mammy to be able to work out how much of his wages he was spending in the pub each week, although she had a pretty good idea. He wouldn't even tell her how much he earned. Whenever she wanted to get something for the flat he would always ask her whether she could get the Alexandras to pay, or questioned whether we really needed it. He was used to living the bachelor life and only spending money on himself, and he didn't see the need for Mammy to buy things for the flat, while she wanted nice plates, cups, towels and a few pieces of furniture. She wanted to live in a home, not a hovel.

It didn't take long for her to use up her meagre Irish savings, and she had no income apart from whatever Bill was willing to hand over, which simply wasn't enough to meet our needs. I could see how much she hated having to ask him and how uncomfortable he made her feel with his inquisitions. It was soul-destroying to have to justify every little purchase she wanted to make. From the money he gave her each week he expected her to pay for food, household items, my clothes, everything. He believed that since he paid for the food and rent, the rest of his wage packet was his to do with as he pleased. He was a reasonable, easy-going man in so many ways, but he had no idea how to share his life, or his money, with his new family.

'All you do is spend money on him,' he grumbled one day when Mammy asked for something very minor.

He had developed an annoying habit of never referring to me by name. Maybe it had something to do with the fact that I refused to call him 'Dad'.

I could see from the expression on her face that this time he had pushed her too far. I knew her better than anybody else in the world, and I could see that this was the final straw. Sure enough, she went off like a firework.

'Stop being so mean with your money,' she screamed. 'You're behaving like a typical Paddy. You have no concept of what things cost. All you know about is how to spend money on your so-called friends in the pub rather than your own family!'

Once she had lowered the barriers of her self-control everything poured out. She shouted louder and louder until I was worried what Mrs Alexandra would think downstairs. Mammy so rarely lost her temper, but when she did she was a different woman. I hadn't seen her like this since the night she fought with Bridget Murphy at the hostel.

Happy Families

'You can keep your drinking money for all I care,' she shouted. 'If I'd known then what I know now I would never have come to London. I've had it up to here with your meanness. And another thing, stop referring to my son as "him" – his name is GORDON!'

She paused for breath, leaving Bill blinking and silent. For a moment I thought she was finished, but she wasn't.

'Why can't you be more like Mr Green?' She wanted to know. 'He supports three children and owns his own house. You certainly wouldn't find him in the pub every night. I'm absolutely sick of feeling like I can't ask you for money for everyday necessities. I never have enough from you for the barest essentials. I'm going to get myself a job because I just can't rely on you to take care of us. Oh, and another thing – don't EVER turn your back on me again when you take money out of your back pocket. You can fuck off and keep your money.'

With that she grabbed my hand and marched us both out of the room. I glanced back from the doorway. I don't think she can ever have spoken to him like that before, because he looked shell-shocked, standing staring after us as we left, rendered speechless. Mammy had brought him face to face with his faults and his responsibilities as the head of our little household.

Once outside the front door Mammy strode towards Finsbury Park without saying another word. I had no idea where we were headed and it seemed best not to ask for now. I trotted silently along behind her. I trusted her completely but wondered what was going through her mind. Thoughts were racing through my head at all the possible outcomes of this explosion, and I silently prayed that everything would be OK, that this wouldn't be the end of their relationship.

We must have walked aimlessly for about half an hour before I dared to say anything. 'Could we go to the Greens and have a cup of tea with Kit?' I asked.

Mammy thought about it for a second. She obviously wasn't ready to go back home yet and we didn't have any money to do anything else, so this seemed like a good option. Kit drank more tea than any woman I had ever met in my life. Going back down our street we actually bumped into Kit on her way home from shopping and as it happened she invited us in for a cup of tea anyway.

For the rest of the evening the two of them sat in Kit's kitchen talking while Kit kept Mammy supplied with endless cups of tea and cigarettes. I began to feel less anxious now that she had stopped shouting and seemed to be talking in a reasonable voice. She didn't mention the fight, but I expect Kit could tell she was upset about something.

'I've seen they're advertising a part-time job down the road,' Kit said at one point.

'Where's that, then?' Mammy asked.

'In the shop at the top of the road. The one that takes the laundry and dry cleaning. They're asking for a general helper and window dresser. That might suit you.'

I knew the place she meant. Bill used to take his washing and laundry there before he married Mammy.

Mammy didn't feel ready to go back home until late that night, and I had no clue what would happen between her and Bill when we got there. It was so late he was actually asleep in bed when we let ourselves in. He woke up but didn't dare to ask where we had been. He tried to say a couple of things but Mammy completely ignored him and climbed into my small bed to sleep with me. I could see he was shocked. He obviously had even less of an idea what was going through her head than I did. I suspect he was worried that his marriage might be over already.

Over the following days Mammy cooked and cleaned as normal but refused to talk or even smile at him.

'How long do you think she's planning to keep this up for?' he asked me when we were alone for a moment.

'You've upset her a lot,' I said. 'I've no idea how long it will take.'

'Do you want to go to the picture house with me?' he asked. I thought it was sweet of him to offer and I really wanted to go, but I didn't think that I should just at that moment.

'No thank you,' I said politely. He nodded his head as if he understood and went to the pub instead.

The next day Mammy went to the laundry shop and applied for the job. She secured herself an interview with the area manager, who ran a chain of shops including this one. She didn't tell Bill anything about it. I liked the fact that she seemed to be taking control of the situation and finding a way round the problem.

'I'm going to my interview this afternoon,' she told me as she saw me off to school a few days later. 'Meet me outside the shop after school and we can go food shopping together.'

When school was over I hopped on a bus and got as far as I could before the conductor realised I hadn't paid for my ticket, and then jumped off and walked to the shop. Through the window I could see that Mammy was still inside talking to a man. I waited outside and prayed it was going well. After a while she came out.

'Come and meet Mr Davies, Gordon,' she said, ushering me into the shop to meet the manager. He was a very posh, polite man who talked like the RAF pilots in black-and-white war films. He wore a dark three-piece suit and glasses and had a small moustache. Ironically he looked a little like Bill. He seemed a bit plump to me, and I noticed he ate a lot of biscuits. I also noticed the way in which he looked Mammy up and down as we talked, which she didn't appear to notice. I could tell from the way he looked at her that he really liked her.

'Would you like to start on Monday morning, Mrs Lewis?' he asked. 'I'll meet you here and show you the ropes.'

Her beaming smile said it all. I felt so relieved to see her happy again.

'It's only part time,' she said once we were outside, 'and it doesn't pay very well, but it's what I need for now.'

'Bill said you wouldn't have to work once you were here,' I said.

'I know,' she smiled, 'but it seems it's just not meant to be.'

That evening she started talking to Bill again.

Three months after starting her job Mammy received a letter from her brother, Christie, telling her that Granny had passed away. Another death to take in. It seemed like they were coming one after another, though Mammy wasn't completely surprised by the news. She told Bill and Mr Davies that she would need to go to Ireland for the funeral.

'Can I come with you?' I asked, thinking this would be a good chance to see Joseph and Connor again.

Happy Families

'No, Gordon, you can't have the time off school,' Mammy said, 'and we can't afford two fares. I'm afraid I'm going to have to go on my own.'

I couldn't stop myself from crying. I felt so afraid that she might not come back, leaving me and Bill together in London.

'Don't be crying, Gordon,' she said, giving me a cuddle. 'You'll be just fine with Bill and I'll only be gone for five days.' Before she left she asked Kit to keep an eye on me and make sure I didn't get into trouble.

The moment she had gone the flat seemed strange and empty. Bill and I had lived together for less than six months, I felt I hardly knew him and he certainly didn't know me. He was awkward around me and struggled to make conversation. In fact we barely spoke to each other the whole five days Mammy was away. I wasn't used to being with him on my own, since most days I only saw him if I stayed up late at night, and even then he didn't talk much, preferring to read his *Daily Mirror* at the kitchen table. The next morning he went to work as usual and I went to school. Afterwards I had my dinner with the Greens and watched television until Bill came to collect me. For the first couple of days the Greens invited him over to watch television and have dinner with them. I couldn't believe he was actually watching television; he seemed to be enjoying it so much he had difficulty switching it off until I told him I was tired and wanted to go home to bed.

'Why don't you go out and buy a television set of your own?' the Greens suggested to him one night as we were leaving.

That Saturday evening after work he came straight home to collect me from the Greens, where he had dropped me off earlier that day. Then for dinner he cooked me the one dish he knew, which was breakfast. It was the greasiest meal I'd ever eaten. On the Sunday he cooked it again, and again. I was starting to feel sick.

'I'm going next door for my dinner,' I said when he served up the fourth fry-up,that evening'and to watch television.'

When I got home later Bill told me he'd made a decision. 'I'm going to rent you a television set, Gordon,' he said. It was obvious that he now wanted one as much as I did and he was also hoping it would be a good way to win me over. This time he kept his word. We went out together the very next day and rented a black-and-white set.

When Mammy returned home I was more than pleased to see her and bombarded her with questions about everything she had done and everyone she had seen.

'I saw Lily and Christie and Dennis,' she said, 'and all the rest of the family.'

'How are Joseph and Connor getting along?' I asked. 'And all the mothers and Sisters at Regina Coeli?'

'There was no time to see anyone else while I was there,' she said, picking up a letter that was waiting for her on the kitchen table.

I couldn't understand how she could have gone all the way back to Ireland and not gone to see everyone at the hostel. Did she simply not care about our old friends any more, now that she had a husband, I wondered as she opened the letter. She read it intently and then sat down with a thump.

Happy Families

'It's from Mr and Mrs Alexandra,' she said. 'They have requested that we should vacate our rooms within four weeks in the New Year.'

'Why?' I asked. Why did letters always seem to bring bad news?

'They don't give a reason,' she said, dropping the letter on the table. 'They just want us out.'

Bill was furious when he got home and she told him the news, but Mammy was strangely calm and accepting.

'I suspect they were never keen on children to begin with,' she said. 'I've been half expecting this to happen for a while. Why don't we look into buying our own flat, or even a little house?'

'No, you need to have the money for a deposit to do that,' Bill said. 'I've got no savings. Besides, I don't want to buy a property and have the responsibility of having to look after it. It would mean we'd have to buy furniture too, which would be more money. I'll find us somewhere else to rent when I next have some free time.'

I could see that she was bitterly disappointed, but I could also see that there was no way he was going to be changing his mind. To my relief she obviously decided that she didn't want to have another row.

Chapter Twelve
Hard Times

Mammy didn't seem to be as upset about moving out of our flat in the Alexandras' house as I was.

'I always knew we weren't welcome here,' I heard her telling Bill.

I knew exactly what she meant, but I had got used to living next to the Greens and I felt I had just got my bearings in the area. Moving house was going to mean that I would have to adjust all over again to a whole new environment and all the upheaval that would inevitably involve. Before we had to move, however, we were going to be able to share our first Christmas together. Like all children I desperately hoped it would snow.

'I'm going to be working away in Germany for five months in the New Year,' Bill told Mammy one evening.

'You'll be away for five months?' She obviously didn't like the idea, but knew there was no point in complaining. 'We'll be needing to find a place quickly, then,' she said, 'so we can move in before you go.'

Hard Times

I doubt if Bill wanted to move any more than I did. He hated change or anything that disrupted his routines or was likely to cost him money. He was completely familiar with all the pubs in North London and wasn't going to want to move too far from them. He even used them as reference points for his property searches.

The date when Bill would be disappearing off to Germany was approaching fast, and Mammy was nervous he wasn't going to put enough effort into the search. She probably didn't trust his judgement when it came to choosing somewhere for us to live either; so she decided she would do a bit of research herself, even though she had hardly any spare time now that she was working.

'Let's go and look at what's being advertised in the local shop windows,' she suggested to me one cold December evening. I was able to read a little myself now, although English was still my worst subject, so I joined her in scanning the various handwritten and typed cards that were on display in the shops.

'Mammy,' I said after a few moments, 'what do they mean by "No wogs"?'

'Don't ever use that word, Gordon!' she said. 'That's a terrible thing to say.'

'But it says it there,' I said, pointing to one of the cards. 'And there!' I'd spotted another. 'And there!'

'Oh my Lord,' she covered her mouth in horror. 'That's horrible.'

'But what does it mean?'

'It means the advertisers don't want black people living in their accommodation. It's disgusting.'

'It says "No Irish" on that one,' I pointed out. 'And that one.'

'I just don't understand it,' Mammy said, shaking her head in despair. 'I don't understand how people can be so narrow-minded.'

I was completely puzzled by the whole thing. Surely we looked no different to English people. Why should they be frightened of us? I had noticed there were many more people of different races in London than there had been in the small white world I had inhabited in Dublin, but it had never occurred to me that there were people who had a problem with that. I could see that this was as much of a surprise to Mammy as it was to me, a side of London she had not seen before and definitely did not like.

'I can't believe people are allowed to post such obscene things in shops windows like this,' she said, and we hurried home to get warm.

Her search didn't get any further than that, and two weeks before he left for Germany, and a week before Christmas, Bill realised he couldn't put it off a moment longer.

'Come on, Gordon,' he announced, waving the local paper with its classified ads pages. 'Let's go find a new flat.'

We simply went around knocking on doors of anyone who was advertising. On many occasions the moment Bill opened his mouth and spoke the answer would immediately be, 'Sorry, it's gone.'

'It's my accent,' he explained the third time it happened. 'As soon as they realise you're Irish they don't want to know.'

I knew he was right because I'd seen the cards in the windows, but I could also see that in many people's eyes I was a problem as well. They took one look at a small boy and imagined all the noise and disruption I would cause. I did my best to look angelic, smiling till my face ached, but it obviously wasn't convincing anyone. We went out for three evenings in a row but never even got in through anyone's front door. I could see that Bill was beginning to lose interest in the whole process. Apart from anything else, the time we were spending tramping around the streets knocking on doors was eating up his precious pub time. I began to worry about what Mammy and I would do if nothing had turned up by the time he left for Germany.

On the fourth evening the small ads led us to a five-storey house not far from where we were living. A small man in his late sixties opened the door. He spoke in a heavy London accent.

'We've come about the two rooms to rent,' Bill said, but before he could get any further a woman's voice started shouting angrily from somewhere inside the house. The man shouted back, equally angrily, and the argument continued to go back and forth for about five minutes while we stood silently on the doorstep, waiting for the inevitable rejection.

'Come in,' the man said eventually, 'I'll show you the rooms.'

Without another word he started up the four flights of stairs to the top floor and we followed behind, passing numerous other doors with strong cooking smells emanating from them as tenants prepared their evening meals.

'You need to make your mind up quickly,' the man said when we finally reached the top. 'They'll go fast.'

He unlocked the door and led us into a large main room with a kitchen along one side. There was a little table in the corner and a double bed in the middle of the room. Two windows overlooked the street outside and there was a small wardrobe in the other corner. The room was smaller than the two rooms we were currently living in.

'You have your own gas and electricity meters,' the man was saying as I looked around, 'and you'll need to keep them fed with coins, otherwise you won't get either. It's important if you want to keep warm!'

'How long have I got to decide?' Bill asked.

The old man looked him up and down, sizing him up like a salesman. 'The sooner you decide the better. If you don't want it just say. There are lots of people coming tomorrow and it will be gone by the evening.' This guy was obviously a professional landlord, not like the highly strung Mrs Alexandra. 'If you want to give me cash up front it's a done deal.'

'The ad said it was two rooms,' Bill said, looking around.

The man went to a curtain which was hanging against one of the walls and pulled it across, separating the kitchen area off from the bed. He said nothing.

'Let's bring Mammy here, first,' I suggested, being pretty sure that she would not be giving this place her seal of approval, and I certainly didn't think she would like the landlord any more than I did. The man raised his eyes and shrugged as if he had no more to say on the subject, and I could see that Bill was under pressure, wanting to get back home in time to catch Clint Eastwood in *Rawhide*, our favourite western series. Bill was just as hooked on television by then as I was.

Hard Times

'OK,' Bill said, pulling his cash out and, without even turning his back to me, counting out the necessary notes before handing them to the man. As we walked home I had a horrible sinking feeling in the pit of my stomach.

'Bill,' I said after a while, 'I'm not sure Mammy is going to like those rooms. They're smaller than what we have now.'

'Oh, it'll be fine, Gordon,' he assured me. 'It'll only be for a short while, just till I get back from Germany. Then we'll find something more suitable.'

It sounded like he was trying to reassure himself as much as me. When we got home and told Mammy we had found somewhere she was relieved, although she had a lot of questions about the rooms, wanting to know the size and other details. Bill was not forthcoming with information and did his best to avoid discussion by turning on the television. I could see that Mammy was a little worried, but she was too preoccupied with her job to find the time to check the flat herself and so she obviously decided she was going to have to trust Bill. Since he had already paid the rent in advance it was a done deal anyway.

The build-up to Christmas was really exciting and I couldn't wait to experience my first festive season in London, especially when they started to forecast snow on the television.

'I hope Father Christmas will bring me lots of presents,' I told Mammy and Bill, even though I had secretly worked out that he didn't exist. My theory was that if I pretended that I believed, they were more likely to spoil me. On Christmas Eve, Bill played Father Christmas. He and I had been getting a lot closer, and Mammy had even suggested that I might like to start calling him Dad, but that was still a step too far for me. Knowing that I loved cowboy films he had built me a wooden fort, with a house inside it where the cowboys could have their coffee. He had also bought me a small train set. They were the best Christmas presents I'd ever received and I gave both him and Mammy a big kiss to show how grateful I was.

Over Christmas the snows started to fall heavily and continued for a solid week with hardly a break. I had never seen anything like it. It was truly magical, turning the whole city into a Christmas card, quietening the noise of the traffic and making everything look clean and beautiful. On Christmas Day, Mammy and I went to church for Mass and when we got back home she started to prepare our Christmas lunch.

'Take Gordon out to play in the snow,' she told Bill. 'And lunch will be ready at about one thirty.'

Bill did his best to keep up with me as I raced through the virgin snow, shouting with joy, but he soon began to lag behind.

'Listen, lad,' he puffed, 'I'll get you some sweets and you can eat them while I pop into the pub for a Christmas drink.'

I knew that meant I would have to wait outside, but I didn't mind because I had a bag of sweets and there were other Irish children in the same position who I could talk and play with as we waited for the men to emerge and take us home for our Christmas lunches.

Bill eventually emerged from the pub. We got back to the flat an hour late but Mammy was too busy to be cross. She'd cooked roast beef and chicken as a special treat. I'd never eaten two types of meat at the same time before and I couldn't believe my luck. It seemed to me like the greatest luxury possible, knowing how hard-up we were. She had also made a Christmas pudding and a delicious Victoria sponge cake. The food was incredible and we ate like kings. Bill cracked open a couple of bottles of Guinness and we settled down to watch *Rawhide*. What a day! It wasn't long before they had both fallen fast asleep and I had sole control of the television. I watched as much as I could before I too was eventually overwhelmed by tiredness and nodded off. The next thing I knew, Bill had lifted me into bed and Mammy was tucking me in. It was the best Christmas ever.

The fun and festivities carried on until New Year's Eve, when Bill and Mammy joined Kit and Mick Green in the pub across the road while I stayed with the Green boys and we had a party of our own, playing games and running wild around their house. It was bliss, but I also knew it was about to end.

The weather men were predicting one of the most severe winters on record, with the snow expected to last until at least March. On the second of January it was time for us to move so we packed our cases. We had four now, one each for clothes and another for bits and pieces. There were also a few pieces of furniture and a couple of boxes of household items. Mammy had arranged for someone who she knew from work, who had a van, to help with the big bits like my bed, while we went ahead in a black taxi. We couldn't walk as the roads were too deeply covered in snow and too slippery for us to be carrying heavy bags and boxes around.

Mammy was noticeably quiet as she concentrated on lugging the heavy boxes up the four flights of stairs, while

Bill carried the suitcases. I ran ahead with the key, excited by all the activity but nervous about how Mammy was going to react to the place. As I opened the door I was hit by a blast of freezing air.

'It's so cold,' Mammy said, putting the boxes down on the table and looking around, taking it all in. 'Where's the second room?'

I demonstrated the pulling of the curtain to show how the room could be divided, just as the landlord had done.

'You call that a second room?' Mammy asked Bill. 'You think a curtain is a reasonable replacement for a brick wall?' She looked panic-stricken and I had a feeling that had I not been there she would have burst into tears.

'Why don't the lights work?' she wanted to know, flicking the switch up and down. 'Why is it so cold?'

'We just need to put a little money in the meters for the heating and the electricity to work,' he explained, pulling out a couple of coins to demonstrate. 'Don't worry about a thing. We'll only be here a short time, till I get back from Germany.'

'Bill Lewis, you are a fool,' Mammy said. 'Have you really agreed to pay more for this room than the other place? Plus this time we have to put money into meters as well? It's going to cost us a fortune. I can't believe you've done this – you should have known better!'

Before Bill could say anything there was the sound of crashing on the landing outside and Alf, one of the laundry drivers from Mammy's work, came in with my bed.

'Cathleen, my love,' Alf said cheerfully, apparently not even out of breath from the long climb up, 'where would you like me to put young Gordon's bed?'

Hard Times

I liked Alf. He was a cockney lad with a cheeky glint in his eye and he obviously like Mammy.

'Just pop it next to the big bed, Alf, thank you.'

'Right you are,' Alf said, giving her a broad wink. 'You have a lovely wife here, mate,' he said to Bill, who was looking distinctly hostile.

Alf trotted back downstairs, whistling happily, and returned a few minutes later with our television set.

'Is there anything else I can do for you lovely people?' he asked.

'No, Alf, you've done more than enough,' Mammy said. 'We really are very grateful. I don't know how we would have managed without you.'

'Yes,' Bill grudgingly agreed. 'Thanks.'

'No problem at all,' Alf gave them both a cheery grin before bounding away down the stairs again, leaving us alone in the chilly silence of our new home.

That night, as we got ready for bed, exhausted from the day's activities, Bill went downstairs to use the toilet, coming back to report that two of the three toilets in the house appeared not to flush. At that moment the lights went out.

'Put some more coins in the meter, Cathleen,' he instructed.

'I fed the meter just two hours ago,' she said. 'This can't be right. These rates are much higher than they should be. I've never paid this much for gas and electricity in my life.'

A few days later Bill left for his five-month stint in Germany, having made an arrangement for his employers to send part of his wages directly to Mammy in cash, to arrive in the Saturday morning post, while the rest was paid to him in Germany. That money was supposed to be for rent, food and heating.

'You won't be needing as much from me now you're working,' he'd said to Mammy when explaining the arrangements he'd made. As usual he was entirely wrong about that. The weather continued to grow colder, with the temperatures dropping below zero. The main power supply for London was affected by the high demand and there were regular power cuts. The room was like a fridge and I found it better to go from school to Mammy's shop, where it was always warmer, waiting for her to finish work so that we could go back to the freezing room together. At least at Regina Coeli we'd had a great big fire in the middle of the dormitory, burning twenty-four hours a day.

'Things will get better soon,' Mammy kept saying when I complained, but to me they just seemed to be getting worse all the time. It was a terrible struggle to manage on her wages and the measly amount the Bill sent, and we had no money at all for treats like sweets or visits to the picture houses. We just existed in a routine of school and work and watching television in our ice pit.

Whenever I was with her in the laundry Mammy would encourage me to pitch in, allowing me to handle the money from customers and giving me the responsibility for giving out any change there might be. I enjoyed it and thought that one day I would like a shop of my own. In the gaps between customers Mammy would ask me how things were going at school and made me practise my spellings and update her on whatever I had learned that day. To be honest, I was never that comfortable when being questioned about school.

Hard Times

Academic progress was proving pretty slow; I found most of the subjects extremely difficult and couldn't quite understand why. The only thing I enjoyed, and was any good at, was PE. But I had started to make friends at last.

I was only just ten but I behaved older than my years, probably because Mammy talked to me like an adult most of the time. She only treated me like a child when I misbehaved and needed to be told off. On my tenth birthday she took me to Wimpy for the first time. I ordered a burger and chips, followed by a Knickerbocker Glory ice-cream – and thought I had landed in Heaven.

'Can we come here every week?' I asked Mammy.

'We don't have the money for that, Gordon,' she laughed. 'If you want to come here regularly you'll have to find some money yourself.'

For the first time it occurred to me that this was the only way forward. I was going to have to find ways to make my own money, because however hard Mammy worked she was never going to make that much, and we certainly couldn't rely on Bill's generosity. With my stomach still comfortably full of chips and ice-cream I started to apply my mind seriously to the idea.

Every Saturday morning, after Mammy had gone to work, I would wait by the door for the postman so that I could sign for the special delivery of cash from Bill's employers. The rent would then be paid to the landlord the same day. One Saturday, however, the postman uttered the fateful words, 'Just a postcard for you today, I'm afraid.'

He handed me a postcard from Bill in Germany.

'What about the special delivery?'

'Hasn't turned up today, I'm afraid. I'm sure it'll be here on Monday.'

As he went jauntily on with his rounds he had no idea of how devastated I was by the news. This was a disaster. I knew the rent was due and I didn't want to worry Mammy, so I decided to go straight to the landlord myself and confess that we would be a couple of days late with the payment. It was a daunting prospect as the two of them were a scary couple, never smiling and as cold as the rooms they rented out. Their arguments were a constant background noise in the house, and we would often hear the woman screaming at the top of her voice. I tried to avoid them at the best of times, and this was definitely not the best of times.

Taking a deep breath I knocked on their door. The landlord opened it and glared down at me.

'What do you want?' he demanded.

'Our rent money didn't arrive in the post this morning but the postman says that it will probably arrive on Monday morning, so we won't be able to give you this week's rent till then.'

As I finished, his wife came screaming out of the kitchen brandishing a long knife. I was sure she was going to stab me. 'Tell your mother we will not wait till Monday. Tell her to have the rent by tonight or you'll be sleeping on the streets!'

She slammed the door in my face, leaving me shocked and speechless and imagining Mammy and me wandering the streets that night in search of a doorway to sleep in.

I ran straight to the shop in a blind panic, only to find that it was full of customers and I had to wait, panting for breath and trying to compose myself, until they had left. As soon as the shop was empty I blurted out the whole story of how we were about to be turned out onto the streets, destitute and freezing.

'Calm down, Gordon,' Mammy said. 'She can have her money.'

Every day Mammy had the job of cashing up the day's takings. Without a moment's thought she took what she needed from the till.

'We'll replace it on Monday when Bill's money arrives,' she said when she saw me watching her with wide, fearful eyes.

As soon as we got home, Mammy knocked on the landlord's door and his wife opened it.

'I've brought your money,' Mammy said, 'but I would thank you not to go scaring the wits out of my son again.'

'I was only joking with him,' she cackled.

'You were definitely not joking,' I retorted indignantly. 'You were deadly serious.'

'He's a cheeky little Irish boy,' she snapped at Mammy, her face returning to its usual grimace, 'with too much to say for himself.'

'As you have our deposit,' Mammy continued politely, 'you could have been more understanding of our problem, particularly as it is the first time it has ever happened.'

The woman slammed the door in our faces again and as we walked away up the stairs we could hear the two of them starting to argue loudly once more. After an anxious couple of days the postman did bring the necessary envelope on Monday morning and Mammy was able to replace the cash in the till before anyone else had even noticed it was missing.

I soon learned to hate the snow which I had been praying for so fervently a few weeks before. All the pipes in the house had frozen and we had to go into the street to get our water from special taps in the pavement. Four times a day I had to carry buckets across the icy streets between heaps of dirty snow in order to fill them and then lug them all the way up the four flights of stairs. It was agony. My shoulders and back would be aching and I would always end up slopping the cold water down my legs. We never used the filthy bathrooms in the house anyway, preferring to wash ourselves over the kitchen sink, so we had to boil the freezing water on the oven. The situation continued for weeks, and I wished with all my heart that we had never left Dublin.

Sometimes at night we would run out of coins for the meters and had no light or heat. We would then huddle together in bed in the pitch black, trying to keep each other warm. It was hard to get to sleep when even our bones felt cold. I missed Dublin and Regina Coeli and my friends, and I knew Mammy was unhappy too. She had admitted that she found London a hard place to live in. Bill had left us alone and cold and miserable, fending for ourselves. He'd promised me we would have a garden and I would have my own bedroom, but neither had ever materialised and I felt like we couldn't trust him any more. One night I couldn't contain myself and broke the golden rule of never mentioning our previous life.

'Mammy,' I said as we lay together, shivering in the dark, 'we should move back to Regina Coeli. At least we would be warmer ...'

She heard me out, but as soon as I had finished she made herself very clear.

'We are never going back to Dublin, Gordon,' she said, 'not under any circumstances. We have to make the best of our lives here in London. Dublin is a tough place too, you know.'

I thought I could detect a tremor in her voice, as if she might be about to cry, and so I said no more. I didn't really understand why she was so upset, so I changed the subject and started talking about my latest favourite subject, John F. Kennedy. I had seen him on the news a lot and I had decided that I liked him even more than the Pope because he was better looking, young and charismatic. I was also under the misapprehension that he was President of Ireland, because I had heard them talking about him being Irish. Once I had exhausted that topic I moved on to the Beatles, who were a new band at the time, just emerging from Liverpool. I really liked their music, their hair and their clothes, and I thought they were Irish too.

'Stop talking now, Gordon,' Mammy said. 'Go to sleep.'

The only good news at the time was that Mammy had been offered a promotion to shop manager, and it came with a small pay rise, which would help to feed the ever hungry meters. In April the weather finally started to warm up and our spirits rose a little too. I had started to help her out at the shop every Saturday and enjoyed the work and dealing with the customers. Bill's money kept arriving every Saturday morning and Mammy was hoping that he was managing to save a bit from his wages so that we would be able to move quickly when he got back.

'He's getting his food and accommodation paid for over there,' she said, 'so even he should be able to save something.' I had my doubts, based on everything that had happened so far.

When Bill arrived home at the end of May he seemed genuinely pleased to see us. He had bought me a cowboy gun and a warm jacket that almost fitted me, which was an achievement since he had no idea how fast children my age grew.

'I've got something for you too,' he told Mammy, handing her a tiny parcel with a twinkle in his eyes.

When she pulled out the tiny baby doll underwear I thought he had made another mistake with the sizing. 'They're a bit small too, aren't they?' I said. 'Maybe you should have got a bigger size, and not so see-through.'

They both giggled like naughty school children. I was completely puzzled. I had expected Mammy to tell him off for wasting his money, but she seemed quite happy about it. I could tell she was thrilled to have him back home as we all told each other everything that had happened to us since he left.

After he had been home a few days, Mammy explained to him very calmly how difficult it had been with the money and the meters, and for once Bill seemed to understand the seriousness of the situation. She told him about how cold and damp the room had been and that a room with a curtain was a miserable place to live.

'I'll have a word with the landlady,' he said, 'and ask her to change the tariff so we aren't spending so much cash every day.'

The woman listened much more politely to Bill than she would have done to Mammy or me before giving her response.

'If you don't like it,' she said, 'you can move out.' She then slammed the door in her usual manner and started screaming at her husband. I could see Bill was shocked by the rudeness and realised that Mammy hadn't been exaggerating the problem. When it came to handing over more money from his wages, however, his position had not changed. It was not long before he was back in the pub every evening, flushing his spare cash down the drain. It was obvious that he cared nothing about the creature comforts of life and still didn't have a clue about the rising costs of raising a growing child. I could see that Mammy was bitterly disappointed by his attitude and his set ways, but she must have decided that there was no point in lashing out as that didn't get them anywhere, apart from making things uncomfortable around the house.

That was why she had gone out and found herself a job, no doubt. She had realised that it was pointless hoping that Bill would ever change. He was a stubborn Irishman in his fifties; he was never going to alter his ways now. She had to accept his flaws or it was basically 'game over'. They did still have rows about money, but they never got any closer to agreeing, and each time she raised the subject she risked tearing them apart. The only way forward if we wanted to be happy and have peace in the family was for her to find another way round the problem, one which didn't rely on him.

One thing that had changed with Bill since he had been away was that he suddenly seemed to be taking an interest in my education. He now wanted to hear about everything that went on at school and what I had learned, which was a problem. Each time he asked a question I tried to talk my way out of it and change the subject, so that he wouldn't find out that I hadn't progressed at all since arriving in London and was continuing to struggle in class. Bill was a learned man and had been well educated in Dublin. He had wanted to become a surgeon, but his father had not been able to afford to send him to medical school and so he had become a master joiner instead.

He started by trying to ascertain my competence in Maths, and wasn't impressed, but it was only when he saw my first school report that he realised just how badly I was doing in virtually every subject. He fell entirely silent as he read it and I could see that he was totally flabbergasted. Mammy was less surprised, having known for some time how bad I was academically. Eventually Bill finished reading and looked up.

'Why is he so backward?' he wanted to know. 'He's failed in every single subject apart from Religion and PE.'

Now there was no escaping his questions about school and what I was supposed to have learned by this stage. It was plainly obvious I had learned nothing and I could see that he was genuinely worried about me.

'Don't worry, Bill,' I said with all my usual confidence, 'I'm going to make it, just like JFK.'

'JFK?' He couldn't believe what he was hearing.

Hard Times

'The Irish President,' I said, thinking I was helping him out.

'You think JFK is the President of Ireland?' he said, his astonishment turning to horror. 'Do you know nothing at all?'

'He's Irish,' I said, my confidence wavering slightly. 'I've heard people saying it.'

'His grandparents were Irish,' Bill said, rubbing his brow hard as if to ward off an impending headache, 'but JFK is American, Gordon. He is President of the USA.'

This did come as a surprise and I was very sad to see how disappointed he was in me and how worried he was by my undoubted ignorance. I really wanted to find a way to impress him and make him proud of me.

'I need a drink,' he said, hauling himself out of his chair and heading to the pub.

It would be many years before my dyslexia would be diagnosed and it finally became clear why I struggled so much with schoolwork during those years. At the time, having given the matter serious thought, Bill decided that the best thing would be to move me to a Protestant school.

'He needs to get away from all that religious nonsense,' he told Mammy.

I was horrified, but Bill was insistent and to my amazement Mammy went along with it. I began to wonder if she might have converted secretly behind my back.

'I've not been paying enough attention to your education, Gordon,' she said, 'what with everything else that's been going on. Bill's right to suggest you need a change.'

I had just started to make good friends at the school and now I was going to have to start all over again, facing yet further upheaval in my life. To my amazement, however, my new school actually did work out better. There were children of every faith, race and background, which made it much easier to make friends because I didn't stand out so much. I soon settled in, and the teachers were more attentive and made sure I followed what was happening in the classes. That in turn made me more attentive. They seemed to make the subjects more engaging and explained things far better than in the previous school. I started to enjoy subjects like History, Social Studies and Domestic Science, which in the past I had always thought were boring.

I started attending a different Catholic church where some of my friends, including Gerard Green, were altar boys, and I was asked if I would like to become one. Most Irish parents liked the idea of their children serving Mass, but for some reason I wasn't keen on the idea. I had not forgotten the 'men in black' at the hostel who had never seemed to have much time for me or my friends, and who viewed Mammy and all the other women there as sinners.

One Sunday morning, however, after church service, I wandered into the room at the back of the church and found my friends there with Father Michael O'Brien, the 'Big Fella', as they called him. He had just given Mass and was chatting to the altar boys.

'Come in, come in!' he boomed when he saw me, gesturing for me to join them. 'It's Gordon, isn't it?'

'Yes, Father.'

'Your friends have told me about you. I think it's time you joined the altar boys here at our lovely church. Tell me about yourself. Which part of Dublin are you from?'

'The centre,' I said.

'And are you settling all right in London?'

'Yes, Father.'

'Do you like to play, Gordon?' he asked. 'And fool around with your friends?'

It seemed a silly question for a priest to ask, and before I could think of an answer he had grabbed me from the back, wrapping his big arms around me. I could feel his horrible, fat stomach pressed against my back. He put one hand on my chest to hold me and tickled me with the other. But it wasn't funny in the slightest and when I tried to break away he was too strong and wouldn't let me go. To my horror, the tickling hand went down the front of my shorts and grabbed my private parts.

'Get off!' I shouted, knowing exactly what he was up to.

He took no notice, just laughing at me and continuing. To my dismay I saw that my friends were laughing too.

'We have a lot of fun at Mass,' he continued. 'We play games and we do Bible studies.'

Bible studies, my arse, I thought.

'Piss off!' I screamed at the top of my voice, 'and let me go!'

The shock tactic of telling a priest to 'piss off' worked. All of a sudden the other boys weren't laughing any more and he released me like I was a hot coal.

'Little boys must not use such language in the house of the Lord,' he scolded. 'Don't you want to join the other boys to give Mass?'

This man just did not know when to give up.

'I don't give a shit,' I shouted angrily. 'I don't want to be one of your altar boys and I don't want you to touch me ever again.'

With that I stormed out of the church, closely followed by the other boys.

'You shouldn't have spoken to Father O'Brien like that,' Gerard said. 'You used foul words in the church and swore at him.' The others nodded their heads in agreement. I couldn't believe what I was hearing. Had they not seen what he was doing?

'Oh, shut up,' I shouted. 'He was touching my privates. He's got to be queer.'

'You can't say that about Father O'Brien. He's really nice and so much fun.'

'Nice, my arse! Believe me, he's queer. Just watch your backs with him.'

The boys stared at me in disbelief before slinking away. I didn't really care whether they believed me or not, but there was no way I was going to be an altar boy in that church, or even step inside it ever again. I didn't tell Mammy or Bill what had happened, but Bill was pleased to hear about my decision.

'Good,' he said when I told him. 'I think you are too indoctrinated with Catholicism as it is.'

In all the years we lived at Regina Coeli I had experienced no problems with the priests. But the mothers had always warned us about adults, not to be too trusting, and to beware of friendly strangers. After this experience, and with my new experience of other faiths and beliefs, I was beginning to think that perhaps Catholicism wasn't the only way after all.

Chapter Thirteen
A Real Education

Although I was doing far better at the new school than I had at the Catholic one, it was still obvious that I was never going to shine academically. When I tried to read anything, letters would appear all jumbled up to me and completely refused to make sense, no matter how long I stared at them, which meant that I inevitably fell behind the rest of the class. I lacked a basic comprehension of pretty much all my academic subjects.

During the school term I was feeling deeply unsettled about life. I was still wetting the bed frequently, which Mammy was being very understanding about. My London adventure was not fun any more. I felt completely lost and confused, but realised that I must never talk about going back to Dublin to Mammy or Bill. I understood that I just had to make the best of the situation.

I knew that Mammy and Bill wanted me to do well at school and were worried about what would happen to me if I didn't manage to get an education and pass some exams. I also knew there was no chance I was going to be able to turn things round now. I had simply fallen too far behind. I was going to have to find an alternative route to success. It was a huge relief when the summer holidays arrived and I didn't have to sit through any more boring, frustrating lessons.

Most of my friends from school would be going off to the seaside for their holidays, but I knew we didn't have the money for trips like that. I decided that I would use the summer break to find ways of making money instead.

My other plan for the holidays was to prepare to join the Scouts the following term, which was going to involve buying a uniform. Based on my previous experiences with Bill I anticipated that it would be a battle to get him to pay for it and so I wanted to have some money of my own stored away, just in case.

Bill and I were getting on well; he had even promised to take Mammy and me to the theatre to see my first ever live performance. As with everything else, however, he was all talk and no action and I swallowed my disappointment, telling myself that I had to learn not to get my hopes up when he made promises like that.

I spent a lot of my time talking about pop music, which was one of my new enthusiasms, telling Bill how much I wanted my own transistor radio so I could listen to people like the Beatles, the Rolling Stones and Dusty Springfield.

'This modern music's not worth listening to,' he would grumble. 'It's just a load of noise.'

I knew that meant I had no chance of getting him to pay for the radio, which meant I needed to make enough money for that as well. Without telling Bill, Mammy offered to pay me a little pocket money in exchange for cleaning the room while she was at work. It was a good start, but it was only pennies and I knew I was going to have to think of more ways than that if I wanted to buy a transistor.

When school finished I would be at home on my own in the mornings after Mammy and Bill had gone to work. I would get my own breakfast, wash and dress and then, once I had cleaned and tidied, I would have the glorious freedom to do whatever I wanted for the rest of the day. There was no Bridie to look after me now, so Mammy had to trust me, she had no choice. Since the main reason she had moved out of Dublin was in order to have more control over me, that must have been a worry to her, but she just got on with it. In our early months in London we had spent a lot of time together and had grown much closer. She had imagined that she would be able to stay at home with me all the time, which was why she had been so reluctant to get a job again. Like me, however, Mammy wanted some of the good things in life, like a home she could be proud of, and she understood now that she could not rely on Bill to provide that and was going to have to find alternative ways to make money.

With the luxury of so many hours of freedom came the need for someone to share them with me. I had met a boy called Eamonn Keane who lived nearby. He had been born in England but his parents were Irish, and distant relations of the Greens. Eamonn was very different to me. Where I was short and stocky he was enormous in every way, mainly because of the amounts of food that he consumed. Also, unlike me, he loved to read – the Green boys referred to him as 'Bookworm'. I hated books, but for some unknown reason we liked each other a lot and he was very happy for me to teach him how to play Dare.

I loved to play silly games like knocking on people's front doors and running away. I used to play this trick on people two or three times in a row. Sometimes I would go into a public phone box and call the Fire Brigade, telling them there was a cat or a child stuck up a tree, or a fire. Sometimes I would vary it and call the police in my strong Irish accent, giving them false stories about how my parents were fighting so violently I thought they were going to kill one another. I would then hide and watch to see if a police car would turn up to investigate. It was huge fun and Eamonn joined in happily.

His mother, known by everyone as 'B', was a very strict woman, and just as large as her son. If she had ever known what a terrible influence I was on him she would have stopped him from seeing me immediately. She had his life completely mapped out for him. He was going to do well at school, get into university and then have a glittering professional career. I was only allowed to play with him until she called him in to study, but I was grateful for that. If Eamonn was busy I would make my way over to the Green boys and would lead them astray instead.

That summer I started to enjoy life in London more because I could do exactly as I pleased, much the same way I had in Dublin but without the watchful eyes of the Sisters and Bridie. I was my own boss and that was just the way I liked it. Some mornings we would go to see the latest children's films, and on Saturday mornings we went to see the black-and-white *Batman* series at the Astoria, our local picture house in Finsbury Park. I had thought Ireland was a great place to see films, but London was much better. For one thing, English children were much quieter and more polite when watching films. If I started to shout and jump up and down like I did in Dublin the others would tell me to 'shut up' and 'sit down'. I soon learned to be quiet.

After a film I would walk round to the laundry shop to see Mammy and grab something to eat. I was getting to know the regular customers and was beginning to realise that Mammy had a lot of male admirers. The shop wasn't big but it was always busy and popular with locals. The players from Arsenal Football Club often came in to drop off their laundry and chat with her. Sometimes, if I managed to look cute enough, I struck lucky and scored free match tickets from people like Bob Wilson, the goalkeeper.

'Would you like to come to watch Arsenal with me?' I asked Bill one time. 'I've got free tickets.'

'I don't want to be wasting my time watching a bunch of grown men running around a football pitch kicking a ball about,' he replied. 'I'd rather have a pint in the pub.'

To my surprise his lack of interest was in stark contrast to Mammy, who started to watch football on television with me and became a big fan as she recognised the players who came into the shop. I began to wonder if Bill's attitude was sparked by jealousy.

There were three other shops close to the laundry. To the right was my favourite, the sweet shop, run by a nice old couple, Cyril and Gina Solomon, who had no children of their own. Cyril was quite short, slim, with almost no hair and always wore a cap. Gina was on the large side and wore glasses.

'Gina eats too many sweets,' Cyril used to joke, but I didn't see how that could be possible.

On the other side an old man called Mike ran a small jeweller's shop. Like Bill he wore a dark suit every day. He had long grey hair, spoke very little and worked all the time.

'He's a kind man,' Mammy used to say.

On the other side of Mike's shop was what was known locally as a 'special shop'. No one would ever explain to me what it really was. It just had a couple of medical-looking things in the window and everything else was blacked out. I would hear customers talking to Mammy about it and giggling, but they always clammed up as soon as they saw I was listening. The shop was run by Lew Goldsmith, another small man with heavy, magnifying-type glasses. He too wore a cap all the time, whatever the weather. Some people said he wore a wig, but no matter how hard I stared I couldn't work out if that was true. Lew never wore a suit and although he was younger than most of the men in the shops he looked old to me.

'That man doesn't know the first thing about how to look smart,' Bill would grumble every time he saw him in the street. I knew there was more going on in that shop than met the eye, and I was determined to get to the bottom of the mystery sooner or later. If he had no customers Lew would hang around outside, and whenever a man walked past and glanced at the window display he would strike up a conversation with him. He seemed to be very good at talking to men and getting them to go inside. I noticed, however, that no women ever went in or came out. He always said hello to me when I went past. I would try to peer past him and into the gloomy interior but I could never see anything. Lew's special shop intrigued me, but it wasn't as important in my life as the Solomons' sweet shop.

I already had my Saturday job in Mammy's shop, and a week into the holidays Alf asked if I would like to work in the van with him. I jumped at the chance. I went with him to all the different shops in North London, collecting and dropping off the laundry. Working with Alf was exactly what I wanted, giving me the opportunity to explore the city and discover new places in the comfort of the van, with the added benefit of earning a wage.

I didn't understand half of what he was saying because of his cockney accent, and he had just as much trouble with my Irish accent, but it didn't bother either of us. Every time he caught sight of an attractive woman he would call out to her.

'Hi, sweetheart! What are you doing later?'

I laughed at his brazen pick-up technique, but to my amazement a lot of the ladies would respond positively and get into a conversation with him.

'It's my charm,' he grinned when I commented on his success rate. 'If you use charm in your everyday life you'll be able to get whatever you want. You mark my words.'

At every laundry shop we stopped in he would always try for a few sneaky kisses from the ladies behind the counters, and again he was surprisingly successful. Women seemed to love the way he flirted with them, many of them making us cups of tea once we had finished the job. I had never drunk so much tea in my life. There were one or two, of course, who did not succumb to his 'charm'.

'Old battle axe,' he would say cheerfully once we were out of earshot. 'I didn't fancy her anyway.'

I knew I could learn a lot from watching Alf.

My job was to help collect the dirty laundry and then deliver the clean laundry back to the customers. Some days it felt like hard work but I honestly didn't care. It beat being at school and I felt I was learning about life at the same time.

'See this as part of your life experience,' Alf said one day, 'working with me.'

'I'd like to be a van driver,' I said, 'like you.'

'You can do better than this, my boy,' he replied. 'You have your whole life ahead of you. Take my advice; you don't want to end up a van driver like me.'

This was the first time anyone had given me practical advice about my future and I appreciated it. I liked Alf, and that meant I actually listened to what he was saying. I liked his laid-back attitude and the fact that nothing ever seemed to faze him. He always had a smile on his face and a jolly disposition. He got things done and got away with a great deal by being friendly and charming. He was a smooth operator and it looked like a clever way to get ahead in life. I absorbed all I could from being around him.

Bill was not happy with me working and earning a wage, partly perhaps because he didn't like Alf being part of Mammy's life.

'You should be using the holidays to study,' he said when we were alone together one day, 'and try to catch up a bit on all the things where you are falling behind at school.'

'But you never give me any pocket money, Bill,' I said, feeling brave because Mammy wasn't there to tell me to be quiet. 'Mammy and I had so little when you were away in Germany, we couldn't even feed the meters to stay warm or keep the lights on.'

My directness obviously shocked him and I could tell from his expression that I had hurt his feelings. But he didn't scold me for being so cheeky because he knew I was just telling the truth.

'I was never given pocket money when I was your age,' he said eventually. 'I don't see why you think you need so much money.'

We were so far apart in so many ways. He was actually old enough to be my grandfather, so things were bound to have been very different in his day. He believed in the importance of academia and in working within the system. I, on the other hand, was street smart and dodged every system going. It was likely to be a long time before either of us started to understand the other.

Whenever I was helping Mammy around the shop I could see that she loved her job and was a 'people person' like me. She was very well liked by the customers and as a result her shop took more revenue than any of Mr Davies's other outlets. Like Mammy I would chat with the customers at every opportunity, and some of them gave me great insights into London people and life. There were two old Jewish gentlemen who came in every week who I particularly liked. Mr Gold and Mr Cohen had a completely different way of looking at life to anyone I had ever met before. They were orthodox Jews, and they thought I was Jewish too because of my surname, and I didn't disillusion them because Bill was always telling me how smart, witty and savvy Jewish people were and I secretly wished I was a Jew myself, especially when I found out that Brian Epstein, who had launched the Beatles, was one too.

As the summer holidays drew to a close I had to start thinking about school again, and I dreaded it. The only thing I was looking forward to was joining the Scouts and getting my uniform. Wednesday night was Scouts night and I was especially excited about meeting the Scout Leader because he was black, the first black person I had ever met. I was so curious, I even wanted to touch his skin to see if it felt different to mine. I tried to persuade Eamonn to join the troop too, but he said he was too busy with his studies. I think it was probably more to do with being self-conscious about his size.

I had managed to save enough money to pay for the uniform myself if Bill made the same sort of fuss as he had over the school uniform, and I stashed the cash in my pocket for backup. As we went into the shop I saw Bill checking the price tags on the trousers, tops, hat, socks and scarf that I needed.

'Is the Scouts a religious operation?' he asked me.

'It's Catholic,' I admitted, knowing what he thought about religion. To my relief he just nodded and made no comment. When we got to the cash desk I waited casually for him to pay, pretending not to notice how much it had all added up to. To my amazement he counted out the money in front of me without making any fuss, and I left the shop a very happy little boy indeed.

One Tuesday night, the week before term started, Eamonn and I were wandering in the streets near his home and passed a Protestant church which had a small hall adjoining it. We had passed it many times before without giving it a second glance, but that evening we could hear the sound of loud laughter emanating from inside the hall.

I stopped and cocked my head to one side, immediately curious. 'Can you hear that?'

'Yes,' Eamonn said.

'What do you think's happening in there, then?'

Eamonn shrugged, looking a little nervous at what I might be about to suggest.

'Come on,' I said, ignoring his protests. He had no idea that I had been inside a Protestant church before and knew that it was not the scary sort of place that Catholic children were led to believe. He hung back as I quietly pushed open the door and peered inside.

The hall was dark apart from a black-and-white image flickering on a screen, and it took my eyes a few seconds to get used to the gloom. When they did I saw the room was full of old people and their laughter was the only sound. On the screen a small man with a walking stick and bowler hat was waddling around the screen in a funny way. He was dressed like a tramp.

'Come on,' an agitated Eamonn whispered from behind me. 'How much longer are you going to be?'

'Wait,' I hissed. 'I want to see this film.'

He leaned over me and peeped inside, making the door move and attracting the attention of one of the women, who came over to ask what we were doing.

'We're enjoying the film,' I said. 'Can we come in?'

'Yes,' she said, smiling kindly, 'but don't disturb the other people.'

We slipped into the back row, our eyes transfixed by what was happening on the screen. When the film finished, the lights came on for five minutes while a man changed the reel on the projector. Then they were turned off again and another black-and-white film came on. It was Laurel and Hardy, who I recognised from films I had seen in the picture houses in Dublin.

When the second film finished the lights went on again and the lady came back to see us.

'Are you two all right?' she asked. 'My name is Hetty. Would you like to stay for some tea and cakes?'

I couldn't believe what I was hearing. First they showed us free films and now they were giving us tea and cakes – what a result! Eamonn looked a little uncomfortable about being in a Protestant hall, but the minute he spotted the table with plates of cakes and biscuits he changed his mind and started eating impressive amounts. A couple of old ladies came over to chat to us, asking us where we lived and whether we had enjoyed the films. I talked at my usual high speed, and I could see from their expressions that they hadn't been able to understand a word I was saying. I assumed it was because of my accent, but I also noticed that some of them had strange, distorted, high-pitched voices.

'Do you know who it was in the first film?' one of the women asked. 'It was Charlie Chaplin. Many people think he is the funniest comedian of all.'

I agreed with that. I couldn't wait to see him again.

'Have you had a nice night?' Hetty asked as people began to leave. 'Would you like to help putting away the chairs and tables?'

A Real Education

Wanting to show my appreciation of her kindness I started roaring around at full speed.

'Young man,' she laughed, 'go slowly with the chairs. It's not a race.'

Eamonn laughed at me for being told off, but I didn't care because everyone had been so nice to us.

'Our mammies will be wondering where we are,' I said once all the chairs were stacked. 'We didn't tell them we were going to be this late out.'

'You'd better get a move on and hurry home,' Hetty said.

When I got back Bill was still at the pub and Mammy was sitting on her own, waiting for me and looking worried. I was just telling her what Eamonn and I had been up to when Bill came in and overheard.

'You've been in the Protestant hall?' he asked, clearly pleased to hear it. 'That's the Tuesday Hard of Hearing Club. Didn't you notice they were all wearing hearing aids?'

No wonder they hadn't been able to understand what I was saying. They must have been trying to read my lips and I had talked far too fast for them to follow. Everything made sense now.

'There's only two people there who can hear anything,' he went on. 'One of them would have been the Hetty woman who talked to you.'

'I'd like to go back next week,' I said, 'to help with the tables and chairs.'

'Are you actually wanting to go there to help the old people,' Mammy asked, exchanging an amused look with Bill, 'or to get free cake?'

'To help the old people, Mammy,' I said in a tone which I hoped expressed my indignation at such a suggestion.

What I didn't realise then was that the old people I would get to know at that club would change my life forever.

Chapter Fourteen
A Hard Day's Night

Bill still disapproved of all the groups that I loved, although he was willing to concede that the Beatles did at least 'look smart' because they wore suits. He couldn't understand how any of the groups were allowed to appear on television when they had such long hair.

I would have loved to be a musician myself, but unfortunately I wasn't able to play a single instrument and had no idea how to read music. That didn't stop me making up tunes in my head and then memorising them. Bill and his brother Eddie both worked on film and theatre sets and it was a constant source of frustration to me that Bill didn't manage to get tickets for the shows he was working on. They had actually worked together on the set of *Cleopatra*, the big-budget film where Elizabeth Taylor and Richard Burton first got together. Eddie had the job when Bill came to England and managed to get his brother employed as well. When I heard that Bill was going to be working on the set of the Royal Variety Show the year that the Beatles were due to play, I begged him to get me a ticket.

'What do you know about the Royal Variety Show?' he asked, surprised that I knew anything about anything.

'The Beatles are going to be on it,' I explained.

'It won't be possible to get tickets for that,' he said. 'It's only on for one night and tickets are always like gold dust. I can't understand what all the fuss is about personally.'

The big night arrived and we sat down to watch the show on television. As expected the Beatles stole the show, with John Lennon telling the people in the stalls to clap their hands and the people 'upstairs' to rattle their jewellery, a joke which seemed incredibly cheeky at the time. They then sang 'Twist and Shout' and I knew that seeing them live was the one thing I wanted to do more than anything.

Later that year a miracle happened. Mrs Brown, one of Mammy's regular customers, had heard me talking about the Beatles when she was in the shop chatting to Mammy. She worked at the Astoria in Finsbury Park where the Beatles were booked to perform.

'Would you like these, Gordon?' she asked one day, passing over two tickets to the show.

I couldn't believe my eyes. There was nothing in the world I wanted more. 'Oh, thank you, Mrs Brown,' I said, probably with tears in my eyes. 'Thank you. Thank you. Thank you.'

I couldn't think how to demonstrate the full extent of my gratitude, and Mrs Brown beamed happily to see how much joy she had been able to give me. The next problem was who to take with me, since all my school friends were as keen as I was. Then to my amazement Bill said he would come with me.

'I thought you didn't like their music,' I said. 'I thought you thought it was just noise?'

'You're too young to be going to something like that on your own,' he said.

'OK.' I didn't mind, although I thought he was far too old to enjoy something like this. As long as I got to be there myself nothing else mattered.

When we arrived at the Astoria the street outside was complete chaos as hundreds of young people surged around the theatre in the hope of catching a glimpse of their idols. Many of them didn't have tickets and I could have sold mine a hundred times over for a handsome profit, if I had been willing to part with them, but no amount of money would have induced me to do such a thing. 'Beatlemania' had arrived and the whole world seemed to have caught it.

'We need to get to the door,' Bill said, taking a firm hold of me and forcing his way through the crowd. There was a line of policemen holding everyone back, including us.

'A bit old for the Beatles, aren't you, mate?' one of them joked to Bill. 'And he's a bit young, isn't he?'

We took no notice, continuing to push our way through until eventually we reached the lobby. Bill looked shell-shocked. 'I need a drink,' he said. 'You go on in.'

I handed him his ticket and made my own way into the auditorium, swept along on the euphoria of everyone around me. It was the most electric atmosphere I had ever encountered. The curtain was about to go up when Bill sank into the seat beside me, grumbling about how rude and unruly young people were. Looking around I could see that he was by far the oldest person in sight.

When the Beatles finally ran out onto the stage the audience went wild, leaping to their feet, cheering and screaming.

'Excuse me,' Bill said to the girls in front of us, 'would you sit down please, we can't see a thing.'

They completely ignored him and I climbed out into the aisle to get a better view while Bill scuttled off back to the bar with his hands over his ears. They sang all my favourite songs, including 'Can't Buy Me Love', 'A Hard Day's Night' and 'Please Please Me', and by the end of the show I was completely certain that I wanted to be involved in the world of music when I left school.

'All that screaming,' Bill muttered, shaking his head to try to clear his ears as we made our way home afterwards. 'I don't think my hearing will ever be the same again.'

I didn't care what he said; it had been the best night of my life so far.

The teachers at the Protestant school were much more relaxed in their approach to education than any of my previous teachers. Now I could easily pretend to be ill and they would happily send me home without any questions being asked. In fact I was ill so many times that it was noted in my dreaded report card.

'Gordon is a sickly child, who has missed many lessons throughout the term and has consequently performed poorly in most subjects.'

A Hard Day's Night

Bill was puzzled by this revelation of my weak constitution. I could see that I wasn't fooling Mammy but, to my relief, she held her tongue.

Because I had worked so hard throughout the summer holidays I'd managed to save quite an impressive sum. I wanted Bill to know how industrious I had been, partly because I was very proud of my achievement and partly because I wanted to show him that I could save money, even if he couldn't. Bill was kind to me in many ways, but I thought his meanness was unkind to both Mammy and me and that made me angry.

Towards the end of the holidays I made my way down to the Abbey National Building Society with everything I had saved and enquired about opening a savings account. I thought that if I were to show Bill that I had a savings account it would both embarrass him and show him how much better with money I was than him. The cashier looked at the money I had laid in front of her and then looked down at me.

'I'm afraid you need an adult to sign the paperwork,' she said.

Disappointed not to be able to handle the whole thing myself, I took the paperwork up to Mammy at the laundry and told her my plan.

'That's very impressive, Gordon,' she said, looking at the amount I had managed to save. 'Very impressive indeed.' I glowed with pride as she signed the papers and then scurried back down to the Abbey National with them.

When Bill got in that evening and was eating his dinner I showed him the savings book and I could see that he was even more impressed than Mammy. I knew for a fact he had never had such a thing.

'I'm saving up to buy a transistor,' I told him.

'That's very good,' he said, reaching into his back pocket. To my amazement he gave me some more money to add to the total.

'You should take a leaf out of Gordon's book,' Mammy said as she watched, 'and save some of your wages in the building society each week.'

As usual he carried on eating his dinner and pretended he hadn't heard. Mammy and I exchanged glances but said no more. I think we had both realised by then that he was never likely to change his habits after so many years of only having to please himself. Nothing more was said about us looking for somewhere better to live, which he had promised to take care of once he got back from Germany, and our lives kept on in the same routine all through the following year.

Every Tuesday I would go down to the 'Old Ladies' Club', as I called it, helping to set up for the films or the bingo or the card playing evenings. There were a hundred or more members of the club, sixty-five of whom would come to all the meetings and most of whom I got to know over the following months. I loved talking to them and hearing their stories about what London was like when they were young and how they had been bombed in the war. Whenever they organised outings to the seaside they would always ask me to come along to help. There were socials with other clubs, and at one of them I heard Hetty explaining to someone that I was their 'lucky mascot'. When they told me they were organising a jumble sale and asked me to help I could hardly contain my excitement.

'Would you distribute some posters for us?' Hetty asked. 'Put them up in local shops and places like that?'

'Of course,' I said, taking a large handful. The following day after school I started going into shops asking if I could stick the posters up. I was shocked by how many of them said 'no' and began to feel pretty dispirited. Towards the end of the afternoon I came across Lew standing outside his 'special shop' in his usual pose, looking bored, leaning against the wall with one of his knees bent up, smoking and passing the time of day with anyone who passed.

'What have you got there, lad?' he asked.

'Posters for a jumble sale,' I said, 'but no one will let me put them up.'

Lew chuckled. 'You don't want to be asking people for their permission,' he said, 'just do it and apologise later if they complain. People always like to say no, but most of them are too lazy to take the things down once they are up.'

'OK,' I said, 'I'll do that.'

To ensure that I continued to earn money during term-time I had taken on a new evening paper run. It started when I heard a friend talking about it in the school playground.

'The newsagent wouldn't give me the job,' he complained. 'He said I was too young.'

The next day I went to see the same newsagent and applied for the same job.

'How old are you?' he asked.

'Thirteen.'

I saw the man do a double take, but he must have been desperate because he decided to believe me and gave me the job anyway.

'The round is divided into two,' he explained. 'The first part is a row of eight houses up the big hill on the side of the park. The second part is the council estate at Manor House. So make your way up the hill first and then come back down to do the main delivery. Can you start straight away?'

'Yes,' I said, delighted to think that I would be earning money immediately. He pointed to the bag which was standing ready in the corner of the shop, packed with the evening papers. I walked confidently over and picked it up in one hand but it didn't leave the floor. Recovering my dignity I put two hands to the job and managed to heave it up onto my shoulders and stumble out of the shop, followed by the newsagent's anxious gaze.

Getting up the first hill with the full weight of the bag was a horrible experience, but I made it and by the time I was coming back down the bag was a little lighter. Over the following evenings I also discovered that the customers on the council estate were much nicer to me than those on the hill, who seemed to constantly complain that I was late. In contrast everyone on the estate was polite and pleasant to me as I passed, and my last customer was an old lady who liked to chat and would offer me a cup of tea. She always had a radio or record player going in the background. Sometimes I would return the favour by picking up her milk or bread for her as she couldn't walk very well.

From the first day I vowed to myself that while keeping the council estate customers happy I would find a way of getting rid of the people on the hill. My first tactic was to roll their papers up as tightly as possible and then jam them hard into the letterboxes, so they would tear them when they tried to take them out. Then, when it rained, I would deliberately leave the papers hanging outside the letterbox so they would get soaked. The plan started to work almost immediately, with several of the people on the hill cancelling their orders, making the bag much lighter. The newsagent, however, was starting to smell a rat.

'I only seem to have two customers left on the hill,' he told me. 'What's going on?'

'That's strange,' I said, opening my eyes as wide as they would go and vowing to myself that I would be rid of the last two by the end of the month. I decided to reverse the order in which I did the round, so that by the time I reached the hill I only had two newspapers left to carry. Two weeks later the final two cancelled their orders.

Mr Gold and Mr Cohen advised me to read up about business and the world of commerce. I took their advice and started reading the business pages of any newspaper I could get my hands on as I walked from house to house, despite being the slowest reader in the world. None of it made sense at first, but gradually I began to understand bits and pieces, and I developed a strong interest in the entertainment industry because I could link it with the things I really knew a lot about: television, films and pop music. Who needed school? I was studying at the University of Life!

I was now enjoying the work and wanted to make more money, so I asked if I could do a morning shift as well.

'What about getting to school?' the newsagent asked.

'They don't mind,' I said. 'They like us to do things like this. They call it work experience.'

I could see he believed me. I wasn't surprised. I was discovering that I had a knack for persuading people of whatever I wanted them to believe. It wasn't long before I was able to buy the transistor radio that I so longed for, and I would listen to pop music whenever I could. In those days there wasn't much on during the day, but at night Radio Luxembourg, the first commercial radio station, came on air. After school I would go into the record shops and listen to music in booths for as long as I could before being challenged.

'Do you think you are ever going to actually buy a record?' the manager of the record shop would enquire.

'Maybe next time,' I would reply, although I still didn't own a record player. My taste in music was moving to the new sound of Tamla Motown from the US. I couldn't get enough of it, much to Bill's puzzlement.

Being in the shop with Mammy I had noticed how much she enjoyed talking with people and how much pride she took in her work. She had a number of admirers among the customers. There were several who she always spoke fondly of, and each time they came in the shop I sensed that she perked up and had an extra sparkle in her eye. There was one particular guy, a policeman called James, who regularly dropped in for a chat as he went about his rounds. I noticed that he never brought in any laundry. When I first saw him in there in his uniform I panicked, assuming he was grassing me up to Mammy for something, but after a few visits I relaxed, realising he was just a friendly man who enjoyed

Mammy's company and a cup of tea. He never stayed more than about fifteen minutes, but afterwards Mammy's mood always seemed to have lightened.

Mammy needed all the cheering up she could get at that stage in her life, worn down as she was by living for more than two years in the same horrible room, constantly scraping around to afford anything. She had disappointment written all over her face, and her inner strength seemed to be dwindling at the same rate as my confidence was building as I settled into London life.

I often overheard her and Bill talking late at night, when I was supposed to be asleep, and it was obvious he had no intention of changing anything. The life he had suited him perfectly. He was away abroad a lot for work, breezing back home each time with a couple of presents for us and expecting everything to be fine. And when he was in London he still spent most of his time at work or in the pub. Mammy never said as much to me, but I knew she was sad that Bill had not delivered on all the promises of a better life that he had used to lure her over from Dublin.

I really wanted to help but had no idea how to go about it, so I sought advice from the person who knew the most about our situation, Kit Green. We were sitting in her kitchen drinking tea and having the usual conversation about school and friends, when she must have realised that I had something else on my mind.

'What's troubling you, Gordon?' she asked, putting the kettle on for another brew.

I told all about our troubles with our landlady, who was constantly threatening to throw us out, and how depressed

Mammy was with the room and how disappointed she was that we hadn't moved.

'You know,' Kit said when I had finally finished, 'my friends Joe and Josephine, who came over here from County Mayo, are about to buy a house and will be moving out of their rented house in Manor House. It would suit you and your Mammy well.'

This seemed like a perfect solution and I felt my heart racing with excitement at the thought that I might have stumbled across a way forward for us. I immediately wanted to race home and tell Mammy all about it.

'I'll pop into the shop tomorrow and chat to your Mammy about it,' Kit said. 'Maybe we could go and see the house together and I could introduce her to Josephine.'

The moment I got home I told Mammy all about it. I didn't want to build her hopes up too much in case it didn't work out, but at the same time I wanted to make the most of the situation.

'If this works out,' I said, 'and I have found us a new home, can I have a dog in return?'

Mammy laughed. 'That sounds like a fair deal to me, Gordon.'

A few days later, after Mammy had closed up the shop, she, Kit and I caught a bus to Manor House. Bill was working abroad again, so we didn't have to worry about persuading him to miss a few hours in the pub. We walked for about six minutes from the bus stop until we reached a row of very cute old two-storey houses in a picturesque street with a small group of shops at the top. Glancing up at Mammy's face I could see that she liked what she saw as much as I did.

A Hard Day's Night

Josephine, who was pregnant with twins, invited us in and made tea after showing us around. There were two bedrooms, a front room, a bathroom with no bath and a very small galley kitchen, all located on one floor. The rooms looked a little run-down and were in need of a great deal of work, but the smile on Mammy's face showed that she could see the potential. It was like I had suddenly got the old Mammy back. Josephine, like Kit, seemed keen to help us in any way she could to get the house.

'I'll make an appointment for you to see the agent who looks after the property for the landlord,' she promised.

On Mammy's next half-day Kit, Josephine, Mammy and I all got a bus to Whetstone to visit the agent. I had insisted on going, even though it seemed a ridiculously long journey, and had made an effort to wear my very best clothes, just like Mammy. We both wanted to make the best impression possible. It also gave me another excuse to skip school for the day. The agent was an elderly Englishman who started off by making a joke about all the Irish people in the room.

'Can you afford the rent?' he asked Mammy.

'My husband and I both work,' Mammy said. 'We have two incomes. We won't let you down.'

'Cathleen is a very reliable person,' Josephine assured him. 'And she needs a good home for her lad, here, Gordon.' I gave my award-winning smile as he looked over at me, hoping that I was projecting a picture of innocence.

'Well,' he said, 'that all sounds fine. The rent will be the same as Josephine and her husband have been paying.' It was the same figure that we had been paying for the room with a curtain, which brought home just how badly we were being ripped off by our current landlords.

'You can move in as soon as we move out,' Josephine said as we made our way back to the bus stop, and neither Mammy nor I could stop grinning at the prospect.

'Don't forget, Mammy,' I said when the other two weren't listening, 'that you promised me a dog if this came off.'

'I won't forget, Gordon,' she said, and I thought I was going to burst with a mixture of pride at having found the house, and made Mammy happy, and joy at the prospect of having my own dog.

The other thing that was exciting me was a forthcoming camping trip with the Scouts, although I was a little nervous because as always there was a fee involved.

'Bill will be back next week,' Mammy said when I mentioned the money. 'You can ask him then. I'm sure it will be fine.'

The moment Bill walked through the door and put down his bag I wasn't able to contain myself and blurted out everything. 'Bill! Bill! I helped Mammy find a beautiful house for us. It was Kit's friends' place and they're moving as they are buying their own house. The agent said we can have the house as long as we can pay the rent and you won't believe it but the rent is the same as this awful place. Imagine! And Mammy said that I can have a dog since I helped find the house.' I paused for a breath before finishing with, 'And can I go camping with the Scouts next week? It's only two pounds …'

'Whoa, not so fast,' Bill said, looking distinctly startled. 'You helped find a house?'

A Hard Day's Night

'Yes,' I said proudly. 'It's in Manor House and it's really nice and it's got two bedrooms and it costs the same as this place.'

'So, have you been good while I was away?' he asked. 'How's school?'

'School's fine,' I said quickly, not wanting to get sidetracked from securing this deal. 'I've been very good. Can I go camping?'

'OK, OK,' he said, 'you can go away with the Scouts. But as for the dog – I can't see how we can accommodate one. They cost a lot of money and they need space and a lot of attention.'

'But Bill, there's a garden at the new house and I will look after it, I promise.'

'No dog, Gordon, end of story. You don't need anything else to distract you from your schoolwork.'

I was pleased to get the camping trip – my first ever holiday, but I felt very cheated about the dog because Mammy had promised me. I didn't say any more because what I wanted more than anything at that moment was a peaceful household. Bill was keen to see the new house and so we arranged to visit again a couple of days later.

'What's at the end of the street?' Bill asked as we walked from the bus stop.

'There are lots of factories and shops,' I said, 'it's a really interesting area.'

Bill knocked on the door, and Joe broke off from chasing his two small children to open it and let us in, welcoming us and telling us to help ourselves and look around.

'Sorry about the mess,' he said. 'It's a bit chaotic with the move and everything.'

Bill skulked around for ages, inspecting the place like he was a prospective buyer, while Mammy and I nervously pointed out all the potential for improvement.

'You could build a nice little kitchen,' she said.

'We could plant flowers in the front garden,' I added, 'and I could put my dog out in the back yard.' I didn't like the fact that he wasn't saying anything.

'Would you like a cup of tea?' Joe asked.

'No, thank you,' Mammy said. 'We can see you have your hands full. I just wanted my husband to have a look around.'

As we walked back to the bus stop Bill eventually broke the silence. 'I'll start looking for somewhere else to live.'

'You are joking?' Mammy asked, exchanging a shocked look with me.

'No,' he said, 'there's too much work to do on this house, Cathleen. Why should I spend my hard-earned money making the place look like a palace for the landlord's benefit?'

He then kept talking, probably to stop either of us interrupting, going off at a tangent about how the country needed a new Labour government to change things. 'They need to be building new houses for working people to rent.'

Mammy was completely horrified. Like me she had assumed he would be relieved that we had done all the work and found somewhere at the same price which was so obviously better. She kept walking, her face set in a grim expression as he rattled on. I could see that the moment she started talking she was likely to let rip and things were going to get ugly. I waited with bated breath. Eventually he fell silent as we stood at the bus stop, waiting for the bus.

'Bill,' she said, with a steely calmness in her voice, 'you may not want to move, but Gordon and I will be, whether you like it or not. Anything is better than the God-awful room we're in now. I simply can't believe that you think it is the right house for us. Yes, this one needs work, but can't you see the potential? And there's all the extra space. I refuse to stay in that money-pit any longer now that we have an alternative. The money we save from not feeding the meters alone will give us something to work with.'

Bill opened his mouth to speak but nothing came out, and Mammy wasn't finished yet anyway.

'You promised Gordon his own bedroom. That never happened. You promised we would be in that place for a short time, but you could never be bothered to find us somewhere else. Now we finally have a great opportunity and you want to just throw it away.'

'But it will cost a lot of money to make this place right,' he protested sheepishly. 'We don't even have enough furniture for it.'

'We can save and get things we need over a period of time, Bill. We need to invest in our home. We can make it work.'

'You can have my savings from the building society as well,' I chirped up. 'And I could get myself some more paper rounds to help out.'

'And Mr Davies has been suggesting that I take the job of supervisor for all his North London shops,' Mammy continued, 'which would mean a pay rise.'

We were going at him from both sides and I could see that he was panicking, retreating into silence while he tried to work out what to do. By the next day he seemed to have thawed a little, although he still didn't like the idea of having to do so much work around the house. Deep down he probably knew that the move was going to mean a lot of changes to his comfortable routine.

'So,' Mammy said when he next raised the subject of how much it would all cost, 'how much did you manage to save while you were in Germany?'

Bill kept reading his paper, saying something about politics in the hope of deflecting her.

'Bill!' Her voice grew louder and more insistent. 'How much have you got saved?'

After a couple more attempts to avoid answering he gave in and confessed that he had nothing. It had all been spent.

'What?' Mammy screamed. 'Nothing saved at all? I'm so disappointed in you, Bill. Gordon and I scrimped and scraped around in this hovel all those months, living on the measly sums you gave us, and you never saved a penny? Without my wages we wouldn't have survived the winters. How could you do this to us? Was it all spent on drink? It was, wasn't it? Admit it!'

Bill sat frozen in his seat, silently staring at the newspaper spread out in front of him. Mammy took a few deep breaths, getting control of herself before continuing in a quiet but altogether more threatening voice.

'I don't care how we do it but we *will* move to the new house and we *will* make it work. You *have* to do the work around the house since we don't have a penny to pay other people to do it.'

A Hard Day's Night

From that moment on Mammy took charge, realising that there was no other way to get us out of the mess that Bill had landed us in. I could see that her show of strength had made him feel insecure, as he realised that she might not need him after all. The insecurity seemed to make him paranoid, and he started to walk past the laundry after work on his way home or to the pub, peering in to see who she might be talking to. If she was chatting to male customers he would come inside and hover in the background, glowering and pretending he was reading his newspaper. One day, while he and I were watching television on our own, he casually asked me who the men were that Mammy was always talking to in the shop.

'Oh, they're just customers,' I replied, 'except for James – he just comes into the shop for a cup of tea.'

'James? Who's James?'

'He's the local policeman,' I said, my eyes still on the television. 'He often drops in for a chat.'

'I see.' Bill fell silent for a moment, but I could tell he was thinking and not concentrating on the programme. 'Exactly how often does he drop in?'

'Most days,' I replied innocently, still not aware of the possible connotations of the conversation we were having.

Later that night I noticed that Bill was being distinctly cold towards Mammy, barely speaking. Over the next few days he spent even more time than usual in the pub, but Mammy no longer seemed to be bothered. It was almost as if she was relieved to have him out of the way so she could get on with her moving plans. She assumed he was behaving like that because he was sulking about having to move.

Two weeks later he went back to Germany and I noticed that they didn't even kiss one another goodbye. For the first time I started to worry that things might just be about to get worse.

Chapter Fifteen

Lessons

Seeing that Mammy had completely made up her mind that we were going to live in the new house, Bill climbed down and agreed to the move. If he hadn't, then I'm pretty sure the relationship would have been over, and I know he loved her too much to allow that to happen. He even set about building her the kitchen that she so desperately wanted.

I tried to do my bit as well and decided that the house's sooty grey brickwork needed cheering up. I knew Mammy liked the colour yellow, so I bought some cans of the brightest canary yellow I could find and re-painted the front of the house from top to bottom while they were both at work, which gave me another good reason not to bother going to school. I could tell she was surprised when she came home, but I couldn't quite work out if she liked the colour or not. Bill rolled home from the pub later, a little the worse for wear, and did a classic double-take as he approached the front door.

'Has Gordon painted the house?' he slurred as he came into the kitchen.

'He has,' Mammy smiled, 'which was very kind of him, wasn't it?'

Bill squinted his eyes as if trying to concentrate his thoughts. 'Is it a very bright yellow?'

'Yes, Bill, it is a little bright,' she said. Some of the other tenants did comment on the 'vibrancy' to her, but she just smiled and said, 'yes, isn't it beautiful? My son painted it for me.'

Mum had accepted her promotion to supervisor of all fifteen laundries. It meant she was managing a lot of staff and initially faced resentment from some of the English women. It wasn't long, however, before she earned their respect, because she was so good at the job, and she went on to gain a reputation as one of the best supervisors they had had. She had a wonderful way with people, always patient, empathetic and kind. I learned a lot from watching how she dealt with people.

'I am so delighted that your mother has agreed to take the job,' Mr Davies told me next time I saw him. 'So, when are you going to join the company too, Gordon, so we can keep it in the family?'

'I'm going to be a DJ on one of the pirate radio stations,' I informed him.

He was clearly not impressed. 'You do know it's illegal to broadcast music from those pirate ships, don't you?'

He went on to tell me that Mick Jagger looked like he needed a bath and the Beatles weren't much better. He was just about to start on Tom Jones, who apparently looked 'disgusting' in tight trousers, when Mammy jumped in and told him it was time to shut up the shop. No one slated her Tom. I was glad to get away.

I never did settle at school, continuing to play truant and skipping the lessons I hated the most, but never getting found out – that's how good I was! I didn't believe I would ever be truly happy until I was the master of my own destiny and out of the suffocating atmosphere of education. My failure at school led to me having the usual sorts of teenage run-ins with both Mammy and Bill. The nearer I got to school-leaving age the more worried Bill became about my future. He suggested that I consider carpentry, since it had always given him a good living, but I wasn't interested. I didn't even bother to turn up to woodwork class at school. I knew I wasn't cut out to be a craftsman.

Bill did eventually agree to take me to work with him on a job at the Drury Lane Theatre. It was a fantastic day for me and while I was waiting for Bill I was able to explore the whole place, finding no end of spooky back staircases and hidden doors. There were lots of people working on the stage in a variety of capacities. Bill was in charge of the joinery and there were electricians and lighting people as well. Over it all, however, was the producer, who was the one shouting out the orders to everyone else, making the decisions.

'Wouldn't you like to work somewhere like this?' Bill asked during lunch break.

'I'd like to have his job,' I said, nodding towards the producer.

'You need to have a university education for that,' Bill laughed, 'and your face has to fit. You need to be realistic about what is possible in life, Gordon.'

I didn't argue, just ate my sandwich, but I was quite sure that there was no reason I couldn't end up doing a job like that. The good news was that Bill and I had grown a lot closer, due to his decision to travel less and do more work in London. He was able to get free theatre tickets to all the West End shows and was happy to give them to me, although he couldn't understand why anyone would want to go and see such things, preferring as he did to spend his evenings drinking in the pub.

Although I dreaded the subject of education and qualifications coming up, I liked that he was taking an active interest in my life. He was constantly nagging and lecturing me about planning for the future, but I was coming to realise that he only did it because he cared and was worried about me, like a proper dad.

I felt that I could talk to him about pretty much anything, apart from sex, and of course this was one of the fatherly things he wanted to do. I could see how embarrassed he was to have to raise the issue of contraception and I pretended I didn't know what he was talking about to avoid the issue. In fact I was learning all I needed to know from Lew in his 'special shop'. It had started one afternoon when he was standing outside his shop as usual and I had paused for a chat, trying to look past him into the shop.

'How's business doing?' I asked in my best grown-up voice.

'Oh, very bad,' he said in his best North London Jewish accent. 'No money out there. It's a Wednesday, my boy. Very quiet.'

We kept talking for a while and he asked me how old I was.

'Fourteen,' I lied, 'nearly fifteen.'

'Really? Well, son, you don't look fourteen. You look more like ten to me.'

'It's my baby face, Lew, that's why. Can I have a look round inside your shop?'

I knew I was pushing my luck and I could see that Lew was uncomfortable. 'I'm not sure that's a good idea, son. You really are too young and your mother would kill me if she knew I'd let you in.'

'I won't tell her if you don't,' I wheedled, 'come on, Lew, let me in.'

'All right, come in … but don't you dare ever tell your mum or dad you've been inside …' With that he threw a quick glance left and right to make sure the coast was clear and then stood back to let me dive inside. I couldn't believe my luck. The shop was smaller than I'd imagined and packed with boxes of all sizes from floor to ceiling.

'I do a lot of wholesale business with people who are in the retail business,' he said, and I nodded wisely, as if I understood the business. I started picking up things and asking what they were for. He was as good a teacher as Alf and started to explain about condoms, oils, creams, lubricants and his 'toys', which made me snigger. He seemed to know so much about his customers and what they liked and didn't like. Looking upwards I saw some sexy magazines displayed on a top shelf.

'Can I have a look at them?' I asked, pointing up at them.

'No, son,' he said, 'I'd have to take off the special protective film and then re-cover them afterwards.'

'Why are you selling those?' I asked, pointing at some whips and canes stacked in the corner.

'Well, some people like to be a bit kinky when they have sex.' He stopped talking and looked at me again. 'How old did you say you were again?' I thought I detected a flicker of panic in his eyes.

'Fourteen.'

'OK, you've been in here long enough. Out you go.'

I was disappointed, because clearly there were a million other interesting questions to be asked, but I didn't want to push my luck too far. I also realised I had a rather obvious erection in my shorts and was going to need to cool down before I went in to see Mammy in the laundry shop.

My first introduction to 'the birds and the bees' had been at Regina Coeli, where we all loved playing 'doctors and nurses'. I guess because there were always older children around we grew up faster than other children. The older ones would often be encouraging the younger ones to kiss each other on the lips, and we would be daring one another to show our genitalia and compare the differences. It was more done in a spirit of inquisitiveness than lust.

Bill still didn't believe we should have a dog, but Mammy's nephew, Denis, who was living in London as well, decided that he would take things into his own hands and honour the deal with me on their behalf, presenting me with a big, beautiful, sweet-natured mongrel.

'I'm going to call him Brandy,' I told Bill, 'since it's one of your favourite drinks.'

'Just don't expect me to be walking the thing,' Bill said, realising that he had been out-manoeuvred.

Over the coming weeks, however, Brandy's cute smile and gentle temperament won Bill over and one evening, when I was out, he actually took Brandy to the pub with him and enjoyed the experience so much it became a regular event. Most of the day, however, Brandy would be following me around to the laundry shop, onto the bus and the underground, where I'd carry him up and down the escalators. He even did the paper rounds with me. Brandy became a well-known local character.

One day I arrived home from school to find a letter addressed to me lying on the doormat. It was official looking, with a typed address. In my experience letters seldom brought good news and I immediately assumed it was from the school and would be about my high levels of truancy. I decided to open it and check, and then quickly squirrel it away before Bill or Mammy spotted it.

Cautiously pulling the letter from the envelope, I was surprised to see that the heading at the top said *Evening News*, which was one of the two London evening newspapers at the time. The body of the letter informed me that I had been short-listed for the 'Teenager of the Year Award'. I had to read it several times to make sure that I had understood correctly. I had never even heard of this award and was certainly not aware that I had been entered for it. The letter went on to invite me to attend an interview at the Town Hall at which the final two would be chosen.

I proudly showed the letter to Mammy and Bill, who were as amazed and thrilled as I was.

'Who could have nominated me?' I wondered.

'Maybe it was someone at the Hard of Hearing Club,' Mammy suggested, but none of us actually had a clue.

The following Tuesday I arrived a little late at the club. As I walked in, all the old ladies and gentlemen started to applaud and Hetty came over with a broad grin on her face.

'Miss Orchard thinks a great deal of you,' she said, smiling at one of the old ladies I was particularly friendly with, who was clapping like mad, 'and she put you forward for the Teenager of the Year Award. It was her idea, her way of showing you how proud she is of you.'

Then they all came over to shake me by the hand and thank me for all the hard work I had done for them over the previous years. It was very nice but a bit puzzling since it had never seemed like hard work to me. If it hadn't been for them I would still never have seen the sea or been on any holidays apart from scout camp, I had seen any number of films with them, eaten vast amounts of cake and biscuits and made a lot of friends. It seemed like I should be the one thanking them.

Bill said he would like to come with me to the interview. I would have preferred to go on my own, but Mammy told me that he really wanted to be there for me and deep down that made me happy.

'Do you want to come too?' I asked her.

'I don't think teenagers really want to turn up with their Mammies, do you?' She smiled and I was grateful to her. She appreciated that I wanted to appear as grown-up as possible.

Lessons

Bill and I found ourselves sitting alongside other nominees and their parents, waiting to be interviewed, and eventually it was my turn to go in on my own and face a judging panel of two women and three men sitting behind a large desk. They seemed to know everything about my involvement in the club from Miss Orchard and Hetty, who had given them a written account of everything from the first day I poked my head around the door of the church hall with Eamonn. All the other members had sent in letters of support.

'It seems you have a large fanbase, Gordon,' one of the judges said.

They then asked me lots of questions about my home life and what kind of things I liked to do in my spare time.

'How long do you plan to stay at school?' one of them asked.

'I would like to leave as soon as possible,' I said, noticing that they were all suddenly taking notes. Maybe I now wasn't such an ideal candidate, but I wouldn't have wanted to lie. I couldn't help thinking that if they ever checked with the school and discovered how little I had been there that would not look good either.

'How did it go?' Bill asked as we made our way out of the building.

'It went well, but I may have lost a few points by saying that I wanted to leave school as soon as possible.'

'Hmm,' Bill said, shaking his head. 'Well, we'll just have to wait and see.'

Four weeks later another letter from the *Evening News* arrived, asking me to return to the Town Hall. I was down to the final two! This time the panel wanted to talk to Bill as well. I wasn't at all sure about that, but he seemed keen, so off we went once more.

Sitting in the same room I listened as they asked Bill a lot of questions and I couldn't believe my ears. He was so complimentary about me, coming out with heartfelt phrases like 'what a wonderful son'. I knew him well enough to be sure that he would not have been able to say such things unless he meant them.

In the end I was chosen as runner-up for Teenager of the Year, and I did wonder whether I had got as far as I did *because* of my remark about leaving school, or whether it was that remark which had stopped me from winning.

'Are you sure you wouldn't like to stay at school for one more year?' Bill asked again afterwards.

'No, Bill,' I said. 'My mind is made up.'

Our next-door neighbours in the new house were the Pozzelli family, consisting of Ollie and Mary and their young son, Ricky. Although Italian like Ollie, Mary had been born in England and had a strong cockney accent and a penchant for fish and chips. By that stage my own accent had changed as well and I had started to use words like 'Mum' rather than 'Mammy'.

My friend at school, Anthony, was Ollie's nephew and they were a stereotypical, larger-than-life Italian family. Despite her own love of fish and chips, Mary was a wonderful Italian cook and I got to eat a lot of meals round at their house.

'No English muck for my Ollie,' she would say, 'only real Italian food.'

Lessons

Ollie had just bought a car and Anthony told me he earned big money in the television industry, even though he only worked three or four long days a week. So far he had failed his driving test four times and was pretty cut up that he couldn't drive his beautiful new car. He was a kind, shy man and I was completely in awe of him for being in the television business and earning so much money that he could buy a car, go on regular foreign holidays and buy things for the house.

I think Ollie liked me from the first day we met, or at least that's what Mary told me as she plied me with plate after plate of pasta. I always made a point of being friendly and polite to neighbours wherever we lived. Ollie obviously earned a lot more money than Bill, even though he was only an unqualified stagehand while Bill was a qualified master carpenter, and I was keen to find out how he did it. One day I bumped into him coming back from work at the television studios. He was carrying some fishing rods he'd been given, left over from one of the programmes.

'I hear they've closed down the pirate radio stations,' he said, knowing that I had set my heart on working as a DJ. 'Do you want to come and see the studios where I work next week?'

By this stage he had finally passed his driving test, and the following week he drove me into work with him at the old 20th Century Fox film studios in Wembley, which had recently been converted into television studios. The security guard at the gate waved us through with a smile and everyone we met was extremely friendly. Ollie seemed to know everybody and I was entranced by the atmosphere, with actors walking around in costumes and technicians moving all sorts of cameras, lighting and sound equipment about. At lunchtime we went to the canteen and ate heavily subsidised tea and cake, and I thought of how much money Bill must have spent in pubs during his lunch breaks over the years.

The day ended with me watching a comedy show being recorded in front of a live studio audience, and I was far more interested in what the crew on the studio floor were doing than the actors on the set. Ollie was impressed by my production knowledge, which I had picked up through watching Bill at work in different theatres. By the time I got home that night I had made up my mind that I was going to work in television, since pirate radio was obviously finished.

The next day Ollie asked if I wanted to go fishing with him and try out his rods. 'Or do you have to go to school?'

'Oh no,' I lied, 'I have the day off.'

When I got up I dressed in my school uniform and waited for Bill and Mum to go to work before changing back out of it and popping next door. I decided that this expedition counted as work experience; I was 'networking'.

My fifteenth birthday arrived and freedom finally lay before me. My self-confidence was total. I knew what I wanted to do with my life and I was relieved to be escaping from a system that I had never fitted into. The teachers that I talked to about my ambitions thought I was mad. Like Bill they didn't think that jobs in the entertainment business were open to uneducated Irish boys like me, but they didn't know about my experiences with Bill and Ollie. They had no idea what actually happened on film or television sets and the job opportunities that existed. People outside the industry just saw the glamour of the finished products and all the publicity surrounding them, but I knew that in reality it was all about hard work.

My real teachers had been the people I had met outside school: Mum, who had understood, encouraged and believed in me; Alf the Flirt, who taught me how to get ahead using charm and personality; Lew the sex shop owner, who taught me to be confident and never to underestimate the general public; while Miss Orchard taught me never to underestimate the kindness of others, and Hetty showed me how important it was to make time for people, no matter what their age or background, and more importantly, to always help people less fortunate than myself; Mr Cohen and Mr Gold, my two old Jewish friends, taught me how important it was to do my research into the television industry, and Ollie found time to teach me what I needed to know about the world of television. My real teachers all had one thing in common: they wanted me to succeed. I was a lucky boy.

One hot summer Sunday afternoon Denis and his girlfriend, Nellie, came over for lunch. Nellie looked a little pale and was very quiet. She didn't want to take off her coat despite the incredible heat, which seemed a bit strange to me.

'Are you all right?' I asked, seeing that she was starting to sweat.

'I'm fine,' she replied, but I could see that she wasn't.

'Are you sure you don't want to take your coat off?'

'No, really,' she insisted, 'I'm fine.'

'Leave Nellie alone, Gordon,' Mum said.

It seemed to me that Denis was stifling a giggle at that moment, but I couldn't work out what might have amused him, so I kept quiet and watched, waiting to see what happened. As I sat watching and listening it gradually dawned on me. I had, after all, seen many pregnant women at Regina Coeli. Knowing that I was forbidden to talk about anything to do with our past, I said nothing – just looked at Mum with what I hoped was a 'knowing' look.

Nellie was a young, innocent Irish woman, far too honest for her own good, verging on naïve. She was a good Catholic and attended church regularly, to the point of even having considered becoming a nun at one stage. Later that day, when Bill took Denis off to the pub for a drink, Mammy took her into the main bedroom to chat, and I was able to hear the conversation clearly through the paper-thin walls. Nellie confessed that she didn't know what to do about the situation, and Mum said something that seemed to come from the heart.

'It happens to the best of us, Nellie, it happens to the best of us. But I promise, things have a way of working out in the end.'

I had been thinking more and more about who my real father might have been and how Mum might have got herself into the position where she had to disappear into Regina Coeli in order to protect her 'secret'. I knew she never wanted me to ask her direct questions about any of it, never wanted to think about those years in Dublin again. But Nellie's condition made it all seem very vivid and real, and I imagined what it must have been like for Mum to find that she was pregnant and alone in the world. In the end Denis married Nellie and it all worked out for her, just as Mum had predicted.

In the last year or so of my school days I played truant so often that I sometimes used to get bored when I found myself alone in the house. One day I decided to see if I could find out anything more about Mum's past before she had me. I was becoming hungry for more information about who I was and what had really happened between Mum and my biological father.

Rifling through all sorts of drawers and cupboards I came across a collection of black-and-white family photos which I had never seen before. There were pictures of Mum and Bill together on his motorbike in Ireland, and another of her wearing a fur coat. There were also lots of his Alsatian, Trigger. Then I found a photograph of a man, with 'Sullivan' written on the back. I had come across that name before in some personal documents that I had unearthed but not been able to understand. For some reason I had a feeling that this man might be my father, but the photo was fuzzy and I couldn't really make out his face.

Chapter Sixteen

The Story of My Mother and Father

I think it is possible that Denis was the only person my mother ever really confided her story to. He had always been her favourite relative, and mine too. I remember when I heard that his brother was training to be a policeman I was shocked that anyone in our family could be such a goody-goody. Denis seemed to have more in common with me. The fact that he brought Nellie to see her when he couldn't have taken her to see his own mother must have meant a lot too. So it was Denis who eventually gave in to my nagging and told me the story of what had happened to his aunt Cathleen after Bill had left for England and before I was born.

Cathleen was still living and working in the Dublin hotel and Bill's letters from England had grown less frequent. In her mind she was coming to terms with the idea that he had probably found somebody else and she might just have to accept that she was not to be the marrying kind. Bill was the only man she had ever loved and she did not expect to meet anyone who would match up to him.

The Story of My Mother and Father

'Life goes on,' her friends and family would say to her, and so it did.

'He was asking for you again at breakfast,' one of her colleagues told her one day when they were taking a cigarette break at the back of the hotel.

'Who was?' Cathleen asked.

'That good-looking fella from Cork. The dark one who looks like that actor, Tyrone Power.'

'The businessman? Mr Sullivan?'

'That's the one.'

She knew exactly who they meant. He was one of the hotel's regular guests and he had asked her out before. He had a cheeky smile and made her laugh with his comments. She liked his forwardness, plus the fact that he had left her a huge tip the last time she served him. She had caught him looking at her several times and was surprised by how pleased she had felt to be the object of his attentions. A few days later she was working in the restaurant when she saw that he had come in for dinner on his own. She felt a little anxious as she approached the table, not sure what to expect; and a little excited too.

'Good evening, Mr Sullivan,' she said. 'Nice to see you here again.'

'Good evening, Cathleen. Please call me John.'

She felt herself blushing. 'What can I get you? A pint of Guinness to start with?'

She could tell his eyes were on her all the time as she went about her work that evening, and they exchanged pleasantries whenever she came to his table. As he was leaving he pressed a tip into her hand and held it as he whispered in her ear.

'I would very much like to take you for a drink some time.'

'Thank you,' she said, pulling away coyly. 'I will think about it.'

The following day he was in the restaurant again. 'I'm still waiting for an answer to that invitation for a drink.'

'The hotel has strict rules about staff socialising with clients,' she said. 'I would lose my job if they found out.'

'Rules are there to be broken,' he grinned. 'Please. Let's be friends.'

'All right,' she said, 'just one drink, but it has to be somewhere a long way from the hotel.'

He suggested a pub on the other side of town, and when she got there at the appointed time she found him waiting outside for her, wearing a hat and smoking a cigarette. When he saw her approaching he quickly stubbed out the cigarette beneath his shoe and lifted his hat in greeting.

'I wasn't sure you would turn up,' he said.

It was a weekday night and the pub was quiet, so they were able to get a table by the window. Cathleen looked around nervously while he went to the bar to order the drinks.

'A bit dead in here tonight,' he said as he returned to the table.

'Good,' she said, 'I prefer it that way.'

The night went well. He had a fund of stories about his work and the people he came across and he made her laugh. She was taken with his worldliness and dynamism. He asked her a lot of questions about herself as well. She talked about her family, but not about Bill.

'I had to wait a long time to get you to come out with me,' he said, 'but it's been worth the wait.'

'Thank you for a lovely evening,' she said as they walked back to the hotel together.

'I would very much like to do it again,' he said, 'next time I'm in Dublin.'

'OK,' she said.

As they reached the hotel they parted ways. He went through the front entrance while she walked round to the back.

Every time he was in Dublin during the following weeks they would meet up on her days off, or in the evenings after she had finished her last shift. Cathleen found herself growing fond of the well-to-do businessman in his smart three-piece suits, white shirts and ties, his polished leather shoes and hat.

He started to talk quite seriously about their relationship. 'I've never met the right woman for me until now,' he told her. 'You have kept my interest for longer than any woman I have ever known.' He even talked about wanting a family one day, when he was not so busy with his work. Once they had been seeing one another for about six months he started to talk about her coming to Cork one day and meeting his mother, although he was always too busy with work to actually make the necessary arrangements. Cathleen told her mother and Lily about the handsome businessman she had met, relieved to be able to reassure them that he was a Catholic as well.

She had not been feeling herself for a few weeks when she decided that she really should see the doctor. He did a few minor tests and informed her she was pregnant. It took her a while to take the news in. In her innocence she had assumed that she was too old for such a thing to happen, and she couldn't even work out if the news made her happy or sad. She couldn't wait to tell John, but at the same time she was nervous about how he would take it. He wasn't due in Dublin for another nine days. When he did arrive he was as delighted to see her as always and they met in the pub as usual.

'There is something we need to discuss,' Cathleen said, and then paused.

'What is it, darling? You know you can tell me anything.'

She took a deep breath. 'I'm pregnant.'

'You are joking.'

She shook her head. 'No,' she said. 'I'm not joking and I am as surprised as you are at my age.'

John was speechless and she could already see that his reaction was not going to be what she had hoped for. The way he was taking the news that he was going to be a father was upsetting her and she wanted to escape. She stood up.

'I'm going back to the hotel,' she said.

He grabbed her hand as she moved away. 'Let me walk you back.'

For the first time in their relationship they were silent all the way back to the hotel. By the time they got there she was unable to stop the tears from running down her face.

'I'm away for the next few days,' he said as they parted. 'I need time to take all this in.'

The Story of My Mother and Father

The next morning he wasn't in the restaurant for breakfast and there was a letter waiting for her. He wrote that he needed to get back to Cork on urgent business and he was very sorry for not seeing her before he left. She was now thinking the worst.

A week later he arrived back in Dublin and told her he had made the trip specially to see her because he knew they had to resolve the situation. During the intervening week she had made up her mind what she wanted to say to him, and now she could do nothing but hope for the best. He arrived in a smart new car.

'I've booked a table at a nice new restaurant on the outskirts of the city,' he told her.

He seemed happy and proud behind the wheel of his new car and she could see he was trying to make it a special night for her. He had always been a man for talking about all the things he was going to do in life, and prided himself on being a man of action, but when it came to talking about the baby he seemed to be a different person. They started with drinks at the restaurant and he talked about taking her to see the new film *The Quiet Man*, set in Ireland and starring John Wayne and Maureen O'Hara, the very popular Irish actress. It was a film she really wanted to see. He continued chatting but she was not really listening, just waiting for him to get to the important questions and answers about their future.

'John,' she said eventually, interrupting his flow of chatter, 'what is it you want from our relationship? Where are you going with it?'

He looked her in the eyes. 'I want to be with you for the rest of my life. I love you very much.'

'Why do you have such a problem with the baby, then?'

'I don't want the responsibility of a baby.'

'If you say you love me and want to be with me forever, why don't you just marry me and accept the baby as part of our family?'

'You don't understand. I just want you, not a baby.'

'Are you saying that if I was to lose the baby you would marry me?'

'Er … yes,' he said doubtfully, 'some day in the future when I am more established in my business. Is it really important to get married? We are having a great time together, aren't we?'

She could see he was trying to charm his way out of the situation, but knew she couldn't allow it to happen. There was no way she would ever get rid of the child that was growing inside her. To start with it was against her religion, but even if it hadn't been she would never have considered such a thing.

'John,' she said firmly, 'I am going to have this baby and you are the father.'

'You are forcing me into a corner,' he said, suddenly furious. 'I cannot accept this and I don't want to be the father of this baby.' He was becoming distraught at what he saw as her stubbornness. 'I am not going to pay for anything to do with this baby and you will not be able to bring it up alone.'

Cathleen knew that this was not something that a man who loved her would ever say. In that moment she realised she knew nothing of his family in Cork or what he did when he went back there. She had fallen for a man she hardly knew. As she started to cry he tried to console her, putting his arm around her shoulders.

'Tell me the truth, John,' she sniffed. 'You have someone else in Cork, don't you?'

He fell back into his chair with a sigh, obviously uncomfortable. 'Yes,' he said, as if summoning all his courage. 'Yes, I am married. I have a wife and two kids. That is why I cannot marry you or be the father of this baby.'

At that moment she knew she was on her own. She composed herself for a few moments.

'I will not interfere in your affairs in Cork,' she said. 'I will not cause you any problems, but you must take responsibility for this baby. I hope you will do the decent thing and support me in this decision.'

'I will Cathleen,' he said, 'I promise. I'm sorry. I shouldn't have reacted like that. It was just such a shock.'

It was too late for his words to make a difference. In those few minutes she had lost faith in the man she had thought she loved. They had hardly touched their food by the time they left the restaurant and few words passed between them on the way back to the hotel.

'I'll be in touch,' John said as she got out of the car.

As she went back to her room in the hotel Cathleen felt as if she had reached the lowest point in her life so far. Once in bed she quietly cried herself to sleep, her brain filled with all the ugly options that now faced her. Should she have an abortion? It would be a hard thing to do in Ireland, since it was illegal and would mean going to a backstreet clinic where anything might happen. She had heard many stories of women dying in such places. She could go to London, where it was legal, but who did she know there apart from Bill? If she decided to have the baby, where would she go once she started to show? The hotel would not want her there and would almost certainly sack her as soon as they found out she was going to be a single mother. Could she even support a child if she had one? How would she pay for all the things that a child would need? It was hard enough to keep herself on the money she earned, let alone a child.

By the next day she had made her decision. She knew that whatever happened she could never get rid of the child that was growing inside her. The first step was to hand in her notice at the hotel and hope that her bump didn't start to show before she had worked out her notice. By the time her final day came round she was in her fifth month of pregnancy and so far no one else had spotted anything.

She had wanted to slip away without any fuss, but her friends were having none of that and were waiting at the back door of the hotel to see her off as she came out with her suitcase. She had hoped that John would send her a little money to live on during the following few months when she wouldn't be able to work, but he had not been in touch since the last time they parted. Wanting to keep him informed of her decisions, she had written to him care of his office in Cork, but had received no reply.

Having virtually no money and knowing that she was going to have to eke out the few pounds that she did have over the following months, she had made enquiries about hostels and a kindly nun had told her about Regina Coeli, leading to her arriving at the doors of the hostel on that cold and rainy night.

The Story of My Mother and Father

Realising that she needed to prepare herself for the possibility that John was hoping to get away without helping in any way, she had been making enquiries about getting legal advice. It was hard to find anyone willing to advise a single mother on how to take care of herself and a child, but she had heard of a Jewish solicitor by the name of Friedman who had a small firm in the centre of Dublin and who took on such cases on a 'no win, no fee' basis. He would look at each case individually and establish if it was strong enough for him to take on. She made an appointment to see him.

The streets were full of early Christmas shoppers as she made her way to his office, reminding her that this was going to be the worst Christmas of her life, the first one that she had not spent at home with her family. She had written to her mother to inform her that the relationship with John Sullivan was over and that she was leaving her job at the hotel. She had suggested that she might even travel to England to try her luck there. She assured her mother that she would be fine and asked her not to worry about her and to forgive her. Having laid this false trail she hoped that she would be able to disappear off everybody's radar until after the baby was born.

Mr Friedman, who seemed a practical and professional man, listened carefully to her story.

'I think it is fair to say,' he said once she had finished, 'that John Sullivan will almost certainly deny he is the father and will demand that you provide some kind of proof. The case is a borderline one. Your best chance would be for me to write to him and inform him that unless he accepts responsibility for the baby he will be summonsed to a hearing at the Children's Court in Dublin.'

'Whatever you think,' Cathleen said, relieved to no longer be totally alone.

'And would you be able to let me have all the letters that he wrote to you during your courtship? If necessary we can threaten to read them out in court and to call witnesses to your many meetings, although hopefully we won't have to and Mr Sullivan will come to his senses.'

The thought of having to appear in court was terrifying, and she hoped that Mr Friedman was right in believing that John would want that even less than she did. It seemed possible that he would respond positively in order to avoid the threat of going to Court and having the affair exposed. She returned to the hostel feeling cautiously optimistic, but as the days turned into weeks and she heard nothing from Mr Friedman, she began to think that her optimism had been misplaced.

Several weeks after the first meeting, however, she heard from Mr Friedman that John had finally made contact. He invited her into the office to talk about it.

'Mr Sullivan claims that you and he were only good friends and had shared a drink occasionally when he was in Dublin,' he said. 'He has denied having a physical relationship with you and claims that he could not therefore be the father of the child.'

Cathleen was deeply shocked that the man she had thought so much of was able to tell such a blatant lie and to betray her so completely.

'I wrote to him again,' Mr Friedman continued, 'informing him that he left me no alternative other than to take the case to court. I reminded him that there would be many witnesses in Dublin who would have seen the two of you together and would contradict his claims that you were no more than friends. I also warned him that his wife might well be called to the witness box as well.'

Cathleen made a sharp intake of breath. This was exactly what she wanted to avoid. She did not want the poor woman who was married to Sullivan to have to go through such an ordeal, but she could see that Mr Friedman had to try everything.

'Mr Sullivan then phoned again,' Mr Friedman continued, consulting his notes as he went, 'and warned me not to involve his family in the case or he would sue for defamation. I replied that we would be very happy if he were to sue, because then the whole story would have to come out in court and everybody would know the truth.'

John Sullivan, however, had apparently decided to take his chances and Mr Friedman received a date from the court for a hearing. Cathleen was tempted at that stage to forget about the whole thing, but Mr Friedman advised her to hold firm. 'He is bluffing,' he said. 'We have to call his bluff.'

Sure enough, a week before the case was due to be heard John Sullivan made an appointment to meet Mr Friedman personally in order to discuss the case. When he arrived at the office he told Mr Friedman that he wanted to make an offer of settlement to resolve the case out of court. Afterwards Mr Friedman wrote to Cathleen asking her to return to his office so that he could fill her in on the offer.

She was becoming increasingly paranoid about walking around the city now that her pregnancy was so obvious for all to see. Wearing loose-fitting clothing, covering her hair with a headscarf and keeping her head down, she hurried through the less frequented streets to avoid making eye contact with anyone. Mr Friedman welcomed her and, after making sure she was sitting comfortably, he told her what had transpired with John.

'You'll be pleased to know that he has seen the error of his ways,' the solicitor told her. 'I think he was so afraid of his family finding out about your affair that he panicked and made some decisions that he now regrets. He says he does not want to avoid his responsibility and hopes that you will accept his apologies for his bad behaviour towards you. He is also offering a one-off payment of £300 to go towards the child's upkeep. He says that is all he can afford.'

'Does he not want anything to do with the child?' Cathleen asked.

'He says that although he would like to be part of the child's upbringing, he knows it would be impossible to keep it a secret. He therefore does not want any association with the child, nor does he want his name to be on the birth certificate. He will not want any contact with you either after the settlement, as he feels it is best for both you and the baby.'

Mr Friedman handed over a document which he had drafted, stating the conditions for both parties to agree and sign. Cathleen read it.

'Does it have to be signed in John's presence?' she asked.

'It won't be necessary for you to see him unless you want to negotiate for better terms.'

'That won't be necessary,' she said. 'I do not want to see him again. I am happy with the settlement for the baby but I never want to see John Sullivan ever again.'

The Story of My Mother and Father

The relief of knowing that it was over, and she would not have to go to court, compensated a little for the fact that the settlement would not be enough to see her through the bringing up of a child. It would, however, help until she was able to get back to work.

'It was brave of you to agree to bring this case to court,' Mr Friedman said as she signed the papers. 'Many women would not have had the courage.'

She nodded but said nothing as she handed the papers back.

'The money will be paid once the baby has been born alive,' he continued. 'I will deduct my fee and you can collect the remainder of the money from me as soon as you feel able.' That would mean £150 for her and £150 for Mr Friedman. (This was worth about £4,000 in total in today's money.)

This was the story that Denis had told me that night in the restaurant when I had insisted on finally knowing the truth. Armed with that small amount of information I had contacted a private detective in Dublin, a former policeman called Donovan, who had been injured in the line of duty and had set up in business on his own. After making a number of enquiries he had discovered that John Sullivan was still alive. On my last morning in Dublin I was waiting in the hotel lobby for Donovan to pick me up and take me to see my father.

Despite having gone over all the questions a thousand times in my head, I was still not at all sure whether I wanted to meet him or not. Did I want to introduce myself to him?

Did I want to confront him and demand to know why he had abandoned me and my mother? Did I want to make sure that he felt guilty? Or did I just want to satisfy my own curiosity about what my biological father was really like?

Donovan arrived at the agreed time to pick me up. He seemed to be using the front passenger seat of his car as an office, with road maps spread out, so I climbed into the back. I didn't feel like talking, my head too full of memories and anxieties about what I was going to find at the end of this journey. We drove in virtual silence through the beautiful countryside peppered with small villages that can't have changed much in a hundred years. From time to time I nodded off.

'We should be there in about ten minutes,' Donovan said, and I felt my heart rate quicken.

For so many years I had been planning what I would say to my father if I ever met him, but now that the moment was approaching I wasn't sure what I wanted to say. I wasn't even sure why I was there. We drove slowly down a tree-lined road in a well-to-do area. The houses were large and the gardens well tended. There were nice cars parked on the driveways, all clean and sparkling in the sun. Most of the gates were open. In the front garden of one house there was an old man playing with a little girl. Donovan slowed down as we approached and rolled down the electric windows. There was a car standing in front of the house with the doors open, as if they were preparing for an outing. The little girl was running around, screaming with laughter and shouting out 'Granddad!' as he pretended to try to catch her, allowing her to escape his clutches at the last moment.

'That's John Sullivan,' Donovan said. 'I'll wait here for you.'

I didn't move, just sat staring out the window. The car attracted the little girl's attention and she came running towards us, assuming we must be visitors. Sullivan hobbled after her. Still I didn't move or speak, unable to think of any words to say. He caught her as she reached the pavement, holding her back with both hands and smiling at me.

'Hello,' he said. 'Can I help you? Are you looking for someone?'

No words came and I shook my head. 'Let's go, Donovan,' was all I said and the old man and the girl watched for a few moments as we drove away, then he released her, following as she ran back up the drive.

'Are you all right?' Donovan asked.

'Yes. Can you take me to the Wicklow Mountains?'

We drove back towards Dublin and on to Wicklow, the area where Mum and Bill spent happy times together when they first met, away from everybody and everything. I directed Donovan to a small, ancient church and asked him to wait for me while I made my way to the cemetery at the side where Mum and Bill's tombstones stood side by side in a joint plot. I read the inscriptions:

'Cathleen Lewis, devoted wife and loving mother', and
'William Lewis, devoted husband and loving father'.

Standing looking at the graves, I remembered the moment when I had been most proud of them. Bill's brother Eddie had a daughter, Janet, and we were all invited to go to her wedding in London. I would have been about fourteen. The groom was from London, so half the guests would be English and the other half would be mostly Bill and Eddie's family, including the four sisters that I had heard him talk about so disparagingly over the years – the women who had refused to accept the possibility that he would marry a Catholic girl, and had refused to even meet Mum. Bill had had nothing to do with any of them since leaving Ireland more than fifteen years earlier.

I was excited at the thought of meeting Bill's family for the first time, all these people who did not even know that I existed, and as the day drew closer I began to wonder how Bill would react to them. He hated them so much for the way in which they had kept him and Mum apart, and now they were all going to be together in one room for the first time.

Eddie was a proud man and wanted his daughter's wedding day to be perfect. It was going to be a long night, filled with eating and drinking and celebrating. I had never been to such a formal event before, where so many people were dressed up in their best. Mum was looking beautiful and far younger than her years with her light blonde hair slightly pinned up and a simple, dark blue dress. She must have been nervous at the thought of meeting Bill's sisters, but she didn't show it. She looked as calm and serene as always in the church, where we were anonymous among the crowd.

After the service I walked with Mum into the rooms where the reception was to be held. There were children running around everywhere and a sea of faces that I had never seen before, all gathering into groups, chatting and greeting one another. No one greeted us or called us over. No one knew who we were. It was like we were invisible as we moved through the crowd. I could see Bill and his three brothers all chatting and drinking in the bar area. Mum cast him an anxious look. We both knew what he could be like once he had a bit of drink inside him and his natural reserve and inhibitions started to slip. It looked like a very typical Irish get-together for the men, all of whom had met Mum in London and gave us a warm welcome as we joined them.

I noticed Eddie and Bill moving away from the group to a far corner of the large room, deep in conversation. Eddie seemed to be trying to reason with Bill, putting his hand on his shoulder as if to restrain him. Both of them were glancing round the crowd. Eddie looked anxious, while Bill seemed to be calmly taking in the lie of the land and seeing who was where as he sipped steadily at his drink. I got the impression that they were talking about their sisters, because I'd heard them discussing the subject in London many times, particularly the older ones, Annie and Susie – 'The Evil Sisters', as Bill called them, cheerfully admitting that he could have happily killed them for what they had done to his relationship with Mum.

The live band was already playing music in the background and there was a sense of excitement in the air as everyone prepared for a good evening. More and more people were pouring in through the doors.

'You mustn't let the past upset you,' Mum was always telling Bill when he started going on about his sisters after he'd had a few drinks, and her willingness to forgive and forget had helped to soothe his anger a little when they were far away from Ireland, but now he was back in the same room with them it might not be so easy. Watching him firing increasingly angry looks around the room I was pretty sure that he was now spoiling for a fight and Eddie must have sensed the same thing, which was why he had taken him to one side to try to reason with him. Mum could also see the danger signals and went over to them.

'Don't start anything, Bill,' she warned, 'or I'll leave the wedding.' The tone of her voice was much more serious than I was used to. I could tell she really meant it.

Because I loved cowboy films so much it reminded me of the famous showdown in *High Noon*, with our hero, Bill, against the four evil sisters. I couldn't wait to meet them for myself. I had seen photos of them so I thought I knew what I was looking for, but obviously they had aged greatly since then. There were so many old people in the room I couldn't work out who was who. I assumed all four of them would be together but I couldn't see a group fitting that description. I slipped away from Mum and moved surreptitiously around, listening in to conversations until I overheard someone talking about Jenny and Sara. I knew those were the names of the two younger sisters and worked out which ones they were. They were sitting alone together at a table for four. I guessed they must be waiting for the other two.

I sidled over to the table without Bill or Mum noticing and sat down next to Jenny.

'That seat is reserved,' she said, looking me up and down. 'What side of the family are you from?'

'The Lewis side,' I said, with my broadest smile.

The Story of My Mother and Father

'We are also on the Lewis side,' Jenny said and it seemed that I was now welcome to stay at the table with them. I used every ounce of charm I had ever learned from watching Mum and Alf and other grown-ups, and I could see it was working.

'You sound like a nice young Englishman,' Sara said.

'Can I get you ladies some drinks?' I enquired.

'You must have a lovely mother and father to thank for your good manners,' Jenny said.

I told them I lived nearby in London and made up some stories to distract them from asking any more personal questions. After a few minutes Annie and Susie arrived and I stood up to allow them to take their seats.

'Thank you,' Susie said. 'And who might you be?'

'He is one of us, Susie,' Jenny informed her. 'A Lewis. He has been entertaining us with stories of life in London and offering to fetch us drinks and all.'

Mum must have sensed danger because she appeared beside me with a beaming smile. 'Good evening, everyone,' she said, resting a warning hand on my shoulder. 'Is everyone enjoying themselves?'

'This is my mum,' I said, 'or should I say Mammy?'

They all laughed and I watched and felt the tension building as they scrutinised Mum, trying to work out who she was.

'What is your name?' Susie asked.

'Cathleen,' Mum said without a flicker of emotion. 'Cathleen Lewis.'

She continued to smile as the sisters exchanged glances, all immediately realising exactly who we were and unsure how to deal with such a volatile social situation. I couldn't imagine what was going to happen next as I watched their faces freeze. Mum continued to smile calmly, looking each of them in the eyes, saying nothing. After what seemed like an eternity of stunned silence they recovered themselves and made polite, wedding conversation for a few minutes. I stayed quiet, listening and watching intently, waiting to see what would happen next.

Out of the corner of my eye I could see Bill approaching the table with a face like thunder, walking past the dance floor, taking no notice of anyone who greeted him, his eyes fixed on us. This, I thought, is it! As he came closer the sisters saw him too and visibly stiffened. Mum glanced at him as he drew close, still smiling but with a warning in her eyes, reminding him silently that if there was a fight she would be leaving. He stood for a few moments staring down at his sisters, all of whom were now sitting bolt upright, partly defiant and partly nervous, as unsure what their brother would do next as I was. Eventually he spoke.

'Can I steal this beautiful woman away from you for a dance?' he asked, and I noticed that the band was playing Elvis's 'Love me Tender', their favourite song.

He took Mum's hand and led her onto the dance floor. They exchanged smiles, both knowing what the other was thinking, and held each other tight as they slow danced around the floor. I stood with the silent sisters, watching, able to see just how happy my parents were, realising that theirs was a true love story.

www.secretchild.com

Acknowledgements

I would like to say a big thank you to Yew Weng Ho, without whose help and creativity I would not have written this book.

Also not forgetting my 'teacher with the ruler' Soot Ng, whose patience has no bounds.

Moving Memoirs

Stories of hope, courage and the power of love…

If you loved this book, then you will love our
Moving Memoirs eNewsletter

Sign up to…

- Be the first to hear about new books

- Get sneak previews from your favourite authors

- Read exclusive interviews

- Be entered into our monthly prize draw to win one
  of our latest releases before it's even hit the shops!

Sign up at

www.moving-memoirs.com